The Power of Past Greatness
Urban Renewal of Historic Centres in
European Dictatorships

 FÜR GESCHICHTE
UND THEORIE DER ARCHITEKTUR
UND PLANUNG

Schriften des Architekturmuseums
der Technischen Universität Berlin
(Papers of the Architecture Museum at the
Technical University of Berlin)

Schriften des Bauhaus-Instituts für Geschichte
und Theorie der Architektur und Planung
der Bauhaus-Universität Weimar
(Papers of the Bauhaus Institute for the History
and Theory of Architecture and Planning at the
Bauhaus-Universität Weimar)

The Deutsche Forschungsgemeinschaft
(German Research Foundation, DFG) has
financially supported this publication.

Harald Bodenschatz / Max Welch Guerra (eds.)

The Power of Past Greatness

Urban Renewal of Historic Centres in
European Dictatorships

Harald Bodenschatz, Christian von Oppen,
Steffen Ott, Christiane Post, Piero Sassi,
Max Welch Guerra

Contents

The Urban Renewal of Historic Centres* in the Service of European Dictatorships

Harald Bodenschatz and Max Welch Guerra

* The German word "Altstadterneuerung" has no precise equivalent in English. "Altstadt", sometimes translated literally as "old town", will be translated in the following as "historic centre", or occasionally as "historic core". The meaning of "historic" is explained in more detail in the text: as a rule the historic centre is that part of a town or city that was founded in the Middle Ages. That is what is normally associated with the German word "Altstadt". "Stadterneuerung" is translated by "urban renewal", although this term is often associated with demolition and new construction. In the case of the dictatorships examined by us it does in fact mainly mean demolition and new construction. In the text the word "redevelopment" is also used, with the same meaning as "renewal". "Behutsame Stadterneuerung", i.e. urban renewal that does not focus on demolition and the displacement of population but, rather, on the development of the existing building stock and the preservation of the social composition of the neighbourhood, is translated as "cautious urban renewal".

In the European dictatorships in the first half of the 20th century the historic centres were regarded as shabby, as marring the desired image of a magnificent new city. This led to the considerable demolition of the historic building stock, particularly, but not only, in the capital cities of the dictatorships. The redevelopment of historic centres did not always mean the complete obliteration of the old towns, however. The aim in many cases was also preservation and often the cultic presentation of historical testimonials to past greatness. This was true of the capital cities but also of small and medium-sized towns of particular historical importance, the preservative redevelopment of which also served touristic objectives. It is revealing to see which historical layers were regarded as worthy of preservation and which were not.

In the following, selected examples of the redevelopment of historic centres under the dictatorships in Italy, the Soviet Union, Germany, Portugal and Spain are presented. This selection is not accidental. We systematically address urban development in the dictatorships that were established in Europe between the two world wars. Simply because of their often long duration these dictatorships launched particularly extensive, remarkable urban development projects. Both their planned and their implemented interventions in the historic centres provide a revealing insight into both the urban development characteristics and the socio-political characteristics of the individual dictatorship.

First of all we examine the redevelopment of the historic centres in the capitals, to which particular attention was paid and which illustrates the specific individual mixture of motives. In Spain, the special case of the city of Barcelona is also discussed. In addition, we bring examples from Italy, Portugal and Spain of the urban renewal of historic centres in small and medium-sized towns, which followed their own logic and – primarily, but not always – also served the demonstration of past greatness. For the Soviet Union and Germany the exemplary case of the capital city is discussed. The order of the chapters is based on a historical criterion: the order of the individual initial stages of the project-intensive redevelopment of the historic centres.

The sample of selected cases allows an overall view of the practices of urban renewal of historic centres under the dictatorships, a dimension that has been paid little attention until now in the historiography of urban development. It was, however, precisely the measures for the redevelopment of their historic centres that decisively characterised the capital cities and the smaller towns, and still characterise them today, even though hardly any of the visitors or residents in the historic centres are aware of this.

This book discusses the connections between historic centres, urban development and dictatorships that took shape in an eventful and painful period. None of these terms is completely unambiguous, however. Their interpretation is very varied, often disputed and subject to historical change. It is thus itself an important subject of scientific analysis. Our results should be understood as a contribution to the improved, i.e. more differentiated, comprehension of the three terms.

"Historic centre" is not a clearly defined term. It is a negative or positive programme and a spatial category, and both of these change with political disruptions and even in the course of one form of rule. In Europe today, "historic centre" is often understood as the part of the centre of a city that was built in the Middle Ages, but occasionally also as parts of the city that were built later, and sometimes the entire pre-industrial city. In the following, the area of a town or city is usually described as the "historic centre" that lies within the boundaries of the medieval city. Rome is a prominent exception: here the area of reference is the city wall of ancient Rome since medieval Rome had shrunk considerably in comparison. In Moscow the area within the present-day Garden Ring is regarded as the historic centre.

We understand *urban development* not only as planned and built urban development form. We also include the relationships and the processes that made this form possible and that led to this form, as well as the messages and the material effects which the urban development form implies. In this sense, the form is the nucleus of urban development but it can only be understood if it is regarded not only as a form. Finally, our understanding of urban development includes its function as a historical testimonial, the meaning of which changed even during the existence of the form of rule that gave birth to it. This concerns the scientific classification as well as the attributions in the course of remembrance policy disputes. This is especially true in the periods of political history that follow, particularly if we are dealing with the products of dictatorial relationships.

Concerning the term *dictatorship*, we focus on an open association, understood as the antonym of parliamentary democracy. In contrast to the 20th century approaches to totalitarianism theory we do not assume any intrinsic similarity. For us dictatorship is a working concept, the configuration of which is made clear by the developed examples. We therefore turn our gaze away from the history of ideas and the history of political systems and towards urban development. We follow the movement of the subject matter, which also means paying attention to internal contradictions, inconsistencies and discontinuities as well as questioning one or the other traditional interpretation.

The states chosen here – with the exception of Stalin's Soviet Union and Hitler's Germany – also pursued urban development in Africa. They founded urban bases there, in some cases centuries ago, which they often developed further in the 20th century, and reshaped existing settlements and towns of the indigenous population. We have ignored this special field because it requires its own research and publications that place the policy of urban renewal in the colonies of the three dictatorships in the context of worldwide colonial policy.

The urban renewal of historic centres is not a speciality of dictatorships. It already began when historic towns became "old towns", primarily from the mid-19th century onward. It played a particular role in dictatorships, however. In dictatorships a very large number of historic centres were redeveloped, and a wide programmatic and practical range of historic centre redevelopment evolved there. The displacement of unwanted population groups and functions, the creation of modern places of residence and employment for loyal middle classes, the demolition of old buildings that were considered to be substandard, the planning of new buildings intended to express the greatness of the dictatorship, the expansion and enlargement of major streets and squares, the construction of new streets and squares not only for the benefit of motorised vehicles, the preservative renovation of testimonials of a construed historical importance – all of these objectives played a role to different degrees depending on the individual dictatorship, and within each dictatorship depending on place and time. The urban renewal of historic centres as an important policy field within urban development was founded in the period of the European dictatorships following the First World War.

The authors and the editors of this volume have conducted research on urban development in dictatorships for many years. Comprehensive results were published in 2003: "Städtebau im Schatten Stalins" (edited by Harald Bodenschatz and Christiane Post, main authors: Uwe Altrock, Harald Bodenschatz, Susanne Karn, Steffen Ott, Christiane Post, further contributions by Benjamin Braun, Heike Hoffmann and Franziska Träger); 2011: "Städtebau für Mussolini" (edited by Harald Bodenschatz, main authors: Harald Bodenschatz, Daniela Spiegel, further contributions by Uwe Altrock, Lorenz Kirchner and Ursula von Petz); 2019: "Städtebau unter Salazar" (edited by Harald Bodenschatz and Max Welch Guerra, main author: Christian von Oppen, further contributions by Uwe Altrock, Harald Bodenschatz, Kathrin Meißner and Max Welch Guerra); and 2021: "Städtebau als Kreuzzug Francos" (edited by Max Welch Guerra and Harald Bodenschatz, main author: Piero Sassi, further contributions by Uwe Altrock, Harald Bodenschatz, Jean-François Lejeune and Max Welch Guerra). Before that, and in parallel to it, the editors of the current volume examined the

legacies of the national socialist dictatorship and those of the other, quite different, dictatorship in Germany, namely the GDR. See for example 2016: "Weimar, Modellstadt der Moderne? – Ambivalenzen des Städtebaus im 20. Jahrhundert" (Harald Bodenschatz with support from Max Welch Guerra).

In addition, a first synopsis of urban development under various dictatorships in the first half of the 20th century in Europe by the current editors should be pointed out, which resulted in the publications in 2014: "Städtebau und Diktatur in Europa: Sowjetunion, Italien, Deutschland, Portugal, Spanien" (special issue of Forum Stadt 1/2014, edited by Harald Bodenschatz and Max Welch Guerra) and 2015: "Urbanism and Dictatorship. A European Perspective" (Bauwelt Fundamente, edited by Harald Bodenschatz, Piero Sassi and Max Welch Guerra), in both of which Christian von Oppen also participated.

The following texts are mainly based on the research mentioned above, published by Verlagshaus Braun ("Städtebau im Schatten Stalins") and DOM publishers (the remaining volumes). The contributions presented here have in part been considerably revised for this publication. The past and present authors of the individual sections on the redevelopment of historic centres are named in the index.

This book represents the first attempt to examine the urban renewal of historic centres in the period of Europe's dictatorships during the first half of the 20th century in a common context. The editors regard the comparison of such experiences as providing considerable insights that help us to better understand the history of urban development and the history of Europe in the 20th century.

References

Bodenschatz, Harald (ed.): Städtebau für Mussolini. Auf der Suche nach der neuen Stadt im faschistischen Italien. Berlin 2011

Bodenschatz, Harald / Post, Christiane (eds.): Städtebau im Schatten Stalins. Die internationale Suche nach der sozialistischen Stadt in der Sowjetunion 1929–1935. Berlin 2003; Russian edition: Боденшатц, Харальд / Пост, Кристиане (сост.): Градостроительство в тени Сталина. Мир в поисках социалистического города в СССР. 1929–1935. Санкт-Петербург 2015 [Bodenshatts, Kharal'd/Post, Kristiane (sost.): Gradostroitel'stvo v teni Stalina. Mir v poiskakh sotsialisticheskogo goroda v SSSR 1929–1935]. St. Petersburg 2015

Bodenschatz, Harald / Welch Guerra, Max (eds.): Städtebau unter Salazar. Diktatorische Modernisierung des portugiesischen Imperiums 1926–1960. Berlin 2019

Welch Guerra, Max / Bodenschatz, Harald (eds.): Städtebau als Kreuzzug Francos. Wiederaufbau und Erneuerung unter der Diktatur in Spanien 1938–1959. Berlin 2021

The Urban Renewal of Historic Centres in Mussolini's Italy

Harald Bodenschatz

It is largely undisputed that Italian fascism was a product of the European crisis during and after the First World War – a reaction to collective experiences in that war, to the Bolshevist dictatorship in the Soviet Union, to the difficult political and economic situation in Italy, to the contradictory reforms of the Giolitti era, to the deficits in industrialisation and infrastructure compared to the rest of Europe, to the contradictions between town and country, between North and South, to the class struggles in the cities and in rural areas, to mass emigration abroad and to the disappointments over colonial policy. The general crisis following the First World War was ended violently with Mussolini's accession to power in 1922 and the establishment of a Fascist dictatorship. No-one could have anticipated in the early 1920s that this dictatorship would survive for two decades. Urban development contributed to a considerable degree to the consolidation of the dictatorship.

Following its accession to power, the Fascist regime had to deal with a phenomenon that had been considerably accelerated by the unification of Italy: the process of urbanisation. As had been the case ever since 1870, in the entire interwar period Italy experienced migration from rural areas into the towns and cities, particularly into the cities. This changed the hierarchy of the cities regarding their size: towards the end of the 1920s Milan overtook Naples as Italy's largest city, but was itself overtaken by Rome in the 1930s. With regard to the economy, the industrial triangle Genoa-Turin-Milan was consolidated, whereby Milan was able to expand its role as an economic administration centre. The port of Marghera in the Venice area was established on the basis of private initiative and with the support of the state. The economic development of Northern Italy corresponded to the decline of Southern Italy, in particular of Naples, the most important city in the South.

At first the regime was unprepared for this rapid urbanisation. This changed quickly, however. The two decades of Fascism were a heyday of urban development. In no other European country were as many radical urban development projects realised in the interwar period as in Italy. Only in Stalin's Soviet Union could a similar urban development fever be observed. Above all the reconstruction of the historic centres, compact, urban city extensions and the foundation of new (small) towns and villages were key themes in the regime's Italian urban development. This was accompanied by efforts to develop the coastal areas for mass tourism, an innovation by the regime. Last but not least, we should not forget the urban interventions outside of Italy, in the colonies and occupied territories. There, too, historic centres were reconstructed and expanded, and new small towns and villages were founded. The capital city of Rome stood at the centre of the Fascist dictatorship. Not only the political elites were concentrated here but also the urban development experts, the most important urban development plans and projects, including, particularly, those concerning the historic centre of Rome itself.

Rome: the Evocation of Imperial Greatness

Rome, and in particular the historic centre of Rome, was the arena of the Mussolini dictatorship. But what is the "historic centre" of Rome? The city within the sprawling ancient Aurelian Wall of the second half of the 3rd century? Or, as is usually meant, the medieval city – in the case of Rome a pitifully shrunken, small and unimportant town? Or the powerful Rome of the popes? For the Fascist dictatorship Rome was an inexhaustible reservoir of past greatness, an incentive and model for the future capital of the Fascist empire. This meant simultaneously: cult of the ancient Rome, particularly the Rome of the imperial epoch, neglect of medieval Rome, regarded as powerless, but also reverence for the absolutist Rome of the popes. The specific meaning of this for the reconstruction of the historic centre was repeatedly disputed. The restoration of Rome's ancient centre was continually under dispute during the dictatorship, by no means only behind the scenes but also in the public sphere. The concept of the "thinning out" of historic centres developed by Gustavo Giovannoni (*diradamento*), perhaps the most important concept for the renewal of historic centres that was developed in Europe in the early decades of the 20th century, awakened considerable interest but was rarely applied.

Beginning of the Reconstruction of the Historic Centre in the 1920s

The reconstruction of the historic centre of Rome had been a central theme in urban development since the unification of Italy. In the Fascist epoch, too, it was considered necessary to clear the way for modern traffic and to eliminate unhealthy housing conditions. The reconstruction was now additionally spurred on by the objective of excavating monuments from ever more glorified antiquity. The fact that in the course of urban reconstruction the poorer social classes were driven out of the historic centre was not only accepted but – with a view to the upgrading of the historic centre – welcomed. Following the establishment of a new municipal government in Rome controlled by the central state (*Governatorato*) in 1926, the publicly supported urban renewal projects in the historic centre first concentrated on the "freeing" of the archaeological zones, the areas of which were systematically expanded by wholesale demolition.

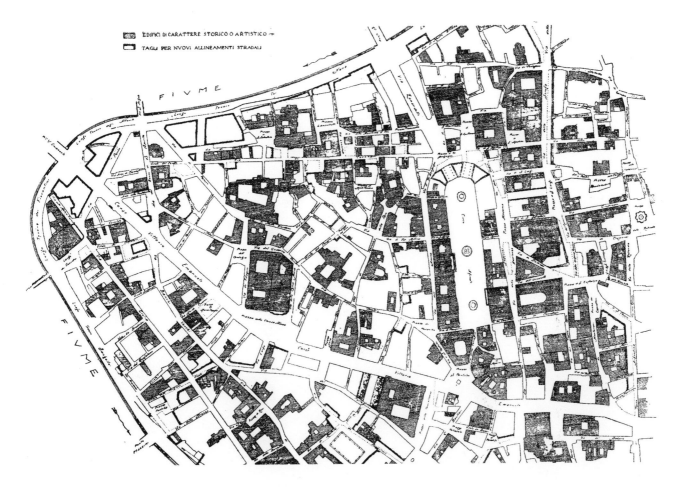

"Renewal project for the Renaissance quarter in Rome: example of cautious thinning out (diradamento edilizio) and careful planning of the routes of new streets without impairing the character of the quarter", presented in the documentation of the International Housing and Town Planning Congress in Rome 1929. [Source: International Federation for Housing and Town Planning 1929, p.354]

The most wide-ranging and extensive measures concerned the sacred centre of ancient Rome, the Capitoline Hill.[1] The densely built-up, historic urban areas on the Capitoline Hill, the Palatine Hill and the Forum Romanum had already been removed step by step in ruthless projects following Italian unification. In 1920 a commission, in which Gustavo Giovannoni also participated, advised the complete "isolation" of the Capitoline Hill.[2] The policy of demolition in order to free ancient monuments was not an invention of the Fascist regime, but rather, to quote the almost apologetical statement by Umberto Broccoli, *Sovraintendente ai Beni Culturali* of the City of Rome (2009), it was a "natural daughter of the dream of architects and archaeologists, who were in love with the perceptions of John Ruskin and romantic classicism regarding testimonies of ancient times."[3]

Following the assumption of power by the Fascists, the Forum of Augustus was excavated in 1924–1928 and the Trajan Markets in 1926–1929 – as a prelude to the excavation of the Imperial Forums and the great destruction on the eastern side of the Capitoline Hill. The excavation of the Trajan Markets in particular established the "archaeological fever" so typical of Fascist urban construction. The excavation of the supposed Vestal Temple[4] and that of the temple for the "Fortuna Virile" on the Piazza Bocca della Verità also began in 1924 – as a prelude to the extensive demolitions on the western side of the Palatine Hill. Densely built historic districts sprawled over the western side of the Capitoline Hill. Their demolition began in the context of the excavation and restoration of the Theatre of Marcellus in 1925–1926[5] in line with plans by Alberto Calza Bini. The beginning of the destruction of the popular Piazza Montanara in this connection was

particularly lamentable. This was followed in 1928–1929 by the demolition of the buildings up to the Piazza Venezia and beyond to the Piazza Bocca della Verità.[6] In this context the Church of Santa Rita at the foot of the stairway to the Church of Santa Maria in Aracoeli was demolished in 1928.[7] Many other churches were destroyed – in spite of protest by Gustavo Giovannoni. The obliteration of the Piazza Aracoeli in 1928–1929, against which Giovannoni expressly took a stand,[8] was particularly controversial.

A further excavation area in the historic centre arose somewhat inadvertently: the Largo Argentina[9], which was soon to become a modern centre of the Renaissance quarter. The starting-point was a traffic project: the long intended connecting of the Via Arenula to the Corso Vittorio Emanuele II at the level of the Teatro Argentina. For this purpose the wholesale redevelopment of the historic quarter and the subsequent new development of the area were prepared.

After four previously unknown temples from the republican era were discovered during the demolition work begun in 1926, it was at first unclear what should happen now. The new construction work had already been started, but the Committee for History and Ancient Art of the *Governatorato* recommended that further new construction should be stopped. Antonio Muñoz, inspector general of the department *Antichità e Belle Arti* of the *Governatorato* since 1928, declared, however, that he did not know how the difficult question of financial compensation could be solved.[10] As in all such cases the *Governatore* turned directly to Mussolini. Under the slogan "For archaeology and for hygiene"

1 In the era of the Fascist regime the Capitoline Hill gained almost cult status. Mussolini described it as the most sacred hill "after Golgotha". Cf. Muñoz 1932, p. 8.
2 Cf. Cederna 1979, p. 121.
3 Broccoli 2009, p. 6.
4 The temple was probably dedicated to Hercules Victor. Cf. Touring Club Italiano 2007, p. 476.
5 On this cf. Ciancio Rossetto 1995, pp. 69–76.

6 On the redevelopment of the Piazza della Verità cf. Bianchi 1930, pp. 573–591.
7 Gustavo Giovannoni had proposed without success in 1929 that the church be reconstructed at the foot of the hill – admittedly in a very free form, i.e. considerably altered. In the course of the demolition of the church the remains of a Roman house were found, which can still be seen today but attract little interest. Cf. Giovannoni 1929, pp. 593–605; Cederna 1979, p. 129.
8 Cederna 1979, p. 131.
9 Muñoz 1929, pp. 169–171. Cf. also Messa 1995, pp. 77–84; Painter 2005, pp. 7–8.
10 Cederna 1979, p. 98.

*Archaeological site Largo Argentina, 1929.
[Source: Capitolium 1929, p. 172]*

*Site of the Area Sacra Argentina: "medieval" island with tower and loggia, a free reconstruction from 1932.
[Source: Muñoz 1935, p. 103]*

Mussolini finally decided on 22 October 1928 that there should be no further building activity in the area.[11] The testimonials of the ancient world were excavated in the following six months and the "Foro Argentina" was handed over to the public on 21 April 1929, the anniversary of Rome's foundation. The further regulation of the *area sacra* dragged on, accompanied by internal controversies among the experts, until 1942. Among the curiosities of this archaeological zone that still exist today – in addition to the girthing of the temple complex, that lies far below today's street level, in a strictly rectangular "corset" – is the lonely medieval island with its tower and loggia at the southeast of the square, a typical contemporary artistic invention from 1932.[12]

Accelerated Renewal of the Historic Centre in the First Half of the 1930s

In the 1930s urban development activities continued to be concentrated on the Capitoline Hill and the archaeological zone including the Palatine Hill, the Imperial Forums and the Forum Romanum up to the Colosseum. They served not only to "free" the ancient ruins but also to improve traffic. On the western bank of the Tiber, the Castel Sant'Angelo, testimony to both antiquity and the rule of the popes, was "isolated". In contrast, the most ambitious architectural and urban development project of the regime in the city centre was a failure: the reconstruction of the *Palazzo del Littorio* in the Via dell'Impero.

In the first half of the 1930s the extensive demolition at the Capitoline Hill and in the archaeological zone was continued. In 1932 the Forum of Caesar and the Forum of Augustus were excavated. Whereas in the 1920s, however, the archaeological aspects – the excavation of the Imperial Forums and the Tarpan rock – were dominant, traffic

measures now came into the foreground. With the complex of the Via dell'Impero, the Via dei Trionfi, the Via del Mare and the road along the Circus Maximus at the foot of the Palatine, inaugurated in 1934, the centre of ancient Rome – the Capitoline Hill, the Palatine Hill and the Forum Romanum – was completely isolated and encircled by a ring of wide thoroughfares for motor vehicles – a solution which still continued to be celebrated as "magnificent" in the post-war period.[13]

Following initial consideration in 1928, the construction of the most important street in Fascist Rome began in 1930: the Via dell'Impero, first called the Via dei Monti, which led to the partial covering up of the testimonials to the ancient world that had been excavated in the 1920s. The construction of this grand boulevard alongside the testimonials of imperial Rome was intended to connect two important places: the Piazza Venezia, location of the "Altar of the Fatherland", inaugurated in 1911, the main monument to the unity of Italy but at the same time the main location of Fascist rule with the seat of Mussolini's government in the Palazzo Venezia, on the one hand, and the Colosseum, the "greatest monument of ancient Rome", the symbol of the perpetuity and the strength of the city,[14] on the other. The new boulevard was, however, also intended to satisfy the traffic requirements of the new city.[15] An entire city quarter that was described as "old, sordid", "ugly and unhealthy"[16] was forced to give way to the new boulevard – via expropriation. Again, archaeology was called upon to justify this: "Archaeology [...] has completely eradicated the maze of backstreets and narrow alleyways that led an ugly parasitical existence between the Piazza Venezia and the Flavian Amphitheatre and returned to the eternal sun the Forums of Caesar, of Nerva, of Trajan and of Augustus in a place where until now only dark shadows, dirt and rubbish were

11 Cederna 1979, p. 83.
12 Cederna 1979, pp. 99–102.

13 Zocca 1958, p. 669. The axis Via Druso – Via Amba Aradam (1933) expanded the new street system. Touring Club Italiano 2007, p. 512.
14 Consociazione Turistica Italiana 1941, p. 91; Touring Club Italiano 1947, p. 42.
15 Muñoz 1932, p. 7.
16 Muñoz 1932, p. 30–31; Italienische Städtebaukunst im faschistischen Regime 1937, pp. 9, 21.

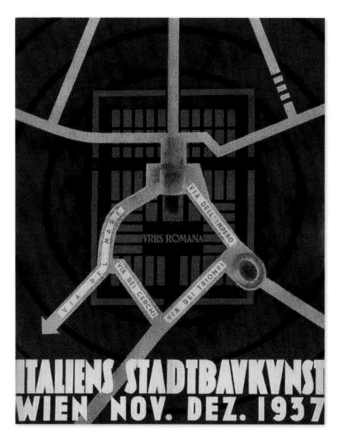

Schematic illustration of the system of new streets in the archaeological zone in Rome on the catalogue cover for the exhibition "Italy's city planning aesthetics" in Vienna in 1937. [Source: Italienische Städtebaukunst im faschistischen Regime 1937]

to be found."[17] Demolitions were often accompanied by extensive restorations. In 1931–1937 the building of the ancient Curia, which had been converted into a church, was also restored to its assumed "original state".[18] The monumental building which was freely reconstructed at that time is admired by tourists today as one of the most important "ancient" monuments of the Roman Forum.

In order for the new boulevard to be built in a straight line, however, it was necessary – without a planning basis – to bore through the Velia Hill. This operation, begun in December 1931, destroyed countless archaeological strata from different periods of antiquity, which were declared to be of little value. The testimonials of antiquity were thus de facto subordinated to the new Fascist boulevard.[19] This is also true of the preserved monuments such as the extensively excavated and restored Maxentius Basilica, which now adorned the new boulevard. On 6 September 1932 the longed-for moment had come: the Colosseum could be seen from the Piazza Venezia for the first time.[20]

The 850 metres-long boulevard was inaugurated on 28 October 1932, the 10th anniversary of the Fascists' March on

17 Buchheit 1938, p. 242.
18 The site had already been bought by the government in 1923. The antique-style facade was finished in 1932. Touring Club Italiano 1938/1947, p. 127.
19 Vannelli 1995, p. 36; Muñoz 1932, p. 14.
20 Cederna 1979, pp. 179, 183–184.

Site plan of the Fori Imperiali with the Via dell'Impero, published in 1938. [Source: Touring Club Italiano 1938/1947, after p. 152]

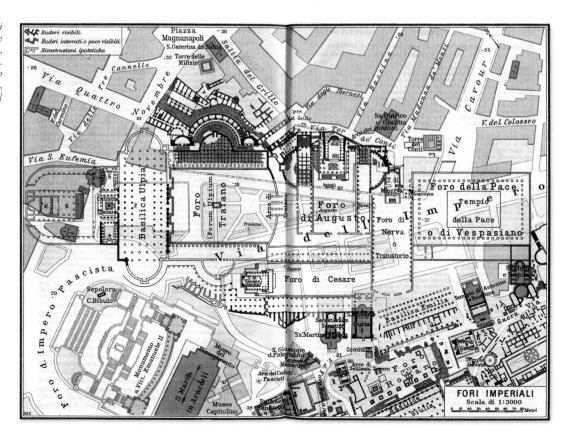

Demolitions for the construction of the Via dell'Impero, August 1932. [Source: Muñoz, Antonio 1932, p. 15]

Rome.[21] This important date for the government enforced a particularly hectic rush for the conclusion of the road-works. 300,000 cubic metres of earth were removed for the construction, including numerous testimonials of ancient Rome. 608 homes had to give way and 1,886 persons were displaced.[22] The Caesar Forums, which had been excavated at great expense, were also largely forced to disappear again: 76,000 sq.m. of a total of more than 80,000 sq.m. had been excavated, of which 64,000 were buried again for the construction of the boulevard.[23] Ninety-seven per cent of the Trajan Forum disappeared under the earth again, 54 per cent of the Augustus Forum, 85 per cent of the Nerva Forum, 60 per cent of the Caesar Forum and 100 per cent of the Vespasian Forum.[24]

The Via dell'Impero was the most important urban development project of the Fascist regime in the capital city from the point of view of propaganda and the one that received the most attention internationally.[25] Rome had

finally found "its centre", its central parade avenue, the "Via Sacra of the Fascist nation".[26] The new boulevard had a breadth of 30 metres, of which 20 were reserved for motorised vehicles and 10 for pedestrians. The increasing deployment of motor cars, which was inevitable in view of their significance for transport, was immediately celebrated: one year later 6,200,000 motor cars, 700,000 lorries and 270,000 horse-drawn vehicles were counted on the boulevard.[27] At the time of Augustus, so it was said, the Forum was the centre of Rome, in the Renaissance it was the Campo dei Fiori, in the 17th century the Piazza Navona, in the 19th century the Piazza Colonna, and now it had returned to the foot of the Capitoline Hill.[28]

The construction of the Via del Mare, also 30 metres wide, which began in 1929 and was ended in 1932, followed the previously begun excavation of the Capitoline Hill, the Theatre of Marcellus and the temples on the Piazza Bocca della Verità. The new street – in accordance with its name – was intended to cross the Lungotevere Aventino and the Via Marmorata to reach the Autostrada to the Lido di Roma (Ostia). Alongside its course, between the Theatre of Marcellus and the Piazza Bocca della Verità, several new large-scale buildings were erected that document the urban development intentions of the 1930s. The famous Piazza Montanara, one of the most picturesque squares of the old Rome, was completely eradicated, forced to give way to the excavation of the remains of the

21   This march by supporters of the Fascist movement, which led to Mussolini's accession to power in October 1922, actually never took place – at least not in the form construed by Fascist legend. Cf. Woller 2010, p. 93. For an evaluation of this event cf. also Dogliani 2008, p. 24.

22   Cederna 1979, p. 188–189. The number of displaced persons increased in the following year dramatically when further buildings were demolished. Franz J. Bauer speaks of more than 4,000. Bauer 2009, p. 243. Bauer estimates that the total number of persons displaced by the policy of excavating the ancient ruins reached 18,000 by 1936.

23   Insolera 1976, p. 134. The construction of the Via dell'Impero was celebrated by some as "one of the most fortunate examples of contemporary urban development" even after the fall of the regime. Cf. Zocca 1958, pp. 667–668.

24   Costantini 1970, p. 108.

25   Cf. Italienische Städtebaukunst im faschistischen Regime 1937, p. 9.

26   Cederna 1979, pp. 187–188.

27   Cederna 1979, p. 192.

28   Cederna 1979, p. 193.

Foro Olitorio, the vegetable market of ancient Rome.[29] A further result of this reconstruction – in addition to the large-scale demolition of buildings that were, again, declared to have no value[30] – was the isolation of the Church of Santa Nicola in Carcere[31] and of a medieval building complex at today's Via di Teatro di Marcello 5. The church was radically made over in 1934 and even the "medieval" building is an example of the few restored medieval secular structures in Rome in the interwar period: it presents itself as a free "reconstruction" in the style of the Middle Ages with a new facade on the side facing the street. Both buildings serve above all as a framework for the new boulevard. Antonio Muñoz mentioned that it was also considered demolishing the Church of Santa Nicola in Carcere. According to Muñoz this would certainly have been an "act of unjustified vandalism". Here we can again observe the manner in which the dispute over demolition in the historic centre took place: the arguments regarding the lack of value and importance and regarding unhealthiness which were expressed by the champions of demolition, were opposed by accusations of unjustifiable vandalism. Who took which side varied from case to case, and which

arguments would gain the upper hand was not always a foregone conclusion.[32]

The Via dell'Impero was continued at the Colosseum in a southern direction by a third new boulevard, the Via dei Trionfi, previously, and again today, named Via di San Gregorio.[33] This "Victory Avenue" was given its particular character by the Arch of Constantine through which a "victory procession" could march on appropriate occasions – such as that of Hitler's visit to Rome in 1938. It extended from this Arch to the Circus Maximus and was flanked by a fountain designed by Antonio Muñoz. It was 502 metres long and 35 metres wide.[34] The Via dei Trionfi, which was completed a year after the Via dell'Impero, i.e. on 28 October 1933, the anniversary of the March on Rome, completed the isolation of the ancient zone, the most brutal part of which was the wholesale redevelopment on and around the Capitoline Hill. In 1932/1933 the Piazzale del

29 Cf. Muñoz 1932, p. 42.
30 Cf. Muñoz 1932, p. 37.
31 Touring Club Italiano 2007, pp. 481–482.

32 Muñoz 1932, pp. 42–48. Cf. also Motta 1995, p. 64. An even more radical urban development accessory was formed by the two medieval buildings reconstructed further south (*Casa dei Pierleoni* and *Casa dei Crescenzi*). Cf. pp. 65–66. The Church of Santa Omobono, already designated for demolition, could be saved.
33 Muñoz 1933, pp. 521–547.
34 Cederna 1979, p. 194.

Demolitions for the Via del Mare at the Theatre of Marcellus, 1932.
[Source: Capitolium 1932, p. 523]

"The medieval house" on the destroyed, famous Piazza Montanara – an example of renewal by "restoration" and the radical isolation of a group of medieval buildings on the Via del Mare, 1932.
[Source: Muñoz 1935, p. 85]

Colosseo was made over.[35] In order to facilitate traffic, and despite the protests of archaeologists, two prominent testimonials of antiquity that were located between the Arch of Constantine and the Colosseum were removed: the base of the Nero Colossus and the Meta Sudans, the remains of an ancient fountain.

All these activities changed the meaning of the Via dell'Impero, as they facilitated traffic from this street in the direction of the Caracalla baths and thus towards the sea. The original Via dei Monti had de facto become a new Via del Mare, putting the importance of the other Via del Mare in question.[36]

Via del Mare, in the background the excavated Theatre of Marcellus, mid-1930s.
[Source: Bardet 1937, p. 249]

At the beginning of the 1930s the Piazza Venezia – the "geometrical centre of the city"[37] and its traffic hub – had also become the political centre of Rome, and indeed of the whole of Italy. Its name was changed accordingly – to Foro Italico.[38] As the "heart of Rome", said Mussolini in 1932, it was at the same time the "heart of Italy".[39] Antonio Muñoz spoke of "a new *Umbilicus Urbis Romae*" (lat: navel = centre of the city of Rome).[40] The Piazza thus eclipsed the old political centre that had been created following the unification of Italy, on the Piazza Colonna, which had already been strengthened as a traffic hub by the construction of the Via del Tritone. The urban development activities in the area surrounding the Piazza Venezia – the construction of the new roads, particularly the Via dell'Impero, which also had to absorb the traffic from the Via Cavour, as well as from the Via del Mare – meant that the Piazza Venezia increasingly became a traffic hub of the first order, i.e. a traffic hell.

The central square, formed by means of demolition as a large open space after Rome had been designated the capital of the new Italy, was dominated – if not downright deprived of life – by the monument for Vittorio Emanuele II that was erected in 1885 and inaugurated in 1911.[41] Compared to this huge monument the great *Palazzo Venezia*, the most important building on the square, appears quite unassuming. The palace was radically restored in 1924–1930, was the seat of the Fascist Grand Council (*Gran Consiglio del Fascismo*) from 1929 to 1943 and the seat of the Prime Minister (Mussolini) from 16 September 1929 onward.[42] The Piazza Venezia had thus become the new central point in Rome, the venue for grand celebrations and demonstrations[43], the "national political Forum"[44]. It faced toward the

35 Zammerini 2002, p. 11.
36 Cederna 1979, p. 194.
37 Touring Club Italiano 1938/1947, p. 62.
38 Cf. also Muñoz 1932, p. 8.
39 Quoted in: Muñoz 1932, p. 8.
40 Muñoz 1932, p. 8.

41 The monument for Vittorio Emanuele II was further extended under the Fascist regime – particularly after the interment of the "unknown soldier" in 1921 (to 1925) and in the context of the placement of the Museo del Risorgimento (1924–1935), both according to plans by Armando Brasini. The huge monument was by no means exclusively regarded as positive among experts in the Fascist era. The attempt by several architects to "romanise" the colour of Vittorio Emanuele's monument, which they regarded as un-Roman, was, however, rejected by Mussolini in 1931. Cf. Cederna 1979, p. 83.
42 Insolera/Sette 2003, p. 21.
43 Zocca 1958, p. 652.
44 Ravaglioli 1996, p. 38. Cf. also Beese 2016, pp. 227–234.

Bird's-eye view of the Colosseum, the "most magnificent monument of ancient Rome", and the Forum Romanum with the Via dell'Impero and the Via dei Trionfi, which was inaugurated in 1933, along with the Arch of Constantine (top right), c. 1941. To the left of the Via dell'Impero was the planned location for the Palazzo del Littorio. [Source: Consociazione Turistica Italiana 1941, Fig. 121]

seat of the head of government, the *Sala del Mappamondo* (hall of the world map), in the upper storey of the Palazzo Venezia, or more precisely: to the leader's balcony in front of that hall. Mussolini delivered his major speeches from this balcony, which – and this was one objective of the new boulevard *Via dell'Impero* – allowed an oblique axial view directly to the Colosseum.[45]

Following the intense debates published in the press in 1929–1930 it was, however, not yet quite clear what should be done with the southern part of the square that had been torn up by the demolitions at the foot of the Capitoline Hill. On 22 December 1931 a commission was formed with the *Governatore*, Senator Corrado Ricci and the landscape gardener Raffaele De Vico, which presented Mussolini with a specific design proposal for the planting of trees. Mussolini agreed and the project was implemented. On 28 October 1932, the tenth anniversary of the March on Rome, the tree

exedra on the Piazza Aracoeli was inaugurated, together with the Via dell'Impero.[46] For this event the entire Piazza Venezia was redesigned, resurfaced and received new lighting. The square now had an expanse of 26,000 sq.m. The distance between the two exedras formed by trees was 207 metres, while the diameter of St. Peter's Square between the porticos only had a length of 197 metres. The composition of the area behind the western exedra, the place covered until recently by the famous Piazza Aracoeli, was regarded at this point in time as a problem still to be solved.[47]

The Castel Sant'Angelo – originally the mausoleum of the Emperor Hadrian – symbolised the double reference to antiquity and to papal Rome in one single structure. Its clearing according to plans by Attilio Spaccarelli meant the demolition – begun in 1928 – of "cottages and barracks" and the exhibition of the isolated structure in a "wonderful, magnificent park", that was inaugurated on 21 April 1934. The park presented the excavated fortifications from the era of Pope Pius IV, which had been buried in 1890.[48]

45 Mussolini spoke a total of 64 times from the balcony of the Palazzo Venezia, including the declaration of war against Ethiopia (2 October 1935), the proclamation of the new empire (9 May 1936) and the declaration of war against France and England (10 June 1940). Cf. Vidotto 2008, p. 163. The Italy of today finds it difficult, however, to find an adequate response to this historical testimony.

46 Cf. Cederna 1979, pp. 142–144.
47 Muñoz 1932, p. 10.
48 Zocca 1958, p. 673.

Composition of a tree exedra, 1932. [Source: Muñoz 1935, p. 180]

The excavated Castel Sant'Angelo. [Source: Italienische Städtebaukunst im faschistischen Regime 1937]

The monumentalisation of the central western bank of the Tiber was not completed with this, however. Between the Castel Sant'Angelo, surrounded by trees, and the gargantuan Ministry of Justice, built according to plans by Guglielmo Calderini in 1899–1911, a large-scale construction for the regime was built according to plans by Marcello Piacentini in 1925–1938 in two stages: the *Casa Madre dei Mutilati e Invalidi di Guerra*.

The most important new building under the Fascist regime was to be constructed on the Via dell'Impero, "the most beautiful of the new streets in Rome"[49], according to the newspaper "*Il Giornale d'Italia*" on 2 December 1932: the *Palazzo del Littorio e della Mostra della Rivoluzione Fascista*, seat of the central directorate and other organs of the Fascist party and museum of the Fascist revolution. A competition for the designing of this large building was advertised on 27 December 1933 not by a Ministry or by the city administration but by the national Fascist party.[50] As was to be expected, many important architects took part. The competition was, however, limited to Italian architects with party cards; foreign architects were excluded. The competition was a highlight in the search for architectural design appropriate to the Fascist era and continues to be regarded today as the focal point of the architectural debates in the Fascist epoch.[51]

The invitation to tender[52] explicitly required the urban planning subordination of the building to the dominant axis of the new Via dell'Impero by excluding the impairment of the view of the Colosseum from the Piazza Venezia. It also required the subordination of the new building to the remains of the Maxentius Basilica by excluding its exceeding the height of the latter (apart from well-founded exceptions for sub-sections). Finally, it was pointed out that the surroundings from antiquity should be paid as much attention

in the search for the architectural form as the representation of the greatness and strength of Fascism, which in turn was placed in the tradition of ancient Rome. In a nutshell, the new building should convey to posterity the message of the Mussolini epoch in a permanent and universal form.

The location was programmatical: the old and the new Rome were to merge on the Via dell'Impero – as a desired symbol of the fact that the Fascist regime embodied and renewed the heritage and the greatness of ancient Rome. The choice of location also conspicuously emphasised that the debate on the question of the new centre of Rome was ended: the axis of the Via dell'Impero with the seat of government on the Piazza Venezia at one end and the Colosseum at the other was now undisputedly the new Via Triumphalis of Fascism.

The location on the Via dell'Impero thus meant rigorous constraints to the freedom of the architectural design. These concerned not only the height of the new buildings but also, above all, their relationship to the boulevard itself. Its axial importance enforced subordination to the linearity of the boulevard. The greatest constraint was the Colosseum, however. As the most impressive embodiment of the greatness of ancient Rome it could not be outshone – neither literally nor symbolically. This meant that the central building of the Fascist party could not take on the role of an urban development baton, of a beacon that could make a long-range impact on the structure of the urban environment. In this respect – decisive from an urban development point of view – the project of the *Palazzo del Littorio* differed from the also unrealised project of the Soviet Palace in Moscow[53] and the (later) Great Hall in Berlin.

49 Ugo Ojetti in: Consociazione Turistica Italiana 1941, p. 21.
50 Competition entries had to be tendered by 15 April 1934.
51 Cf. Zammerini 2002, p. 5.
52 The announcement is documented in: Il nuovo stile littorio. I progetti per il Palazzo del Littorio e della Mostra della Rivoluzione Fascista in Via dell'Impero. Milan-Rome 1936, pp. XV–XXI.

53 Shortly before the submission date for the competition entries, on 3 March 1933, Marcello Piacentini published an article on the competition regarding the Soviet Palace in Moscow in the journal "*Architettura*". In the first round of that competition with international participation there were more than 450 entries. The proposal by Boris Iofan that was finally chosen was acknowledged by Piacentini to be magnificent and original, but without style – just like the monument for Vittorio Emanuele II in Rome, the altar of the fatherland, by the way, Piacentini continued. Iofan's project, he summarised, could not represent the Soviet Union. Piacentini 1934/1996, pp. 193–199.

Enrico Del Debbio, Arnaldo Foschini and Vittorio Morpurgo: Concept for the Palazzo del Littorio, 1933–1934, View of the model for Project A, one of 14 projects chosen in the first stage. This project was favoured by Mussolini. [Source: Il nuovo stile littorio 1936, p. 13]

The choice of location was thus also a trap that the Fascist leaders had laid for themselves in their exhuberant enthusiasm for the new Via dell'Impero. Not only the vicinity of the Foro Romano with the Maxentius Basilica, the new Via Triumphalis, and the Colosseum had to be taken into account but also the other two streets that bounded on the triangular site: the Via Cavour and the Via del Cardello. In addition, a kind of bridge over the Via Cavour to another site was to be constructed. The most magnificent building of the regime was to be erected in this corset, a regime that saw itself as the successor to imperial Rome and that wished, with this building, to show the world with a roll of the drums how Fascism presented itself architecturally and with regard to urban design.

Of the roughly 100 submitted competition entries 72 projects were accepted. All the participants were obviously tormented by the difficult planning conditions. They showed their reverence for the Via dell'Impero – by the parallel positioning of the construction line, by contortions with bends or curves. And they often paid no attention to the relationship with other streets. The stylistically very varied results of the competition were elaborately presented in 1936. At the beginning of the documentation it was pointed out that this competition was the "most outstanding and important artistic project of the Fascist epoch".[54] The debate on the results of the competition pertained almost exclusively to the architectural form, while the urban development dimension was paid little attention. In the end, however, it was this dimension, i.e. the contradiction between the desired representation of the regime and the location, placing severe boundaries on this representation, that led to the abandonment of the location and thus to the failure of the entire competition.

Reconstruction of the Historic Centre in the late 1930s

In the late 1930s the demolition work in the historic centre was continued. That applies to the area surrounding the archaeological zone to the south of the Piazza Venezia too. A major rupture followed behind the Piazza Navona with the construction of the Corso del Rinascimento. Two large-scale projects attracted particular attention: the construction of a cult site near the excavated Mausoleum of Augustus and the neo-baroque opening up of the Via della Conciliazione

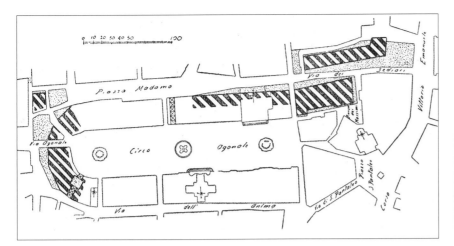

<< *Construction plan for the Corso di Rinascimento, 1935. The shaded areas show the new contours of the street. The planned demolition of the northern front of the Piazza Navona can also be seen. [Source: Architettura. Special issue: Urbanistica della Roma Mussoliniana 1936, p. 64]*

to the east of St. Peter's Basilica. These were the two major zones in the historic centre on which Fascist urban development concentrated in the second half of the 1930s. "The Mausoleum, the Castel Sant'Angelo and St. Peter's Basilica form [...] a homogeneous counterpart to the ancient Rome of the Caesar's Forums – a counterpart that visualises in a truly splendid way the three decisive epochs of Roman architectural history: the Empire, the Middle Ages and the papacy."[55] The two zones emphasised a particularity of Fascist urban development: at its core it confined itself de facto to the emphasising of ancient and – within limits – papal structures, while its own, new architecture at most served – as in the case of the construction of a square around the Mausoleum of Augustus – to provide a framework for the ancient ruins, or – as in the case of the Via della Conciliazione – to pay homage to the St. Peter's Basilica.

Whoever wished to drive south from the Palace of Justice, the most massive manifestation of the new Italy before the First World War near to the Vatikan, could cross the Tiber via the *Ponte Umberto I* and then continue driving on the broad Via Zanardelli that was built before the First World War. But soon he would be abruptly halted: the road ended to the north of the Piazza Navona and there was still no connection to the Corso Vittorio Emanuele. One possibility was the use of the Piazza Navona for through traffic. In the late 1930s a different measure was implemented: a bypass around the Piazza Navona on the eastern side, the Corso del Rinascimento, the breakthrough to which was already contained in the Master Plan of 1931. The name of the new street was based on the quarter that it was to define: the Renaissance quarter.[56]

The construction of the new street, which was completed in 1938 according to plans by Arnaldo Foschini from 1935, required the demolition of numerous buildings and the obliteration of small lanes and squares, in particular the

Piazza Madama. The demolition work began on 21 April 1936. Numerous complicated operations were also necessary such as the moving backwards or the adjustment, with little caution, of historic palaces, the erection of new buildings and the reorganisation of Church and Convent S. Giacomo degli Spagnoli/Nostra Signora del Sacro Cuore. The fact that the northern curve of the Piazza Navona was completely abandoned – due to "static" problems[57] – and replaced by residential and commercial buildings of the *Istituto Nazionale Assicurazioni* (INA) according to plans by Arnaldo Foschini,[58] is hardly noticed today by the many people who visit the famous square. This is due, above all, to the design of the new buildings: only the fronts facing the Via Zanardelli were constructed in the style of the late 1930s, while in contrast the facades facing the Piazza were reconstructed in traditional form, subordinated to the overall appearance of the Piazza Navona. Below the new buildings the remains of the Roman stadium from the Domitian period have been uncovered, the characteristic form of which characterises the Piazza Navona until the present day.

The new street was not originally intended to end at the Corso Vittorio Emanuele but to continue south to the *Ponte Sisto*. The planning of this extension was connected with deliberations concerning the excavation of the huge Roman *Teatro di Pompeo*, which was hidden behind and below the historic buildings on the western side of the Campo dei Fiori – a measure that would have resulted in the demolition of highly valuable historic structures and the obliteration of important historic streets and squares. The controversies regarding this new street led de facto to the abandonment of the project.

The person of Augustus was of central importance in the Fascist construction of the myth of ancient Rome. The reference to Roman antiquity had long been instrumentalised by the Fascist movement to legitimise its claim to power.

Demolition of the northern front of the Piazza Navona, 1937. [Source: Insolera/Sette 2003, p. 117]

55 Buchheit 1938, p. 237.
56 The Corso del Rinascimento 1936, p. 57.

57 Zocca 1958, p. 671.
58 Remiddi/Greco (eds.) 2003, p. 91.

"The Augusteum, smothered by modern constructions".
[Source: Muñoz 1935, p. 476]

Project for the excavation of the Mausoleum of Augustus, 1935. Dotted: demolitions, shaded: demolition and new construction.
[Source: Muñoz 1935, p. 111]

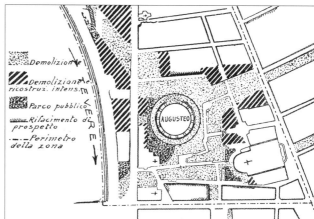

With its territorial expansion and the proclamation of the Fascist empire the regime identified itself increasingly with the heyday of the *Imperium Romanum*, with Mussolini staging himself as the legitimate heir to the Roman Emperor Augustus. The 2000th anniversary of the latter's birthday played a key role in this propaganda: the event was celebrated for a whole year, from September 1937 to September 1938. Against this background it was virtually mandatory to stage the celebrations in an appropriate location – by excavating the Mausoleum of Augustus.[59] In the jubilee year, in addition, there was a conference on the subject of Augustus (start: 23 September 1938), an "Augustian exhibition" (*Mostra Augustea della Romanità*) in the exhibition palace in the Via Nazionale (from 23 August 1937 to 6 November 1938)[60] and the inauguration of the reconstructed Ara Pacis in close proximity to the Mausoleum of Augustus.[61] All these activities were intended to establish a historical connection between Augustus and Mussolini as well as between the Roman and the Fascist Empires. The Mausoleum itself had been largely destroyed in the course of the centuries, the venue had been used as a concert hall since 1908 and had become "the heart of the city's musical existence"[62]. The last performance took place on 13 May 1936.[63]

"An entire city quarter between the Tiber and the Corso Umberto I had to be cleared in order for the Mausoleum of Augustus, the celebrated symbol of the Empire, to be resurrected to its old glory on the occasion of the 2000th birthday of the Emperor."[64] The ruin, which had been "freed" by 1937, was moved to the centre of a new square – the Piazza Augusto Imperatore – that was bounded on three sides by

a closed row of houses with high arcades. The general plan was drawn up by Vittorio Balio Morpurgo and Antonio Muñoz.[65] Originally Morpurgo envisaged the enclosing of the square on the Tiber side, too. The new residential and commercial buildings were constructed by the national Fascist social insurance institute (*Istituto Nazionale Fascista per la Previdenza Sociale*) and the College of the Illyrians (*Collegio degli Illirici*, later of the Croatians) in 1941.[66] The new, wide square with its austere architecture marked by colonnades stood in stark contrast to the surrounding historic buildings. Here, too, the new buildings simply presented themselves as the theatrical backdrop for something much more important – the Mausoleum of the most important ruler of Roman antiquity.

The reference to Augustus was enhanced yet again by another ancient monument, the *Ara Pacis Augustae*. The altar, with a pictorial representation of the *Pax Augustae* following the victories in Spain and Gaul in the year 13 BC, originally stood in the Field of Mars further south of the Mausoleum in today's Via in Lucina. In 1937 further artefacts were salvaged with the aid of a tunnel excavation and the fragments of the reliefs that had been scattered over various collections were restituted either in the original or as castings. After the early concepts for an exhibition on the Capitoline Hill had been rejected, the reconstruction on the western side of the Piazza Augusto Imperatore next to the Tiber was decided upon on 9 February 1937. Morpurgo modified his draft plan and opened up the square to the Tiber in order to place the altar there in a glass pavilion on a rectangular pedestal. On the long side facing the Via Ripetta the *Res gestae Divi Augusti*, the deeds of the divine Augustus, were mounted in line with the surviving text in the Augustus temple in Ankara.[67] The reconstruction according to Morpurgo's plans, the design of which was the subject of dispute[68], was effected rapidly,

59 Cf. on this Brock 1995.
60 On the Augustus exhibition cf. Scriba 1995. The idea for an exhibition came from the archaeologist Giuglio Quirino Giglioli, at that time the director of the "*Museo dell'Impero*". As a member of the Italian parliament Giglioli voted against the race laws in 1938. Major exhibits from the exhibition were utilised for a longer period. They found a new home in the exhibition area E 42 of the *Museo della Civiltà Romana*, opened in 1952, where they can still be seen today. The exhibition was visited by Hitler, Heinrich Himmler and Joseph Goebbels. Quatember 2009.
61 Cederna 1979, p. 209.
62 Brock 1995, p. 133.
63 Brock 1995, p. 129.
64 Buchheit 1938, p. 236.

65 Insolera 1976, p. 130; Cambedda/Tolomeo Speranza 1995, p. 93.
66 Brock 1995, p. 130; Cambedda/Tolomeo Speranza 1995, p. 94.
67 Brock 1995, p. 143.
68 Ugo Ojetti did not like the relatively simple design of the shell structure, which he vilified as a "box". Cf. Cederna 1979, p. 215.

*The excavated Mausoleum of Augustus and the new surrounding square.
[Source: Zocca 1958, plate CLXIV, 1]*

in only 100 days, so that the altar could be inaugurated on 23 September 1938, the final day of the Two Thousand Year celebrations.[69]

As a whole, however, the result of the redevelopment of the area was rather disappointing for the regime: the sparse remains of the Mausoleum were suited only to a very limited degree for an exuberant Augustus cult. All the proposals for its use, including that of a gallery for contemporary art, or ideas such as its crowning with a *torre littoria*, were rejected. On the contrary, Mussolini considered using the gutted cylinder for "assemblies and ceremonies [...] which would attain a great solemnity through the Latin sanctity of the place".[70] With the redesigning of its surroundings and its preparation as an "authentic ruin" the Mausoleum, that had been used continually for centuries, was decommissioned, so to speak. The loss of its continual use turned it into a dead place.

The most important project in the historic centre was the Via della Conciliazione[71], which was to connect the Castel Sant'Angelo with the St. Peter's Basilica – something that had been considered repeatedly since the 17th century[72] but was not included in the Master Plan of 1931. This project was not only an attempt to create a triumphal entry-point to Bernini's St. Peter's Square – symbol of the Holy City of Rome, of the world centre of Catholic Christendom – but also served to celebrate the alliance between Fascism and the Church. It was intended "as a proof of the spirit of universality of this Roman and Catholic Rome, towards which the whole world looks".[73] It was given its name in association with the Lateran Accords, which had been negotiated from 1926 onward and signed on 11 February 1929. "For the State the Lateran Pact is the Ara Pacis of the resurrected empire with the Duce as the new Augustus; for

the Church the Accords represent the modern equivalent of the Edict of Milan (313), with which the persecution of Christians by the State was abolished and the legitimacy of the Christian religion recognised; in this sense Mussolini is a new Constantine the Great for the Church."[74]

In February 1935 *Governatore* Giuseppe Bottai, at the command of Mussolini, awarded a contract to Marcello Piacentini and Attilio Spaccarelli for the "rearrangement of the Borghi", as the quarter to the east of the Vatican was called.[75] The finished project was presented to Mussolini on 20 June 1936 and to the Pope on 28 June 1936, and both approved it. On 28 October 1936, the anniversary of the March on Rome, the demolition work for the new boulevard began – following the necessary expropriations and despite considerable protest, by Gustavo Giovannoni, among others, but with the approval of the Vatican. Once again buildings were described as being of inferior quality, as unhealthy, unworthy huts, the conservation of which was unthinkable. A total of 729 homes were demolished and 4,992 persons displaced, i.e. one third of the residents of the quarter to the east of St. Peter's Square.[76] On 16 September 1937 the name of the street was decided: Via della Conciliazione, Street of Conciliation – an allusion to the Lateran Accords, and on 8 October 1937 the demolition work was completed. The construction of new buildings, including the reconstruction of the altered location, was, however, not completed until after the war, in the Church's Holy Year of 1950.[77]

The New Rome – an Assessment

The reason for the urban renewal of the great historic centre of Rome was primarily a new antiquity cult. Excavation, the "liberation of ancient Rome"[78] became the guideline for Mussolini's development of the historic centre of Rome. The "buildings from the early years of the empire" were of particular interest and their link "with the new Fascist empire".[79] The main focus was the cult of Augustus, with Mussolini presented as his successor.[80] In this context, archaeology rose to become a dominant profession in urban planning. Urban development oriented towards demolition can therefore be denoted as "archaeological urban development".[81] "Archaeology claimed for itself that it had become urban development, and that urban development had become excavation; the archaeologists became

69 Cederna 1979, pp. 213–214.
70 Antonio Muñoz (1938) quoted in: Brock 1995, p. 137.
71 Cf. also Beese 2016, pp. 270–289.
72 On this cf. The rearrangement of the "Borghi" for the access to St. Peter's 1936, pp. 26–27.
73 The rearrangement of the "Borghi" for the access to St. Peter's 1936, p. 27.

74 Brock 1995, p. 143.
75 The rearrangement of the "Borghi" for the access to St. Peter's 1936, p. 26.
76 Cederna 1979, p. 240.
77 Cialoni 2006, p. 57; Zocca 1958, p. 674.
78 Mussolini according to Ugo Ojetti in: Consociazione Turistica Italiana 1941, p. 20.
79 Italienische Städtebaukunst im faschistischen Regime 1937, p. 27.
80 Cf. for example Ugo Ojetti in: Consociazione Turistica Italiana 1941, p. 19.
81 Antonio Cederna described the activity of Antonio Muñoz as *urbanistica archeologica*, archaeological urban development. Cederna 1979, p. 132.

The surroundings
of St. Peter's Square
before the construc-
tion of the Via della
Conciliazione.
[Source: Architettura.
Special issue:
Urbanistica della
Roma Mussoliniana
1936, p. 35]

Marcello Piacentini
and Attilio Spaccarelli:
Model of the approved
project.
[Source: Architettura.
Special issue:
Urbanistica della
Roma Mussoliniana
1936, p. 48]

St. Peter's Square
with the Via della
Conciliazione,
c. 1943.
[Source: Schüller
1943, p. 31]

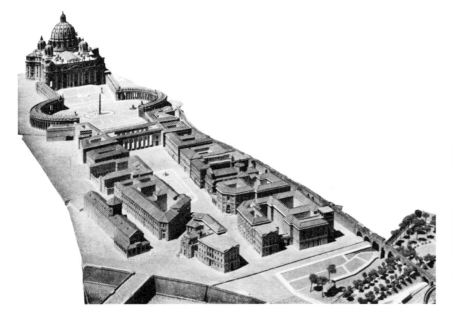

Demolitions next to the monument for Vittorio Emanuele II (Altar of the fatherland): on the left an aerial photograph c. 1900, on the right the same picture with the torn down areas shaded gray.
[Source: Insolera/Sette 2003, p. 54]

inadequate urban planners and the urban planners became inadequate archaeologists."[82] In this climate the central figures of urban development were archaeologists such as Corrado Ricci, Antonio Muñoz and Italo Gismondi.[83]

In the course of the demolitions, above all the little appreciated testimonials of medieval Rome disappeared because the archaeological time horizon ended in 476, the year of the end of the rule of the Western Roman Emperor Romulus Augustus.[84] It was a characteristic of archaeological urban development that it began without a clear objective and without a plan: the demolition work was started although it was unclear how the excavated area was later to be laid out. "It was possible to do anything in the name of archaeology and archaeology quickly served as an excuse and a pretext."[85] There was an evident lack of interest in the scientific documentation of that which had been demolished. A further characteristic was the often extremely liberal handling of historical testimonials. If necessary, churches, palaces and other monuments were moved, relocated or even extensively rebuilt or extended, i.e. "improved".

In addition to ancient Rome homage was also rendered to sacred Rome, the great Rome of the Renaissance and baroque popes. In point of fact the work of these popes served in many ways as a model for Mussolini: the popes cleared medieval buildings away without concern if the urban staging of their construction activities was at stake. They laid new streets through the ancient city, created new squares and improved the utility infrastructure. At the same time they used the ancient remains for their own purposes. Above all, however, they concentrated their efforts on one

large-scale construction that was intended to uphold their claim to the leadership of worldwide Christendom in the era of the Counter-Reformation: St. Peter's Basilica in Rome, the enormous square in front of which demonstrated the theme of the elevation of the individual in a larger religious community symbolised by the arcades of Gianlorenzo Bernini. The city of the 19th century, in contrast, was held in little esteem: "capitalist mass society neither appreciated genuine urban planning nor did it understand antiquity's right of existence. Rome appeared to be becoming a provincial town."[86]

Three areas are representative of the new Fascist centre in a particular way: first and foremost the area from the Piazza Venezia to the Colosseum, the new political and propagandistic centre of the city, then the area between the Castel Sant'Angelo and St. Peter's Basilica, the testimony to the accords between the Fascist regime and the Vatican, and finally the area surrounding the Mausoleum of Augustus, the great importance of which for the regime's cult of Augustus is not reflected in the planning concept, however. Historic districts were torn down not only for these three large-scale projects but also for other excavations and new streets. In particular, one of the largest wholesale urban renewal projects in European urban development was implemented next to the Capitoline Hill.[87] Archaeological importance, the facilitation of traffic and better sanitary conditions were repeatedly named as the reasons for the policy of demolition in the historic centre, as was the creation of new representative spaces. The fact that all these urban development projects, in the final analysis, were of considerable economic importance, must not be forgotten in a city such as Rome with no economic basis of its own.

82 Cederna 1979, p. 71.
83 Cf. Insolera 1976, p. 131.
84 Insolera 1976, p. 132.
85 Insolera 1976, p. 133.

86 Buchheit 1938, p. 233.
87 Cf. The summary in Insolera/Sette 2003, pp. 51–55.

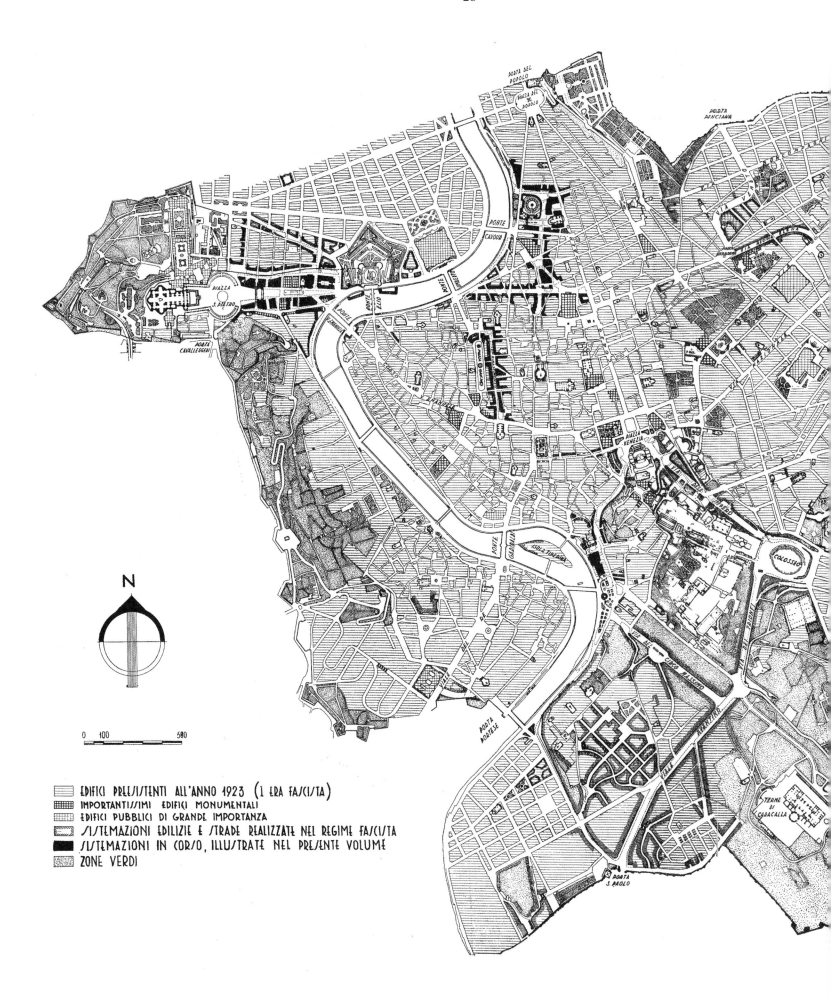

N

0 100 500

EDIFICI PRESISTENTI ALL'ANNO 1923 (I ERA FASCISTA)
IMPORTANTISSIMI EDIFICI MONUMENTALI
EDIFICI PUBBLICI DI GRANDE IMPORTANZA
SISTEMAZIONI EDILIZIE E STRADE REALIZZATE NEL REGIME FASCISTA
SISTEMAZIONI IN CORSO, ILLUSTRATE NEL PRESENTE VOLUME
ZONE VERDI

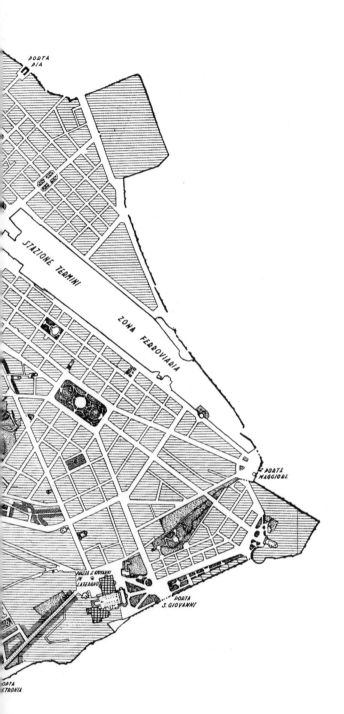

The centre of Rome: the dashed grey stripes show the projects implemented in the Fascist period, the black lines and areas show the planned projects, as of 1936.
[Source: Architettura. Special issue: Urbanistica della Roma Mussoliniana 1936, Table IV]

The urban renewal of the historic centre was anything but consensual practice, however. This was particularly true of the policy of demolition. Virtually every single demolition had its opponents – in the form of specific persons, but also in the form of institutions. A major role was played by the press, which attacked some projects and endorsed others.[88] In support of the waves of demolition the dangers of a dead city, fit for a museum, bogged down in the world of yesterday were invoked and the houses concerned systematically discredited as unhealthy, disgraceful, revolting, derelict, miserable, shabby huts, cottages, shacks with no artistic or historical value whatsoever, while the opponents of the measures emphasised precisely these values. In such an atmosphere certain words gained a particular, positive meaning: "isolation" (*isolamento*) and "liberation" (*liberazione*) of the great monuments from their "unworthy" extensions – often from the Middle Ages, but also from the Renaissance period, and "pickaxe" (*piccone*), as the sign of a demolition policy allegedly oriented towards the future (*sventramenti*). There often existed a programmatic alternative, a milder form of demolition that was advocated in this period with little success by Gustavo Giovannoni, one of the most influential experts on urban development. Giovannoni propagated particularly for the Renaissance quarter a policy of cautious thinning out, of *diradamento*. The demolitions remained controversial up until the final phase of the Fascist regime, even in public. This is demonstrated, for example, by an article in the journal "*Oggi*" of 21 June 1941, in which the carnage among the historical remains in the name of traffic and hygiene is explicitly condemned.[89]

88   Cf. also Zocca 1958, p. 652.
89   Cederna 1979, p. XIV. Positions such as this, fundamentally condemning the policy of demolition, were rare, however.

Brescia: a New Square from One Mould

Brescia, the second most important and richest city in Lombardy after Milan, has an eminent history and its Roman origins can still be experienced today. In the Middle Ages at first a free commune, the city lost its independence in the 14th century and finally became part of the area ruled by Venice in the 15th century. The two stratifications from the Roman and the medieval periods characterised the historic centre of Brescia until in the Fascist epoch a completely new space in the historic centre was broken open: the Piazza della Vittoria, which has remained controversial until the present day.

The reconstruction of the historic centre of Brescia, which began relatively early at the end of the 1920s,[90] was a model project of national importance for the reconstruction of historic centres. It required the demolition, in the heart of the historic centre, of a densely built and – as was always claimed[91] – "unhealthy" and "miserable" area of about 20 closely built blocs of the previous quarters Serraglio (animal market), Granarolo (grain market) and Pescheria (fish market).[92] The most important objective of the re-development was the implantation of a new square, the Piazza della Vittoria (Victory Square) that was laid out in 1929–1932. In an exemplary way an area of mixed use – a city district in which craftsmen and small traders worked and often also lived – was replaced by a modern quarter equipped with offices and service facilities. The director of the wholescale redevelopment was Marcello Piacentini, whose plan was presented in 1928 and approved in 1929. It was based on older plans from the period before Mussolini, which had also aimed at a radical clearing but had never been implemented. Here, too, the dictatorship demonstrated its "efficiency": where previously there had been long debates, plans could now be executed without lengthy vacillation.

The Piazza della Vittoria extended the central system of historic squares in the ancient city of Brescia, in which a new square was fitted in between the existing squares – Piazza del Duomo in the east, Piazza della Loggia in the north and Piazza del Mercato in the southwest. The new square was connected to the old squares by passageways or streets. The new square was to be accessed by three wider streets – the breakthrough of the Corso Garibaldi in the west, the breakthrough of the Via Tosio in the east and the extension of the Via S. Faustino in the north. To the northwest of the Piazza della Loggia Piacentini planned a further large-scale new building complex. The Piazza della Vittoria including its planned access streets and the new building complex to the west of the Via S. Faustino gave no consideration whatsoever to the historical layout of the city, liquidating the central section of the famous Via Alessandro Volta together with several side alleys and calling for new houses and facades along the new streets and squares. Furthermore, the new buildings, especially on the Victory Square itself, were not modest in any way but – at least in relation to the older buildings – quite extensive, even though they were subordinated to the largest buildings, especially the Cathedral. The breakthroughs and extensions for the accessibility of the square were not realised, however.

The "monumental"[93] Piazza della Vittoria provided a stage for the presentation of state and economic institutions. Thus, on the southern side the new building of the *Banca Commerciale Italiana* was constructed (1930–1932) with two storeys for the bank and three residential storeys. This was followed on the western side by the insurance palace of the *Assicurazioni Generali di Venezia e Trieste* (1930–1931). The 60 metre high tower of the *Istituto Nazionale delle Assicurazioni* (1930–1932), also an insurance building but with a restaurant on the upper floors, known as the *grattacielo* (= skyscraper), the first high building of this type in Italy, dominated the western side of the square. Additional new buildings were constructed on the eastern side for the insurance society *Riunione Adriatica di Sicurtà* (1930–1931) and for the *Cassa Nazionale delle Assicurazioni Sociali* (1930–1932). Joined to the latter building was the 37 metre high "tower of the revolution" (*torre della rivoluzione*) with a horseman relief of Mussolini and a large flight of steps that dominated the eastern side of the square. On the north side the square was completed by the mighty Post Palace with a large flight of steps (1930–1931). Several of the new buildings had arcades with cafes on the ground floor. All of the new buildings were designed by Marcello Piacentini. On the western side of the square rose the "statue and fountain of the Fascist era". The giant statue representing Fascism,[94] which was made of Carrara marble, was seven metres high. It was removed after WWII.

Whereas the Piazza della Vittoria and the large-scale project to the west of the Via S. Faustino meant a hard, destructive encroachment into the traditional historic centre, the rest of the planned interventions remained relatively modest and complied more with the principles of cautious thinning out. Marcello Piacentini's plan for urban renewal thus reflected both of the rival strategies for dealing with historic

---

90 Cf. for example Wilhelms 1928, pp. 211–213; on Brescia cf. also Maifrini 1988, Beese 2016, pp. 433–452 and Nicoloso 2020.
91 Cf. for example Foffa c. 1932, p. 5.
92 Sica 1978, p. 474.

93 According to a contemporary characterisation. Cf. Touring Club Italiano 1937, p. 130.
94 Italienische Städtebaukunst im faschistischen Regime 1937, p. 23.

Brescia: Aerial photograph of the Piazza della Vittoria, 1936. [Source: Italienische Städtebaukunst im faschistischen Regime 1937]

centres in the Mussolini period. It also demonstrated the order of importance of the two strategies, however: the new square pushed itself into the foreground. The Piazza della Vittoria was an expression of the changed economic, social and political conditions under the Fascist regime. Although it ruthlessly obliterated the historical layout in the central area, the foreign body was at least – again in comparison to other new squares in historicl centres in the Fascist era – adjusted in its proportions to fit the historic centre and integrated into it. The new square, finally, offered a magnificent arena for the new middle classes that profited from the regime and who found workplaces, cafes and restaurants, and in individual cases even housing, there.

After decades of firm rejection today the square once again enjoys popularity. The Piazza della Vittoria "in Brescia (1928–32) not only produced an architecturally defined space by using deliberately urban types and elements from Italian Renaissance cities, but also displayed a typical mixture of urban functions. Post offices, banks, other office spaces, shops, cafés, restaurants and some dwellings create a mixed use environment which could have emerged and been used in any kind of society, not just under the Italian Fascist regime."[95]

Marcello Piacentini: Master plan for the centre of Brescia, 1929. Violet: historic buildings of national importance, grey: existing buildings, yellow: demolition zone, pink: development areas, green: green zones. In the centre the future Piazza della Vittoria is visible. [Quelle: Rete Archivi Piani urbanistici (RAPu), www.rapu.it]

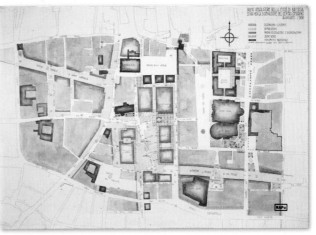

Marcello Piacentini: Partial plan for the centre area of the centre with the new Piazza della Vittoria, 1929. Blue: Historic buildings of national importance, yellow: demolition zones, red: new buildings. [Source: Rete Archivi Piani urbanistici (RAPu), www.rapu.it]

95   Sonne 2005, p. 58.

Bologna: Contradictory Concepts

The university city of Bologna, as the second city of the Papal States with Roman origin, always tended to stand in the shadow of the large Italian cities such as Rome, Milan, Genoa and Naples that were of importance far beyond Italy. Originally a centre of the socialist movement, following the First World War the city became a stronghold of emerging Fascism. After Mussolini's accession to power, however, spectacular building activity at first failed to materialise. Bologna's profile in Fascist propaganda was limited to its railway connections.[96] But it soon became apparent that a great deal was being invested in Bologna too. Large-scale restructuring projects were implemented in the historic centre – above all the construction of a neo-Gothic district and the "systematisation" of the Via Roma.

In the years 1925–1928/32 a spectacular redevelopment project was conducted in the historic centre that was later forgotten: the construction of the neo-Gothic quarter to the east of the main square between the Toschi, Foscherari, Marchesana and Piave streets.[97] At the instigation of the *Podestà,* the mayor[98], the building society SARE (*Società Anonima per il Rinnovamento Edilizio*) was involved in this project. The design was commissioned from the architect Giulio Ulisse Arata, who referred programmatically to the medieval roots of Italian architecture. The aim was the preservative restoration of some of the historic buildings and the replacement of other historic buildings by neo-Gothic new buildings using traditional materials such as stone, brick, terracotta and wood. The renovated district was to have the characteristic atmosphere of a medieval quarter. It included passageways and small squares which had not existed in that form before.[99] In this respect the project represented an idiosyncratic variant of *diradamento*.[100] The result of this great "falsification" was a regionalist urban development – a *Goticità bolognese*, that was conducive to pedestrians and did not fail in its atmospheric effect.[101]

The most extensive urban renewal project for the historic centre in Bologna, however, was the design of the Via Roma (today: Via Marconi), which was also provided for in the *Variante* of the Master Plan of 1929. The task here was "with one incision through the old slum areas, which were exceptionally characteristic, however, and in a certain sense important for the urban landscape, to create space for the

Via Roma [...]."[102] A national competition for this task was announced by the *Podestà* in November 1936 and was decided in March 1937. The subject-matter was primarily the entry of the Via Roma into the Piazza Malpighi including the adjoining zones, an area that was to be redeveloped for health, traffic and economic reasons and turned into a monumental traffic hub.[103] This had been preceded since 1925 by measures to broaden the Via Ugo Bassi.[104]

A total of 19 projects were submitted to the competition, the theme of which was "Felsina 1937". The jury, in which Marcello Piacentini also participated, awarded three equal prizes. The group of Aldo Pini/Alfio Susini/Annibale Vitellozzi/Galliano Rabbi designed a square-like, extended, gigantic T-shaped intersection for the area cleared by large-scale demolition, which was emphasised on the narrow western side by a sombre tower between Via S. Felice and Via del Pratello.[105] The square, that had been torn open for traffic, was to be flanked by buildings, which – like the square itself – lacked any relationship whatsoever to the architecture and the urbanism of the historic centre. The second project awarded a prize, that of the architect Arnaldo degli Innocenti, provided for a tower on the northern side of the square-like extended Via S. Felice. The third prize-winning group (Nino Bertocchi/Piero Bottoni/G. Luigi Giordani/Alberto Legnani/Mario Pucci/Giorgio Ramponi) proposed a row of three 60 metre high residential buildings with green areas on the eastern side of the Via Roma. All of the prize-winning projects embodied insular solutions that either ignored the historic centre or aggressively devalued it and none of them even offered a perspective for the traffic problems.

Following the insular competition regarding the Via Roma, the results of which were not implemented, the city administration decided on 7 January 1938 to announce a competition for a master plan.[106] The major tasks named were the improvement of traffic flow and the redevelopment of the old quarters with bad living conditions. The jury, which included such illustrious experts as Cesare Chiodi, Armando Melis de Villa, Paolo Rossi de Paoli, Marcello Piacentini and Giuseppe Vaccaro, awarded five prizes to the nine competition groups in the summer of 1939. The first prize was awarded to the architect group Arnaldo Massimo degli Innocenti, Domenico Filippone, Goffredo Riccardi, Carlo Vannoni, Mario Zocca under the direction of Plinio Marconi. It proposed numerous demolitions in the historic centre.[107]

96 Italienische Städtebaukunst im faschistischen Regime 1937, p. 35.
97 Penzo 2009, pp. 155–160; Pozzi/Pretelli/Signorelli 2019, pp.173–179.
98 With the legal decree of 3 September 1926, so-called *Podesta,* who were named by the Minister of the Interior, were introduced in all Italian communes as new organs of power. The word *Podestà* is reminiscent of the term for mayors in the Middle Ages. For Rome a special institution had already been created on 1 January 1926 – the *Governatorato*.
99 Mangone 1993, pp. 168–169.
100 Penzo 2009, p. 157.
101 Gresleri 2004, p. 187.

102 Italienische Städtebaukunst im faschistischen Regime 1937, p. 11.
103 Grisanti/Pracchi 1982, p. 73.
104 Gresleri 2004, p. 185.
105 Sica 1978, pp. 457–458.
106 On the history of this planning cf. Note di sintesi per la storia della pianificazione a Bologna, undated.
107 Sica 1978, p. 460.

Bologna was not an outstanding centre of urban development in Fascist Italy. Neither was any particular attention paid to its historical inheritance as an important medieval town nor was the city assigned a new, promising role. In Bologna, however, in the course of time the discontinuities in urban development that were also conspicuous elsewhere could be clearly seen. The different perspectives showed themselves in full force in the two central reconstruction projects in the heart of the historic centre. In the second half of the 1920s the project of a neo-Gothic quarter aspired to strengthen the local environment without taking motor vehicle traffic into consideration, while the project of a new traffic hub on the Via Roma completely negated local traditions and aimed for a car-friendly city. Whereas the project for the new Via Roma was consistent with the long line of destructive wholesale redevelopment projects that did not create any new qualities in the Italy of the 1930s, the neo-Gothic quarter designed by Giulio Ulisse Arata was certainly an interesting contribution to the European history of the urban renewal of historic centres in the 1920s, which – as could also be observed in Siena and Arezzo[108] – uninhibitedly indulged in the cult of the Middle Ages.

108 Tragbar 2009, pp. 189–210.

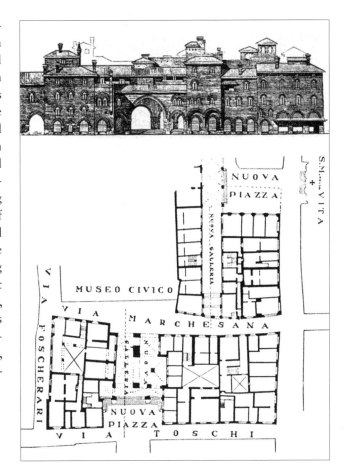

Plan for the facades and layout of the neo-medieval urban renewal project to the east of the main square in Bologna. The facades on the Via Toschi are visible. In the centre is the entrance to a passageway. The layout shows the new squares and passages.
[Source: Bernabei et al. 1984, p. 102]

Views of the neo-medieval quarter to the east of the main square in Bologna. [Source: Mangone 1993, p. 168]

Competition entry of the group Aldo Pini/Alfio Susini/Annibale Vitellozzi/Galliano Rabbi for the systematisation of the Via Roma, 1937. The plan clearly shows the radial clearing and the low spatial quality of the extended T-square. The small dark shape on the crossing of the curved Via del Pratello and the Via S. Felice marks the proposed tower.
[Source: Grisanti/Pracchi 1982, p. 77]

Competition entry of the group Nino Bertocchi/Piero Bottoni/G. Luigi Giordani/Alberto Legnani/Mario Pucci/Giorgio Ramponi for the systematisation of the Via Roma, 1937. The three proposed 60 metre high buildings in a green area are visible.
[Source: Grisanti/Pracchi 1982, p. 80]

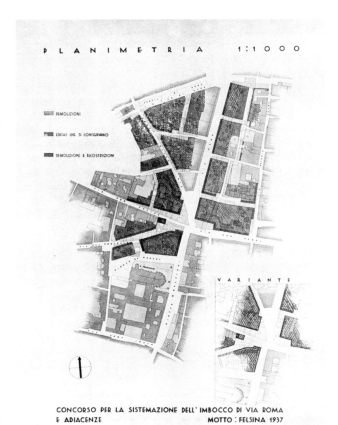

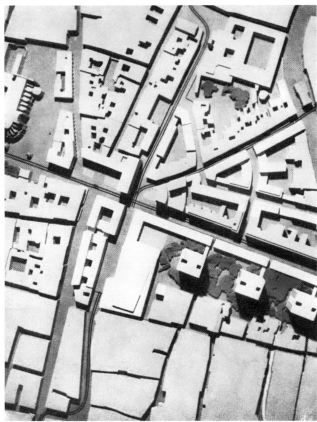

Competition entry of the group Aldo Pini/
Alfio Susini/Annibale Vitellozzi/Galliano Rabbi
for the systematisation of the Via Roma, 1937.
View of the crossing of the Via del Pratello
and the Via S. Felice with tower.
[Source: Grisanti/Pracchi 1982, p. 78]

Naples: Radical Modernisation

Naples played a special role among Italian cities because of its history: the capital of Campania reflected an impressive succession of changing regimes that began with the settlement by Greek colonists known as "Neapolis", then led to its integration into the Roman Empire and was characterised in the following centuries by various dynasties (Normans, Staufer, Anjou, Aragon, Bourbons). When Naples finally became part of the Kingdom of Italy in 1860 its centuries-old privileged role as a capital city and residence of the aristocracy and large landowners ended. The most important city in southern Italy was thus deprived of its political, economic, social and cultural foundations – a tremendous loss, which still remains uncompensated for today.

Around 1900 Naples was still the largest city in Italy, but because of its much lower rate of growth was rapidly overtaken by Milan and then Rome.[109] After the First World War the historic centre of Naples was infamous for its unhealthy living conditions, an extremely high population density and as a breeding ground for disease and infant mortality.[110] The "Neapolitan question" also represented a considerable challenge to the Fascist regime, to which in the final analysis no satisfactory answer was found in the interwar period.[111] The fact that Naples had indeed drawn the attention of the regime is also demonstrated by the fact that Mussolini visited the city five times.[112] Greater Naples even also served the demonstration of a great past: in 1927 the excavation of Herculaneum was resumed on a large scale.

Compared to other major cities in Italy the planning culture of Naples during the Fascist epoch was underdeveloped. This is ascribed to the aversion of the ruling groups to long-term, binding plans, but also to the 1918 policy of annexation, which postponed the drafting of a master plan for the city as a whole.[113] In this situation, the communal administration at first developed isolated projects within the framework of partial development plans. These included selective alterations in the historic centre.

As in other cities, too, in Naples especially in the 1930s projects for the radical redevelopment of the historic centre were implemented, which displaced many poorer residents and tradespeople, and cleared the stage for new institutions to make spectacular appearances on the urban development scene. The most conspicuous project of this type, "the greatest Fascist deed in urban renewal", was the long-planned

wholesale redevelopment in the densely populated historic quarter San Giuseppe-Carità[114], to which several churches from the 16th century, some of them with cloisters, as well as a theatre and several Renaissance palaces fell victim.[115] The old buildings were forced to give way to a modern offices and services district: based on two competitions in 1928 and 1930, the elegant new building of the Post and Telegraph Office (*Palazzo delle Regie Poste e Telegrafi*) was erected here in 1932–1936, designed by the architects Giuseppe Vaccaro and Gino Franzi. The slightly ascending square in front of the Post Office building was dominated by the latter's convexly curved facade. Its entrance portal, carved into almost the entire height of the facade, glazed and clearly divided by a central pillar, remains impressive today.

Opposite the Post and Telegraph Office the building of the provincial administration – less modern in design – was constructed in 1934–1936 according to plans by Marcello Canino and Ferdinando Chiaramonte, as was an insurance building.[116] Further buildings were added, such as the Revenue Office, built in 1933–1937 according to plans by Marcello Canino, the building of the *Banca Nazionale del Lavoro*, designed by Armando Brasini and constructed in 1933–1938, the House of the War Disabled (*Casa del Mutilato*), built in 1938–1940 according to plans by Camillo Guerra and Marcello Piacentini and the Bank of

114   On the prehistory of the wholesale redevelopment in the district of San Giuseppe-Carità since the beginning of the 20th century cf. Cislaghi 1998, pp. 9–38.
115   Döpp 1968, p. 222.
116   Sica 1978, p. 469.

Naples: the Post and Telegraph Office built according to plans by Giuseppe Vaccaro and Gino Franzi in 1932–1936. [Source: Pica 1936, p. 319]

Marcello Canino and Ferdinando Chiaramonte: Illustration of the building of the provincial administration, constructed 1934–1936. The Post Office building designed by Giuseppe Vaccaro and Gino Franzi can be seen on the right. [Source: Cislaghi 1998, p. 90]

109   Döpp 1968, p. 11.
110   Guidi 1980, pp. 125–131.
111   Sica 1978, p. 465.
112   Nicoloso 2008, p. 6.
113   Sica 1978, pp. 465–466.

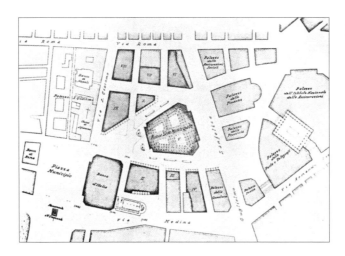

Plan for the further extension of the new offices and services quarter in the district of Carità, 1938. On the right the locations of the dominant Post Office, the massive INA palace, the Revenue Office and the provincial administration are visible, and on the left other projects including the construction of a new municipal building and the Banca d'Italia. [Source: Cislaghi 1998, p. 111]

Naples (*Banco di Napoli*), that was reconstructed according to plans by Marcello Piacentini in 1936–1940.[117]

As a result of all these projects, according to the enthusiastic interim evaluation by supporters of the regime in 1937, the Carità district "has almost completely disappeared and pickaxes are in the process of removing the last remains; and already new monumental buildings are rising up, already the harmonic lines of the new, ultramodern district, the heart of the city, are emerging."[118]

A commission had already been set up in 1933 to take charge of the master plan. Following the completion of its work in August 1936 the plan was examined and endorsed by Gustavo Giovannoni; it was adopted on 21 April 1937 and came into effect on 29 May 1939.[119] The plan was a reflection of the planning culture attained in Fascist Italy at the end of the 1930s and one of the most important master plans of the interwar period.[120] Its explicit and implicit analysis of the status quo was unadorned: the bad living and traffic conditions were denounced, the rough handling of historical inheritance was criticised, as was the extreme lack of green spaces. Inadequate planning and the too great latitude given to private speculators were also pointed out, however. For the historic centre the plan proposed a cautious thinning out of the building density (*diradamento edilizio*), while de facto several radical street breakthroughs and extensions were planned.

Since the unification of Italy Naples was a city with a wonderful past and no recognisable future. This did not change at first in the Fascist era. Only after the proclamation of the new Fascist empire did the "Neapolitan question" appear to have received an answer. Its new role as a bridgehead to the African possessions of Fascist Italy proved, however, to be a blossom with a very short life.

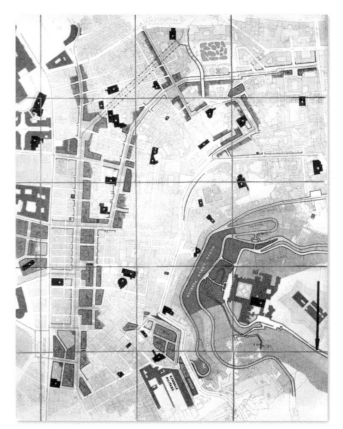

Master plan for Naples, 1939: Detail showing the historic centre. It is completely obvious that here not only "cautious thinning out" is planned, but also several brutal street breakthroughs and extensions (marked in yellow). [Source: De Lucia, Vezio Emilio/Jannello, Antonio: L'urbanistica a Napoli dal dopoguerra ad oggi: note e documenti. In: Urbanistica 65/1975, after p. 8]

117 De Antonellis 1972, pp. 191, 218; Cocchia 1981, p. 30.
118 Italienische Städtebaukunst im faschistischen Regime 1937, p. 25.
119 De Antonellis 1972, p. 187; De Lucia/Jannello 1975, pp. 6–14;
     Sica 1978, p. 470. The plan is documented as a map and as text in
     Urbanistica 65/1975 (after p. 8 and pp. 81–82).
120 Cf. also De Lucia/Jannello 1975, p. 7.

Policy of Urban Renewal

Urban development in Fascist Italy was guided by a whole bunch of objectives, which to a large degree conformed to the international expert debates of the period. One major objective was the redevelopment of "unhealthy" historic centres and their car-friendly conversion to administrative centres. This conversion implied the removal of historic buildings, historic parcels of land and small tradespeople as well as the displacement of poorer residents with the aim of strengthening the tertiary sector, i.e. the administrative functions of the towns or cities. On the other hand, new, more opulent, larger-scale squares and streets were to be created to serve not only representation but also motor vehicle traffic. Free rein was created not only for private transport, however; public transport was also enormously increased. This concept was essentially nothing new but linked to the traditions of European and US American town planning that had enthralled experts around 1910 – in Germany under the heading of *"monumental city"*[121], in the USA under the slogan of *"city beautiful"*.[122] The fact that the construction of such a centre meant the destruction of large parts of the historic centres was not a speciality of Fascist dictatorship but part of an international trend. Especially advocates of urban modernity such as Le Corbusier and Ludwig Hilberseimer saw primarily only shortcomings in the historic centres. In the Soviet Union there was also little appreciation of the older structures, although the traditional ring-radial city structure of the capital, Moscow, was positively commended.

The historic centre redevelopment projects in the Mussolini era were therefore – quite within the context of the international objectives of the experts at the time – very ruthless and not exactly careful. Different variations of wholesale redevelopment can be observed, however: those that created new, utilisable spaces by making a clean sweep – such as the Piazza della Vittoria in Brescia and the new administrative centre in the Neapolitan district of Carità – and those that created desolate, monotonous or traffic-exposed and often over-dimensioned spaces – such as the Piazza Venezia in Rome and the Piazza Malpighi in Bologna.[123] The area to the east of the Piazza Maggiore in Bologna is an instructive example of the neo-medieval remake of a small area – a variation of historic centre redevelopment in the 1920s.

On the other hand it must not be forgotten that in Italy conceptual principles for a more cautious handling of the historic centres were developed by the protagonists of urban development in the interwar period. With reference to the Belgian urban development specialist Charles Buls, Gustavo Giovanonni developed a concept for the relatively cautious urban renewal of historic centres (*diradamento*) before the First World War, which was diametrically opposed to wholesale redevelopment (*sventramento*). Giovannoni continued to pursue this concept throughout the entire Mussolini era. Due to the programmatic and practical influence of Gustavo Giovannoni it was possible very early on in Italy to develop isolated approaches to the preservative redevelopment of historic centres, which have been paid too little attention in the history of European urban development. Giovannoni's defeats in the perpetual dispute over demolition in the historic centres were admittedly much more numerous.

A major objective of the urban renewal of historic centres, particularly but certainly not only in dictatorships, is to provide a reminder of a great past. "Nothing is more indicative for the mentality, for the determination to face the future of a nation than the choices that it makes regarding the epochs of its past: what it presents and honours, what it forgets, what it despises."[124] Margret Boveri praised Mussolini's strategic orientation in 1936 with those words, and in particular his "contempt" for medieval Rome. "Mussolini has clearly shown which epochs of Italian history serve as guides for the Italy of today. [...] And if the Duce lets the high medieval houses between the Tiber and St. Peter's Basilica [...] be torn down today, [...] he is again showing his love of wide spaces. [...]"[125] In contrast, the regime saw itself in the continuity of the Roman Empire, of the papal spiritual world empire and of the "maritime dominion of the imperial cities of Genoa, Pisa and above all Venice".[126] The unparalleled cult of ancient Rome, but also the reference to papal Rome and to the medieval maritime republics, was intended to provide historical legitimacy to the Fascist regime.[127] Just how strongly the dictatorship outside of Rome also related itself to glorious medieval traditions can be seen in the redevelopment of historic centres such as those in Venice or Siena, but also – partially – in Bologna. The possibility of access to many different glorious pasts was a decisive advantage compared to the other dictatorships.

---

121 Cf. Bodenschatz 2009, pp. 28–45.
122 Cf. also Fraticelli 1982, p. 85. Fraticelli emphasises here in particular the relationships between the planning of centres by the young Marcello Piacentini and the US American City Beautiful Movement.
123 On further examples of the urban renewal of historic centres during the fascist dictatorship cf. Enns/Monzo (eds.) 2019.

124 Boveri 1936, p. 165.
125 Boveri 1936, p. 166.
126 Boveri 1936, p. 169.
127 Even the Middle Ages offered a "crystallisation point for national feelings". Tragbar 2009, p. 192. A central role is played here by the cult regarding Dante Alighieri. In this context, above all in the historic centres in the Toscana, projects for the "regaining of the admittedly greatly idealised, medieval townscapes" (p. 190) were implemented – for example in Siena and Arezzo. Cf. Tragbar 2009.

The instrumentalisation of Roman antiquity, above all, led to a particular form of urban development: archaeological urban development. The "liberation" of Roman building remains was intended not only as a reminder of the imperial greatness of ancient Rome, but also to celebrate the Fascist regime as the reincarnation of ancient greatness. In the framework of the growing personality cult of the 1930s and, above all, following the proclamation of the new empire, they were aimed at the staging of Mussolini as the new Augustus. *Romanità* was a defining culture, to which architecture and urban development were increasingly obliged to subordinate themselves. Archaeology was, without doubt, of exceptional importance in this setting. Its influence on town planning was exemplarily embodied in one particular person who was responsible for the redevelopment of Rome, not only from the point of view of archaeology but also from that of urban planning: Antonio Muñoz. On behalf of the Governatorato, the Fascist municipal government of Rome, Muñoz ensured the "liberation" of the Capitoline Hill from "unworthy hovels", and he played a decisive role in the construction of the Via dell'Impero and the Via dei Trionfi. The design of the Mausoleum of Augustus can also be traced to him. Other archaeologists also had a considerable influence on the architectural and urban development discussion, however, including Italo Gismondi.

All the same, it should not be ignored that archaeological work must always be seen in the context of political and social interests. The evocation of Rome in order to legitimise one's own greatness and capital city can also be found elsewhere and in other epochs. "The influencing of archaeological disciplines or at least of individual scientists by historical circumstances is not a phenomenon of Fascist or totalitarian regimes, but part of the complex reality of historical research."[128] Nevertheless, the urban renewal of the centre of Rome in the period of the Fascist regime is an unparalleled climax of archaeological dominance in the history of modern town planning. Without any doubt the "city centre of Rome [...] is characterised today to a great extent by the excavation and construction activities of the Fascist period."[129] It is precisely this dominance of archaeology that allows today's visitors to the eternal city to admire the Roman ruins without realising that these represent the principal result of urban development in the centre of Rome during the Mussolini era.

Whereas the archaeological dimension of urban development is recognised among experts, the social orientation often remains in the dark. Not only in Rome did planning policy aim beyond its grand words at the urbanisation of the middle classes that supported the state,[130] even in the historic centres. At the same time the service orientation of the centres, the formation of a "business city", was strongly encouraged. Thus the regime was able to offer housing and workplaces in an urban environment to the social strata that profited from the dictatorship. The Fascist policy of the urbanisation of social strata that in other countries as a rule sought suburban locations, was accompanied by the forced suburbanisation of impecunious immigrants or poor townspeople, who were often forced to give way to the pickaxe in the centre and seek a new home in the frequently dismal *borgate* (austere outskirts).

128 Quatember 2009, p. 1.
129 Quatember 2009, p. 2.

130 "The middle classes, long the most dynamic segment of society, used the opportunities for advancement that were offered them in 1922 [...]. They were the first supporters of mass consumption and the pioneers of early mass tourism [...]." Woller 2010, p. 113.

References

Architettura. Rivista del Sindacato Nazionale Fascista Architetti (1932–1944)

Bardet, Gaston: La Rome de Mussolini. Paris 1937

Bauer, Franz J.: Rom im 19. und 20. Jahrhundert. Konstruktion eines Mythos. Regensburg 2009

Beese. Christine: Marcello Piacentini. Moderner Städtebau in Italien. Berlin 2016

Bernabei, Giancarlo/Gresleri, Giuliano/Zagnoni, Stefano: Bologna moderna 1860–1980. Bologna 1984

Bianchi, Arturo: La sistemazione di Bocca della Verità e del Velabro. In: Capitolium 1930, pp. 573–591

Bodenschatz, Harald: Städtebau von den neunziger Jahren des 19. Jahrhunderts bis zum Ersten Weltkrieg. In: AIV zu Berlin (ed.): Berlin und seine Bauten. Teil I: Städtebau. Berlin 2009, pp. 13–109

Boveri, Margret: Das Weltgeschehen am Mittelmeer. Ein Buch über Inseln und Küsten, Politik und Strategie, Völker und Imperien. Zürich Leipzig Berlin 1936

Broccoli, Umberto: Preface. In: Via dell'Impero. Nascita di una strada. Exhibition catalogue. Rome 2009, pp. 6–7

Brock, Ingrid: Das faschistische Erbe im Herzen Roms – Das Beispiel Piazza Augusto Imperatore. In: Wissenschaftliche Zeitschrift der Hochschule für Architektur und Bauwesen Weimar 4–5/1995, pp. 129–156

Cambedda, Anna/Tolomeo Speranza, Maria Grazia: La sistemazione di piazza Augusto Imperatore. In: Cardilli (ed.) 1995, pp. 93–97

Capitolium. Rassegna mensile del Governatorato

Cardilli, Luisa (ed.): Gli anni del governatorato (1926–1944). Interventi urbanistici – scoperte archeologiche – arredo urbano – restauri. Rome 1995

Cederna, Antonio: Mussolini urbanista. Lo sventramento di Roma negli anni del consenso. Rome-Bari 1979

Cialoni, Donatella: Roma nel XX secolo. Fotocronaca dal cielo di una città in trasformazione. Rome 2006

Ciancio Rossetto, Paola: Lavori di liberazione e sistemazione del Teatro di Marcello. In: Cardilli (ed.) 1995, pp. 69–76

Cislaghi, Paola: Il Rione Carità. Naples 1998

Cocchia, Carlo: Da un vicolo di Napoli alla Mostra d'Oltremare. In: Lo spazio della città. Trasformazioni urbane a Napoli nell'ultimo secolo. Naples 1981, pp. 25–37

Consociazione Turistica Italiana: Attraverso l'Italia. Illustrazione delle regioni italiane. Volume decimo. Roma. Parte prima. Milan 1941

The Corso del Rinascimento. In: Architettura. Special issue: Urbanistica della Roma Mussoliniana. Natale 1936, pp. 59–61

Costantini, Cesare: Il comune dal 1919 al 1970. In: Roma un secolo (1870–1970). Rome 1970, pp. 103–111

De Antonellis, Giacomo: Napoli sotto il regime. Storia di una città d della sua regione durante il ventennio fascista. Milan 1972

De Lucia, Vezio Emilio/Jannello, Antonio: L'urbanistica a Napoli dal dopoguerra ad oggi: note e documenti. In: Urbanistica 65/1975, pp. 6–79

Döpp, Wolfram: Die Altstadt Neapels. Entwicklung und Struktur. Dissertation an der Universität Marburg 1968

Dogliani, Patrizia: Il fascismo degli italiani. Una storia sociale. Druento 2008

Enns, Carmen M./Monzo, Luigi (eds.): Townscapes in Transition. Transformation and Reorganization of Italian Cities and Their Architecture in the Interwar Period. Bielefeld 2019

Foffa, Oreste: Guida illustrata di Brescia. Brescia c.1932

Fraticelli, Vanna: Roma 1914–1929. La città e gli architetti tra la guerra e il fascismo. Rome 1982

Giovannoni, Gustavo: Attorno al Campidoglio. Per la chiesa di S. Rita da Cascia. In: Capitolium 1929, pp. 593–605

Gresleri, Giuliano: Il Novecento e gli anni trenta. In: Guida di architettura Bologna. Turin et al. 2004, pp. 180–202

Grisanti, Ezio/Pracchi, Attilio: Alfio Susini. L'attività urbanistica nella "stagione dei concorsi" 1928–1940. Milan 1982

Guidi, Laura: Napoli: interventi edilizi e urbanistici tra le due guerre. In: Mioni, Alberto (ed.): Urbanistica fascista. Ricerche e saggi sulle città e il territorio e sulle politiche urbane in Italia tra le due guerre. Milan 1980, pp. 123–150

Insolera, Italo: Roma moderna. Un secolo di storia urbanistica. Turin 1976

Insolera, Italo/Sette, Alessandra Maria: Roma tra le due guerre. Cronache di una città che cambia. Rome 2003

International Federation for Housing and Town Planning. In: International Housing and Town Planning Congress. Vols. I und II. Rome 1929

Italien aus der Vogelschau. Edizione tedesca. Direzione Generale per il Turismo/Ferrovie dello Stato. Milan-Rome 1936

Italienische Städtebaukunst im faschistischen Regime/ Urbanistica italiana in regime fascista. Exhibition catalogue. Rome 1937

Maifrini, Mariarosa: Tecnici e ammistrazione: i piani di Brescia fra le due guerre. In: Ernesti, Giulio (ed.): La costruzione dell'utopia. Architetti e urbanisti nell'Italia fascista. Rome 1988, pp. 303–324

Mangone, Fabio: Giulio Ulisse Arata. Opera Completa. Naples 1993

Messa, Luigi: La demolizione dell'isolato di S. Nicola ai Cesarini e la scoperta dell'Area Sacra Argentina. In: Cardilli (ed.) 1995, pp. 77–84

Motta, Rossella: Conservazione, demolizione, ricostruzione di strutture medioevali lungo la via del Mare tra piazza Montanara e piazza Bocca della Verità. In: Cardilli (ed.) 1995, pp. 61–68

Muñoz, Antonio: I templi della zona Argentina. In: Capitolium 1929, pp. 169–171

Muñoz, Antonio: Via dei Monti e Via del Mare. Second edition. Rome 1932

Muñoz, Antonio: La Via dei Trionfi e l'isolamento del Campidoglio. In: Capitolium 1933, pp. 521–547

Muñoz, Antonio: Roma di Mussolini. Milan 1935

Nicoloso, Paolo: Mussolini architetto. Propaganda e paesaggio urbano nell'Italia fascista. Turin 2008

Nicoloso, Paolo: Piazza della Vittoria in Brescia. The history and difficult legacy of fascism. In: Jones, Kay Bea/ Pilat, Stefanie (eds.): The Routledge Companion to Italian Fascist Architecture. Reception and Legacy. London and New York 2020, pp. 435–448

Note di sintesi per la storia della pianificazione a Bologna. http://psc.comune.bologna.it/qc_cd/volume4/Vol4_note_di_sintesi_storia_pianificazione_a_Bo.pdf [05.03.2011]

Il nuovo stile littorio. I progetti per il Palazzo del Littorio e della Mostra della Rivoluzione Fascista in Via dell'Impero. Milan-Rome 1936

Painter Jr., Borden W.: Mussolini's Rome. Rebuilding the Eternal City. New York and Houndsmill 2005

Penzo, Pier Paola: L'urbanistica incompiuta. Bologna dall'età liberale al fascismo (1889–1929). Bologna 2009

Piacentini, Marcello: Un grande avvenimento architettonico in Russia: Il Palazzo dei Sovieti a Mosca. In: Architettura 3/1934, pp. 129–140

Piacentini, Marcello: Roma. Bollettino della Biblioteca della Facoltà di Architettura dell'Università degli studi di Roma "La Sapienza" 53/1995. Rome 1996

Pica, Agnoldomenico: Nuova Architettura Italiana. Quaderni della Triennale. Milan 1936

Pozzi, Elena/Prettelli, Marco/Signorelli, Leila: Giulio Ulisse Arata: Urban Renewal in Emilia Romagna. In: Enns/Monzo (eds.) 2019, pp. 171–184

Quatember, Ursula: Archäologie und Faschismus. Das problematische Verhältnis von Archäologie and Politik im faschistischen Italien. 2007. In: http://homepage.univie.ac.at/elisabeth.trinkl/forum/forum0607/forum43rom.pdf [11.04.2021]

Ravaglioli, Armando: La Roma di Mussolini. Fasti e nefasti del regime fascista nella storia della capitale. Rome 1996 The rearrangement of the "Borghi" for the access to St. Peter's. In: Architettura. Special issue: Urbanistica della Roma Mussoliniana. Natale 1936, pp. 26–27

Remiddi, Gaia/Greco, Antonella (eds.): Il moderno attraverso Roma. Guida alle architetture romane di Adalberto Libera. Rome 2003

Schüller, Sepp: Das Rom Mussolinis/Roma Mussoliniana. Rom als moderne Hauptstadt/Roma Capitale Moderna. Düsseldorf 1943

Scriba, Friedemann: Augustus im Schwarzhemd? Die Mostra Augustea della Romanità in Rom 1937/38. Frankfurt am Main 1995

Sica, Paolo: Storia dell'urbanistica. III, 2 Il Novecento. Rome-Bari 1978

Sonne, Wolfgang: Culture of Urbanity. A New Approach to 20th Century Urban Design History. In: Journal of the Scottish Society for Art History 10/2005, pp. 55–63

Touring Club Italiano: Italia Settentrionale. Milan 1937

Touring Club Italiano: Roma e dintorni. Guida d'Italia. Milan 1938, Reprint 1947

Touring Club Italiano: Roma. Guida d'Italia. Milan 2007

Tragbar, Klaus: Dante und der Duce. Zu den politischen Motiven der Umgestaltung historischer Städte in der Toskana. In: Mattioli, Aram/Steinacher, Gerald (eds.): Für den Faschismus bauen. Architektur und Städtebau im Italien Mussolinis. Zürich 2009, pp. 189–210

Urbanistica. Rivista quadrimestrale dell'Istituto Nazionale di Urbanistica (INU)

Vannelli, Valter: Le case dei Mercati Traianei tra la piazza del Foro, via Alessandrina e via di Campo Carleo: premesse su via dei Fori Imperiali. In: Cardilli (ed.) 1995, pp. 25–38

Vidotto, Vittorio: La Roma di Mussolini. In: Gentile, Emilio (ed.): Modernità totalitaria. Il fascismo italiano. Rom-Bari 2008, p. 159–170

Wilhelms, Rudolf: Die Erweiterung der Stadt Brescia. In: Städtebau 9/1928, pp. 211–213

Woller, Hans: Geschichte Italiens im 20. Jahrhundert. Munich 2010

Zammerini, Massimo: Concorso per il Palazzo Littorio. Turin 2002

Zocca, Mario: Roma capitale d'Italia. Istituto di Studi Romani. Storia di Roma. Topografia e Urbanistica di Roma. Parte quarta. Bologna 19

Rome: Italy's Capital City
*In a central location on the bank of the Tiber stands one of the grand new
buildings of the Fascist dictatorship in the historic centre of Rome: the Casa
Madre dei Mutilati (Head Office of the Association of the War-disabled),
crowned by a tower, which was built in two stages from 1925 to 1938
according to plans by Marcello Piacentini, the most influential urban development expert of the dictatorship. This building does not particularly attract the
attention of visitors to Rome despite its vast dimensions as it is subordinated
to two much larger buildings that draw the attention of the observer to
themselves. The first is the Castel Sant'Angelo, which – as an object of the
Fascist veneration of the imperial greatness of both ancient and papal Rome –
was "freed" of the surrounding houses during Mussolini's dictatorship and
presented in a park inaugurated in 1934. The second large building is the
Palace of Justice that was built from 1889 to 1910, a gigantic monument to
the unified Kingdom of Italy.*
[Photo: Harald Bodenschatz, 2013]

Rome: The Modernised Piazza Navona
The Piazza Navona is considered one of the most important squares created
in the Baroque period in general and is one of the main tourist destinations in
Rome. The fact that the northern curve of the square represents an urban development project from the Mussolini period, planned by Arnaldo Foschini, remains a secret to most visitors. It is the result of one of the greatest demolition
plans in the historic centre of Rome during the 1930s, to which the buildings
on the north of the Piazza Navona also fell victim. The aim of the plan was to
improve traffic in a north-south direction by means of the breakthrough of the
Corso del Rinascimento to the east of the Piazza. The fact that this massive
intervention is hardly noticeable on the Piazza Navona itself is due above all to
the design of the new buildings there: only the facades facing north were constructed in the severe style of the late 1930s, whereas the facades facing south
were reconstructed in a traditional form to subordinate them to the overall
appearance of the Piazza. Underneath the new buildings, remains of the former
Roman Stadium from the Domitian epoch were made visible, the characteristic
form of which shapes the Piazza Navona to this day.
[Photo: Harald Bodenschatz, 2010]

Bologna: New Historic Centre
Today's capital of the North Italian region Emilia Romagna possesses one of the most magnificent historic centres in Europe, which has been internationally famous at least since its modernisation at the beginning of the 1970s that was geared towards preservation and social acceptability. Hardly anyone knows, however, that a small part of the historic centre came into existence during the rule of Mussolini: the neo-Gothic quarter to the east of the Piazza Maggiore, the main square of the old city. A spectacular redevelopment project was carried out there from 1925 to 1928/32 at the instigation of the Fascist mayor (Podestà) according to plans by the today largely forgotten architect Giulio Ulisse Arata. The project drew on the medieval roots of Italian architecture. In order to maintain the impression of a Gothic quarter, several historic buildings were preserved and combined with new neo-medieval buildings. The result was a series of passageways and small squares that had not existed in that form before. Today this mini historic quarter from the era of the dictatorship enjoys great popularity.
[Photo: Harald Bodenschatz, 2015]

Naples: Modern Centre
It tended to be the exception among the modernisations of historic centres under the Italian dictatorship that, following considerable demolitions in the old city, new buildings were constructed that contrasted with the surrounding historic buildings so starkly as the new buildings on the Piazza Carità in Naples, the capital city of the Southern Italian region Campania. Following two contests, an "ultramodern" offices and services district was erected there in a historic quarter from 1932 to 1936. This was perceived at the time as the new "heart of the city". The new buildings included the by all means elegant Post and Telegraph Office (Palazzo delle Regie Poste e Telegrafi) according to plans by the architects Giuseppe Vaccaro and Gino Franzi, the building of the provincial administration according to plans by Marcello Canino and Ferdinando Chiaramonte and an insurance building (Palazzo I.N.A.), also by Marcello Canino, an influential architect in the Naples of that time. The, in part very modern, architecture on the Piazza Carità will hardly be connected to a dictatorship by many observers. In front of the insurance building since 1971 there has stood a memorial, designed by the artist Lydia Cottone, to Salvo D'Aquisto, who was executed in Palidoro, near Rome, by the German occupiers in 1943. The sergeant of the Carabinieri, who was born in Naples, shouldered the blame – although innocent – for the putative assassination of German soldiers in order to save 22 civil hostages.
[Photo: Harald Bodenschatz, 2013]

The Urban Renewal of Historic Centres in Stalin's Soviet Union: Moscow

Steffen Ott with Harald Bodenschatz and Christiane Post

Socialist construction in the Soviet Union under Stalin is not usually associated with the urban renewal of historic centres. The testimonials to past regimes, in particular churches and monasteries, were often converted to other uses or torn down without great concern. Added to this was the unpretentious style of building existing in the cities, apart from Petrograd/Leningrad (Saint Petersburg), which was declared to be backward and a testimony to relationships of exploitation that had now been overcome. Finally, socialist urban development was aimed at a new type of city, with new people and new buildings. The old cities had no future. Or so it appeared. A closer look shows, however, that in the capital, Moscow, the model for urban development in the entire Soviet Union, a quite independent type of urban renewal was developed: the conversion of the historic centre – the area within the Garden Ring ("B" Ring) – to a centre for Moscow, for the entire socialist state, even for the world communist movement, a conversion that paid little attention to the existing historic buildings but maintained the fundamental structure of the historic city.

Moscow is conspicuously first and foremost a city of the 20th century.[1] This assessment is somewhat deceptive, however, and eclipses something that should be in the light, that was long neglected, damaged and partially destroyed: the historic, old Moscow, the Moscow of before the October Revolution, particularly the Moscow of before the industrialisation brought about by the railway. Historic Moscow is not only the Moscow of the many traditional churches and fortified monasteries that are paid due attention in every travel guide. Nor is it the wonderful buildings of the Russian art nouveau, known and appreciated by a few enthusiasts. It is the large number of buildings, streets and districts from the time before industrialisation, including the "neo-classical Moscow" that was reconstructed following the city fire of 1812 caused by the Napoleonic invasion. But it is also the fascinating, perceptible, magnificent layout of the city: the system of rings and radial roads with a central heart: the Kremlin. Moscow has one of the largest and most important historic centres in Europe, but also one of the most unknown, culturally least accessible, in the course of the 20th century most run-down centres. Western Europe has forgotten that the Moscow that was first mentioned in 1147 – claiming the title of "The Third Rome" – was one of the largest cities in Europe in the 16th century.

The heart of the historic centre yesterday, today and tomorrow is the Kremlin, which was fortified in its present form between 1485 and 1495, and the neighbouring settlement of Kitai-gorod, which was fortified from 1534 to 1538 and transformed into a modern business centre in the decades

---

1 Cf. on the (urban) development of Moscow Pamiatniki arkhitektury Moskvy 1983, 1989a and 1989b. The following two paragraphs are based on reflections in Bodenschatz 1992, pp. 36–37.

following the October Revolution.[2] This nucleus was expanded in an extraordinary way very early on by two concentric "rings": the area of the White City (Belyi gorod), which was surrounded by a wall built from 1586 to 1593 along the route of the present Boulevard Ring ("A" Ring), and the area of the "Earthen City" (Zemlyanoi gorod), which was

delimited by an earthen wall built from 1591 to 1592 along the route of the present Garden Ring ("B" Ring). Today, the Garden Ring marks the historic centre, the previous old city, in the narrow sense. Preindustrial areas of the city – apart from the Kremlin – are to be found above all inside the rings of the previous "White City" and the "Earthen City".

2 The stone city walls of the business centre Kitai-gorod were largely removed in the 1930s.

Moscow after the October Revolution

Following the accession to power of the Bolsheviks, the Second All-Russian Congress of Soviets of Workers' and Soldiers' Deputies passed a Decree on Land on 26 October (8 November) 1917.[3] The property of the crown, the aristocracy and the church were expropriated without compensation and the right of ownership to land in Russia abolished.[4] Further directives such as the Decree on the Socialisation of Land from 6 (19) February 1918 followed.[5] On 20 August 1918, finally, the Decree on the Abolishment of Private Ownership of Real Estate in the towns and cities was passed.[6]

All these measured formed the framework for Soviet urban development, including the urban renewal of historic centres. It soon proved to be the case, however, that they were inadequate. It was neither clear what a socialist city should be nor did institutions and resources exist to realise the socialist city. This did not change fundamentally until the rise of the group around Stalin within the Communist Party and the five-year plans at the end of the 1920s and beginning of the 1930s.

On 16 March 1918 the Extraordinary Fourth All-Russia Congress of Soviets declared Moscow the capital of the Russian Socialist Federative Soviet Republic (RSFSR).[7] The background to the relocation of the capital from Petrograd to Moscow, which was originally intended as an interim

measure[8], was the resumption of war on 17 February 1917 following the abandonment of peace negotiations and the ending of the ceasefire, and the beginning of the February offensive of the German Empire, in the course of which Petrograd was threatened with capture. The evacuation of the government was planned in utmost secrecy. On 11 March 1918 the representatives of the Council of People's Commissars with Lenin at its head arrived at the Nikolaevsky railway station in Moscow.[9]

Following the relocation of the capital, the historic Kremlin, the heart of the historic city, became the seat of the Soviet government. This did not save all the historic buildings. Churches and monasteries were demolished at the end of the 1920s and beginning of the 1930s.[10] Following the death of Lenin on 21 January 1924 the historic ensemble of the Kremlin was symbolically upgraded once again: by the Lenin Mausoleum, the most important new building of the 1920s in Moscow's historic centre, adapted both formally and in colour to the Kremlin. The original – small – Mausoleum of wood was built on Red Square next to the Kremlin wall in 1924, replaced by a larger one in the summer of the same year that gave way to one made of stone in 1930. The architect of the Mausoleum was Aleksei Shchusev.

With Moscow's nomination as the new capital city of the first socialist state came its aspiration to representation and the demand for urban renewal, particularly regarding the historic centre. "In the two centuries in which St. Petersburg was the capital of the Russian Empire there was no occasion to develop Moscow on a large scale. The city comprised a maze of streets and alleyways that was typical of Russian towns with small-scale buildings, often only two or three storeys high. Even the 19th century brought hardly

3 Excerpts from the speeches, decisions and decrees of the Second All-Russian Congress can be found in: Lenin II 1967, pp. 521–541. Regarding the dates it must be taken into account that until February 1918 Russia used the Julian calendar, which at the beginning of the 20th century was 13 days behind the then introduced Gregorian calendar.
4 Decree on Land. In: Lenin II 1967, pp. 536–538.
5 Decree of the VCIK (All-Russian Central Executive Committee) on the Socialisation of Land, published on 6 (19) February 1918. Excerpts in Russian in: Khazanova (ed.) 1963, p. 13.
6 Decree of the VCIK (All-Russian Central Executive Committee) on the Abolition of the Private Ownership of Real Estate in the Towns and Cities, published on 20 August 1918. Excerpts in: Khazanova (ed.) 1963, pp. 13–14.
7 Cf. Moskva. 850 let II 1997, p. 61.

8 Cf. Colton 1995, p. 97.
9 Cf. Colton 1995, p. 97; Moskva. Ėntsiklopediia 1997, p. 39.
10 On the considerable loss of church buildings inside the Kremlin, particularly since the end of the 1920s cf. Moskva. 850 let II 1997, pp. 56–61.

Moscow with fortifications. In the central area the Kremlin and the oldest city district of Kitai-gorod to its east are highlighted. Around this medieval centre there are two further rings of fortifications, which were later to become ring roads: today's inner Boulevard Ring ("A" Ring), which is really only three-quarters of a ring, bordering on the Moskva River at both ends, and the outer Garden Ring ("B" Ring). The entire area within the Garden Ring can be described as the historic centre. The large arterial roads are also highlighted. The map, which was published in 1938, is a part of the comprehensive presentation of the Moscow Master Plan of 1935. [Source: Institut izobrazitel'noi statistiki 1938]*

* This comprehensive and elaborate presentation of the Master Plan dating from 1938 was principally designed by Aleksandr Rodchenko and Varvara Stepanova. Numerous illustrations from this little known magnificent tome will be documented in the following. The pages of the tome are not numbered.

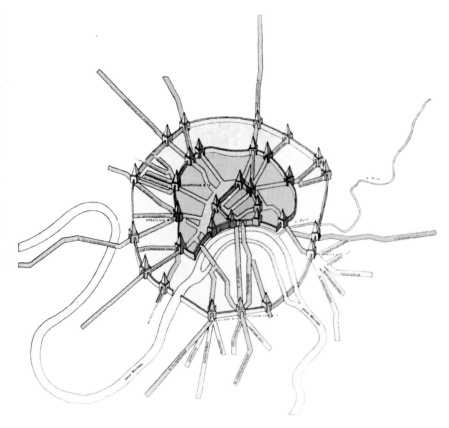

The Lenin Mausoleum on Red Square in front of the Kremlin Wall, before 1928. [Source: Sidorow 1928, p. 31]

any appreciable intervention into the structure of the city but limited itself to the replacement of individual buildings in important locations by new business premises."[11]

One month after the relocation of the government, in April 1918, in the Department of Civil Engineering of the Mossovet (Moscow Soviet) an architectural workshop was set up under the leadership of Ivan Zholtovsky and Aleksei Shchusev, which was commissioned to draw up plans for the reconstruction of Moscow.[12] But the political situation at first made extensive building operations impossible. During the civil war from 1918 to 1921 the depopulation

11 Huber 1998, p. 49.

12 Cf. Khazanova (ed.) 1963, p. 37.

of the cities and a massive flight to the countryside began. In Moscow the number of inhabitants fell between 1917 and 1921 from c. 1.9 million to 1.1 million.[13] Even maintenance activities were neglected.[14]

Up until the first Five-Year Plan (1929–32), lavish plans for the redevelopment of Moscow's historic centre were compiled and drawn,[15] but the instruments and resources for the implementation of the plans were still missing, despite the possibility of appropriating land and buildings. With the first Five-Year Plan, which aimed at rapid industrialisation and the collectivisation of agriculture, the situation with regard to urban development changed radically. The construction of new towns, the construction of huge factories and the

connected works housing estates moved into the foreground. Extensive resources were provided for this. Magnitogorsk was the central project in these years. The older cities, including Moscow, appeared no longer to have a future. Radical plans for their redevelopment were envisaged.

The hasty industrialisation and collectivisation of agriculture lent a dynamic to conditions in the entire Soviet Union in a way that the strategists of the first Five-Year Plan had not envisaged. Millions of people were set in movement and the flight from the land culminated in an urbanisation process of a previously unknown dimension. Particularly the large cities, especially Moscow, experienced an invasion of former farmers. The rapid urbanisation was finally countered with the Decree of 27 December 1932, which tried to come to grips with this mobility by the introduction of domestic passports. The situation in the countryside was particularly bad, however.[16] From 1931 to 1933, and especially in 1932–33, the crisis led to a wave of – regionally varying – famines. Probably 6 million farmers fell victim to these famines.[17]

13 Cf. Moskva v cifrach 1934, p. 13.
14 One example: "In the building season in 1920 in Moscow 3,653 buildings were renovated, i.e. one and a half times as many as in all the other towns of the Soviet republic. Nevertheless, this was extremely few compared to what was necessary: 35,000 buildings urgently required renovation, and almost all buildings needed small repairs." In: Gorzka 1990, p. 105.
15 With the move of the government to Moscow plans for the reconstruction of the new capital were commissioned. The project "New Moscow" (Aleksei Shchusev) emerged from the first plans. In 1925, the city development plan "Great Moscow" (Sergei Shestakov) was drawn up at the behest of the Moscow municipal authorities. In the late 1920s, this was followed by individual plans for urban development such as the "Plan for a new socialist Moscow" by Nikolai Ladovsky.

16 Khlevniuk 1998, pp. 34–35.
17 On the estimation of the number of deaths from famine cf. Hildermeier 1998, pp. 400–401.

The Great Turnaround of Socialist Urban Development

The rapidly changing situation in the countryside and the reactions of the Party leadership also conditioned the debates on urban development in the Soviet Union. The vision of a new "socialist city" appeared to founder in the chaos of industrialisation and the collectivisation of agriculture. Working and living conditions in Moscow were declining for all the world to see. In this situation the Party pulled the emergency brake. It attempted to find a way to overcome the increasing chaos in the capital. To do so, it made institutional changes and introduced measures for the reorganisation of the municipal economy.[18] The model for this accomplishment was Moscow and its organiser was Lazar' Kaganovich, one of Stalin's closest associates. At that time Kaganovich was Secretary to the CC (Central Committee) of the VKP(b), member of the Politburo and First Secretary of the Moscow District Party Committee. The changes in Moscow were prepared and implemented in close cooperation between the Politburo and the Moscow party leadership.[19]

The work of the networked commissions of the Moscow organisations and the Politburo ultimately reached its peak in the famous plenum of the CC of the VKP(b) from 11 to 15 June 1931. In a three-hour speech to that plenum Kaganovich presented his report on the state of the municipal economy and on measures to improve it. Following this report a resolution of the CC of the VKP(b) was passed unanimously.[20]

In the plenum Kaganovich painted a dismal picture of the situation in the towns and cities. Moscow in particular was taken as an example: housing conditions there were unsatisfactory[21], demonstrated by, among other things, the high share (86 per cent) of houses with only one or two storeys[22]. In the case of new buildings, quality had often been neglected in favour of quantity.[23] Energy supply was

18 The municipal economy included the following sectors: housing, water supply, lighting, heating, sewage, urban traffic, external repairs and maintenance, baths, laundries, public eating houses etc. Cf. Über die städtische Wirtschaft Moskaus 1931. In: Kaganovich (c. 1931–32), p. 128.
19 We are grateful to Dietmar Neutatz for informing us about his archive work on these events and for placing his records at our disposal.

20 The importance of the plenum in the eyes of the Party leadership is shown by the foreign language versions of Kaganovich's arguments and the resolution, which were distributed soon after. Cf. among others the German version: Kaganovich (c. 1931–32) and the English version: Kaganovich (c. 1931); on the Russian version cf. Kaganovich 1931.
21 Cf. Kaganovich (c. 1931–32), p. 26.
22 Cf. Kaganovich (c. 1931–32), pp. 27–28.
23 Cf. Kaganovich (c. 1931–32), p. 35.

not guaranteed[24], nor was water supply[25]. The sewage system[26] and road building[27] also left a lot to be desired. Refuse collection did not function as it should.[28] Urban transport was completely inadequate.[29]

The short-term, ambitious goal of urban development was named as "reconstructing the old towns and building new ones".[30] Behind this apparently well-balanced objective, however, lay a clear shift in priorities: while Kaganovich enlarged upon the reconstruction of the old cities in detail, his statements regarding the building of new towns remained very brief.[31] In the discussion on the reconstruction of the old towns and cities one city in particular was singled out as an example: the capital, Moscow. The improvement of conditions in Moscow was regarded as a model for the entire country.

The state of the historic centre in Moscow was described as very unsatisfactory. "When you walk through the alleys and byways of Moscow you get the impression that they were laid out by a drunken man."[32] The revolution had created the foundations for making a clean sweep of these conditions. "If we had had a plan we could already have done a great deal. In Moscow, particularly, we had not, and still have not, a plan for the construction of new streets and the reconstruction of old streets."[33] One thing was certain, however: "We cannot leave small, wretched-looking, broken-down houses in the centre of the city."[34]

Kaganovich's speech was followed on 15 June 1931 by the passing of the resolution of the CC of the VKP(b) "On the municipal economy of Moscow and the development of municipal economy in the U.S.S.R."[35]. With this formal act the change of course was sealed. Specifically, for Moscow the drawing up of a three-year plan for the construction of housing funded by industry for at least 500,000 people and the repair of the entire housing stock in the course of the summer season was proposed.[36] The construction of the Metro (underground railway) was to be started in 1932. The final point in the recommended measures was the

24 Cf. Kaganovich (c. 1931–32), p. 36.
25 Cf. Kaganovich (c. 1931–32), p. 44.
26 Cf. Kaganovich (c. 1931–32), p. 50.
27 Kaganovich (c. 1931–32), p. 55.
28 Cf. Kaganovich (c. 1931–32), p. 52.
29 Kaganovich (c. 1931–32), p. 60.
30 Kaganovich (c. 1931–32), p. 3, cf. also pp. 124–125.
31 Cf. Kaganovich (c. 1931–32), p. 8, 112–113.

32 Kaganovich (c. 1931–32), p. 106.
33 Kaganovich (c. 1931–32), p. 106.
34 Kaganovich (c. 1931–32), p. 107–108.
35 Über die städtische Wirtschaft (c. 1931–32), pp. 126–146.
36 Kaganovich (c. 1931–32), p. 133–134.

"Planning of Moscow". "The Plenum of the Central Committee instructs the Moscow organisations to undertake the elaboration of a serious, scientifically developed plan for the building of Moscow."[37]

The June Plenum of the CC of the VKP(b) represented the pinnacle of the urban development paradigm shift in the Soviet Union. It was geared towards the existing city, the large city, and specifically Moscow. Completely new factory cities no longer primarily embodied the concept of the socialist city, but also, and above all, the modernised, historic large cities, especially Moscow. Important, demonstrative measures for the modernisation of the urban and transport infrastructure and for the improvement of living conditions in Moscow were commissioned – first and foremost the construction of the underground railway. The drafting of a large-scale plan for Moscow was now unmistakeably on the order of the day. The plan was to involve, in particular, the redevelopment of the historic centre. Although the urban structure of Moscow had not yet been decided upon, a tendency towards a ring-radial system was already hinted at.

Whereas in 1931 there were only early, not yet completely clear, indications of the urban development turnaround, following the surviving of the famine winter of 1932–33 a new triumphalism established itself that lent it new impetus. The symbolic mise en scène of the illustrious capital of the Soviet Union was now required. The aestheticism of austerity was no longer in demand but, rather, the exhibition of the proclaimed "victory of socialism". It was particularly necessary to give visible expression to the decreed increase in the standard of living in the towns and cities. This meant focussing on ornamentation, on the aggregation of the arts, on the monumental together with axis concepts and visual connections, the abandonment of construction in rows, a reorientation towards urban, multi-storey buildings, an emphasis on streets and squares, on public spaces, on building facades. Above all, however, the focus was on the redevelopment of the old town, on the construction of a resplendent centre, a showcase of the socialist state.

For the further development of the Moscow Master Plan the remarks of Lazar' Kaganovich in his report on the activity of the Moscow Party Committee and of the Moscow City Committee of the Communist Party of the Soviet Union at the Third Moscow District and Second Moscow Municipal Conference of the VKP(b) on 23 January 1932 are important.[38] In this report new directives for the reconstruction of Moscow were issued, which were intended to have a decisive impact on the urban development of Moscow and to determine the foundations for the future Moscow Master Plan.

A brief outline of the history of the city's development[39] was followed by an assessment of the current situation: "In spite of its tremendous building activities Moscow, as the saying goes, looks like a village. It is time to unfold the building activity and the planned structuring of Moscow in such a way that Moscow ceases to be a large village."[40] Kaganovich did not see any corresponding concepts in the draft plans to date. "There are several variations for the structuring of Moscow. But all of these variations pose the question in a rather abstract, artificial way. [...] We must, in particular, discard two extremes: firstly, conservatism, which aims to leave Moscow inside the limits of the A and B rings in its previous state and to build everything new beyond today's city limits, in the suburbs; and secondly, the aspirations expressed especially by some radical architects. The latter wish to give no consideration to the city in its present form, with all its buildings and its streets. They wish to solve the task of reconstructing Moscow 'resolutely' and 'in a revolutionary way' at any price; they wish to lay out a new system of streets without taking the historically evolved city into consideration."[41] Yet according to Kaganovich's concept the structure of precisely this "historically evolved city" should be maintained, reorganised and developed: "We must [...] interlink [...] the changing of the face of the old Moscow to the historically evolved city."[42]

The mandatory guidelines for Moscow's future Master Plan were thus stipulated: "The reconstruction of Moscow [must], firstly, be based on the historically evolved principle of the radial roads and the ring roads; secondly, we must relieve the congested radial roads and the centre of the city by increasing traffic on the ring roads; thirdly, we must align the roads, widen them, lay out new squares and aggregate the many small streets and alleyways to uniform roads. Fourthly and finally, we must add further storeys to the old houses, build green spaces, embellish the entire city and improve it architecturally."[43]

37 Kaganovich (c. 1931–32), p. 133–134.
38 Kaganovich 1932.

39 Cf. Kaganovich 1932, p. 174.
40 Kaganovich 1932, pp. 174–175.
41 Kaganovich 1932, pp. 175–176.
42 Cf. Kaganovich 1932, p. 176.
43 Kaganovich 1932, p. 179.

The Reconstruction of the Historic Centre of Moscow

On 10 July 1935, in an official act, the Council of People's Commissars of the USSR and the Central Committee of the VKP(b) adopted the joint resolution "On the Master Plan for the Reconstruction of the City of Moscow". Signed by Vyacheslav Molotov, the chairman of the Council of People's Commissars of the USSR, and Joseph Stalin, the Secretary to the Central Committee of the VKP(b), the document[44] contains mandatory directives for the urban development of Moscow. At that point in time the redevelopment of the historic centre had long started and Moscow

had already been turned into a huge construction site with massive demolitions and radical reconstruction activities. In his "Reise nach Sowjetrußland 1934" (Journey to Soviet Russia 1934) Oskar Maria Graf describes his impressions of the reconstruction of the capital city to date: "By and large the Moscow of that time gave the impression of being ugly, unfinished, terribly chaotic and mundanely noisy. [...] Torn up streets, kilometre-long, narrow drainage ditches over which were laid narrow footbridges of planks, and huge mounds of earth. Entire blocks of houses were demolished and entire columns of heavily laden lorries drove the dusty rubble away. Everywhere the lengthy, high planking of the underground railway, which was still under construction,

44 General'nyi plan rekonstruktsii goroda Moskvy 1936.

Master Plan 1935, Moscow's inner city: road plan (excerpt). [Source: Institut izobrazitel'noi statistiki 1938]

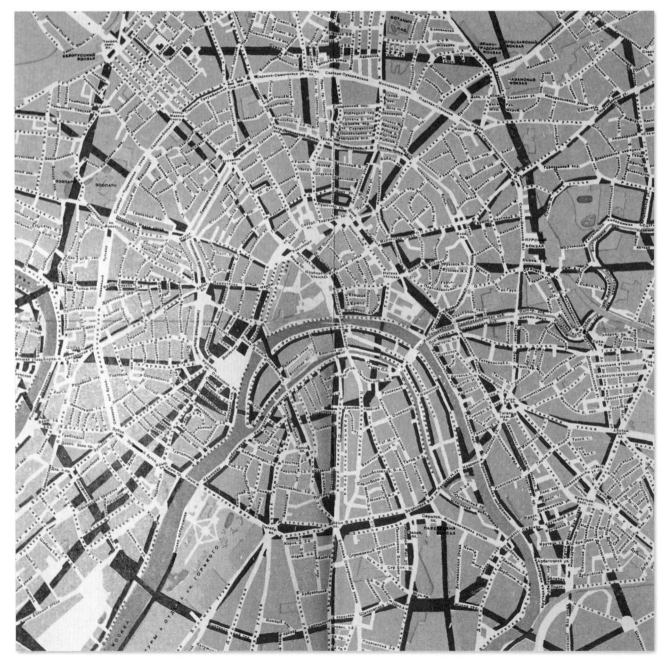

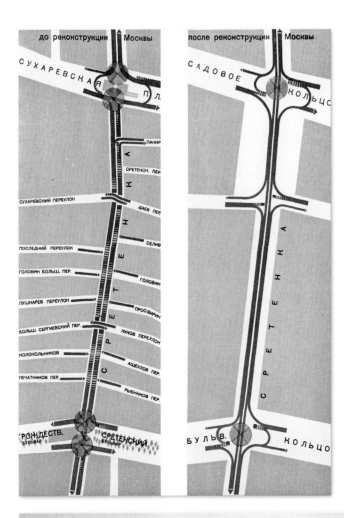

Model representation of the widening of a street before (left) and after (right) the reconstruction according to the regulations of the Master Plan, 1938, showing the section of Sretenka Street between the Boulevard Ring and the Garden Ring. The redevelopment was intended to facilitate the smoother flow of traffic.
[Source: Institut izobrazitel'noi statistiki 1938]

Exemplary representation of the planned simplification of the road network according to the regulations of the Master Plan, 1938.
[Source: Institut izobrazitel'noi statistiki 1938]

Exemplary representation of the reconstruction of a residential district according to the regulations of the Master Plan, 1938: buildings beforehand (left) and afterwards (right); brown roofs: demolition, red roofs: maintenance, ochre: planned new buildings, green: green spaces. The small alleyways disappear.
[Source: Institut izobrazitel'noi statistiki 1938]

The planning of the new Metro aimed at an increased centrality of the heart of Moscow, status as of 1938. [Source: Institut izobrazitel'noi statistiki 1938]

everywhere gigantic scaffolding for future skyscrapers and apartment buildings."[45]

Overlooking the old historic centre, Red Square, which was described as "greatly in need of expansion"[46], was to be doubled in size.[47] In the district of Kitai-gorod, one of the oldest quarters in Moscow, the small buildings were to be demolished to create space for monumental government buildings. In the southern part of Kitai-gorod, in Zaryad'e, which lies between Red Square and the Moskva River, the building of the People's Commissariat for Heavy Industry was planned. For its building site the densely populated area was completely vacated and demolished. Naturally the project of the Soviet Palace was also broached, but

relatively hesitantly. One could almost have the impression that the Palace already existed. Existing radial and ring roads were to be straightened and extended to a width of 30 to 40 metres by demolishing buildings and removing flowerbeds, lawns and trees that narrowed the width of the streets and impeded traffic flow.[48] At all the crossings of the ring and radial roads those buildings were to be demolished that blocked the entry to the boulevards; the spaces created in this way were to be the subject of architectural design. In addition to this, the Metro was to be further extended.[49]

---

45 Graf 1977, pp. 39–40. A similar picture of the numerous building sites and the "construction frenzy" in Moscow had already been described by Franz Carl Weiskopf in his travel report "Zukunft im Rohbau" in 1932. Reprinted in: Weiskopf 1959, pp. 93–97.
46 Kaganovich 1934, p. 53.
47 Cf. Aranovich 10–11/1935, pp. 37–43.

48 Kaganovich commented in 1934 on the demolition of houses for the expansion of streets as follows: "Of course streets will also have to be straightened even if this takes place at the expense of the unusable, one-storey houses. At present, even in the main thoroughfares, e.g. in Gorky Street, next to large, attractive buildings we can see miserable hovels, one-storey derelict cottages, spoiling the look of the proletarian capital city. [...] Where relatively large or new houses are in the way of the widening and straightening of the streets, these houses must be moved. A great deal of experience has already been accumulated abroad in the moving of relatively large buildings over distances of dozens and even hundreds of metres" In: Kaganovich 1934, pp. 40–41.
49 On the architecture of the Moscow Metro in the city centre cf. Meuser/ Martovitskaya 2016; on the construction of the Metro cf. Neutatz 2001.

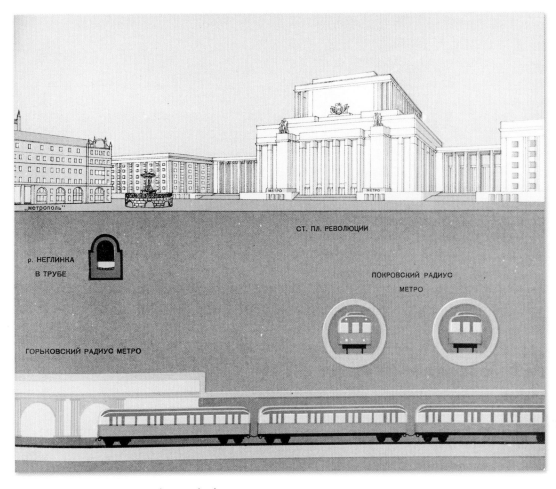

Representation of the Metro using the example of
Revolution Square in the centre of Moscow, 1938.
[Source: Institut izobrazitel'noi statistiki 1938]

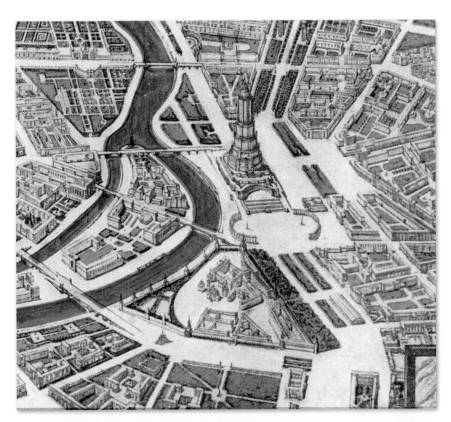

Bird's eye view of
the centre of the new
Moscow. Front inside
cover of the official
publication "Master
Plan for the Recon-
struction of the City
of Moscow" (excerpt),
1936.
[Source: General'nyi
plan rekonstruktsii
goroda Moskvy 1936]

The Palace of the Soviets

The contest for the Palace of the Soviets in Moscow was the decisive step for establishing in professional circles the urban development turnaround introduced in 1931. It was paid the utmost attention not only in the Soviet Union but also internationally. It "was among the most spectacular and representative events in architectural history in the first half of the 20th century. [...] The history of the Palace is linked to the names of great architects such as Le Corbusier, Perret, the brothers Vesnin, Ginzburg, Lubetkin, Gabo, Mendelsohn, Gropius and Hannes Meyer and is at the same time intimately interwoven with the emerging of the architecture of totalitarianism."[50] The contest played a key role in the history not only of Soviet architecture[51] but also of urban development. Two political decisions highlighted this dimension: first, the decision in favour of a location directly neighbouring on the Kremlin, i.e. in the heart of the historic centre, and later the decision for a gigantic statue of Lenin which, together with the excessive emphasis on the verticality of the planned building, established its importance for the entire city. The project of the Palace of the Soviets embodied in an especially pointed way the paradigm change in Soviet urban development: it drew the attention of the public and of professionals away from the new towns and toward the capital city of Moscow, and served to present efficaciously the modernisation of the historic centre of Moscow as a model for socialist urban development.

The preliminary decision to build the Palace of the Soviets was taken in February, possibly even in January, 1931.[52] On 17 April 1931, several leading soviet architects and the architects' associations received an invitation to participate in the drawing up of a programme for the public Union-wide contest for the design of the Palace of the Soviets.[53] The first round of the contest was thus initiated at the behest of the building authority. The preliminary invitation of tenders did not include any major formal conditions or guidelines with regard to content in order not to limit the possible spectrum of concepts at that point in time. The drafts were to be submitted by 1 July 1931.

The location for the Palace of the Soviets was still undecided at first. The participants in the preliminary invitation to tender suggested four different locations. Only on 2 June 1931, shortly before the June Plenum, was the location finally decided upon. In a discussion in the Kremlin in which – in addition to eight soviet architects and

Hannes Meyer – Joseph Stalin, Vyacheslav Molotov, Lazar' Kaganovich und Kliment Voroshilov participated, it was decided that the Palace should be constructed on the bank of the Moskva River on the site of the Cathedral of Christ the Saviour and that part of the construction should be in Volchonka Street.[54] The Palace was to rise up directly next to the Kremlin and had to deal with the existing heights to be found there: with the 81 metres high Ivan the Great Bell Tower in the Kremlin and with the 100 metre high dome of the Cathedral of Christ the Saviour.[55] The choice of location emphasised the ring-radial structure of the city of Moscow, reinforced the status of the Kremlin as central point and at the same time expanded – in fact doubled – it in size. The decision was undeniably a rejection of a radical urban development break with the historic structure of the city. The extraordinary consequences that this choice of location would have, however, were not yet discernible at this point in time.

The result of the preliminary invitation to tender was 15 entries[56], which were presented from 14 July 1931 onward in the All-Union Building Exhibition in the Park of Culture and Leisure, and in the press. The solutions offered were primarily in accordance with architectural modernism, designed as monumental solitary structures with little concern for the historic city. At this point on time the location was less important. The urban development orientation of the Palace played a subordinate role. The planned building complexes could, however, be interpreted as the beginning, or as the motor, of a radical modernisation of the historic centre.

The political importance of the project was emphasised by a new institution that was set up in June 1931 and which was to organise the actual contest: a Palace Building Council equipped with legislative powers and subordinated to the Central Executive Committee (CEC) of the USSR[57]. Members of the Building Council were, for example, Vyacheslav Molotov, Chairman of the Council of People's Commissars since 1931, Lazar' Kaganovich, Kliment Voroshilov, Anatoli Lunacharsky, Avel' Yenukidze und Konstantin Uchanov.[58] The building administration of the Palace of the Soviets now functioned as an executive body. Its chairman was Mikhail Kriukov, and Boris Iofan, the later first prizewinner, was also a member.[59]

A crucial professional role was played from the beginning by the architect Boris Iofan. His concept – still in a modern architectural language – was aimed at restructuring the

50 Ter-Akopyan 1992, p. 185. Cf. auch Kazus' 1997, p. 79. With regard to the contest for the Palace of the Soviets Kazus' speaks of an outstanding procedure in the history of construction in the 20th century.
51 Pistorius 1992, p. 132.
52 Ter-Akopyan 1992, pp. 192–193.
53 Ter-Akopyan 1992, pp. 185–186.

54 Cf. Winkler 1989, p. 140. Igor' Kazus' assumes that Stalin himself took this decision on 2 June 1931. Cf. Kazus' 1994, pp. 53–54. Cf. further Soiuz sovetskikh arkhitektorov (ed.) 1933, p. 123.
55 Cf. Flierl 2000, p. 152.
56 Cf. Borngräber 1987, p. 417.
57 Ter-Akopyan 1992, p. 186.
58 Cf. Pistorius (ed.) 1992, pp. 132–133.
59 Ter-Akopyan 1992, p. 186.

The location chosen for the Palace of the Soviets: the site of the Cathedral of Christ the Saviour, before 1928. [Sidorow 1928, p. 85]

entire surrounding area and subordinating it to the palace. At the same time he already presented two major compositional elements: a domed hall and a tower, elements which in the third round would be amalgamated. The tower was crowned by a statue.

On 13 July 1931[60] the Palace Building Council announced the modified programme for the public all-Union contest, ringing in the second round. The closing date was first set for 20 October 1931 but was later extended to 1 December 1931. In a building administration bulletin for the Palace of the Soviets in September 1931[61] it was unmistakeably demanded that "the building should appear monumental. The choice of appropriate building materials and the number of storeys are left to the architect." Furthermore, "the architectural design must a) correspond to the character of the epoch, i.e. be an expression of the will of the working people to build socialism, b) be aligned to the specific purpose of the building, and c) take into account its importance as an artistic architectural monument of the capital city of the USSR."[62] There was no mention of concern for the existing historic centre.

The second, public round of the contest brought 272 concepts, of which 112 were ideas from laymen and 160 were architectural concepts, of which in turn twelve were commissioned works and twenty-four were out-of-contest entries. Twenty-four concepts were entered by foreign participants, of which eleven came from the USA, five from Germany, three from France, two from Holland and one from each from Switzerland, Italy and Estonia.[63] Commissioned works were entered by – in addition to three Soviet authors[64] – the foreign architects Le Corbusier and Perret (France), Gropius, Mendelsohn and Poelzig (Germany), Lamb and Urban (USA), and Brasini (Italy).[65] The drafts were shown at an exhibition in January 1932.[66]

In the second round, too, architecturally modern concepts were dominant.[67] Among these, Le Corbusier's proposal was paid particular attention – both in the Soviet Union

60 According to Catherine Cooke and Igor' Kazus' the public contest was advertised on 18 July 1931. Cf. Cooke/Kazus 1991, p. 59.

61 Programma proektirovaniia Dvortsa Sovetov SSSR v Moskve 1933, pp. 119–129.

62 Cf. Programm für das Projekt des Sowjetpalastes der UdSSR in Moskau. In: Naum Gabo 1992, p. 205.

63 Cf. Adkins 1992, p. 197. Helen Adkins points out, however, that a question mark should be put on the official number of twenty-four foreign contributions.

64 The following Soviet architect groups were invited: 1. Ivan Zholtovsky, 2. Boris Iofan, 3. German Krasin and the GIPROVTUS-Brigade. Cf. Adkins 1992, pp. 197–198.

65 The Italian architect Armando Brasini was invited – probably on the recommendation of Iofan – to take part in the contest for the Palace of the Soviets as the only Italian architect. Brasini's contribution was historically oriented. In 1934 Brasini was, in addition to Marcello Piacentini, the judge in the contest for the Palazzo Littorio in Rome, a very similar building project of the Fascist dictatorship.

66 Borngräber 1987, p. 419.

67 Cf. Pistorius (ed.) 1992, p. 135.

*Boris Iofan: Contribution with domed hall
and tower in a moderately modern style
for the contest for the Palace of the Soviets,
July 1931. Preliminary invitation of tenders,
first round of the contest.
[Source: Tyrannei des Schönen 1994, p. 154]*

*Le Corbusier and Pierre Jeanneret: Concept for
the Palace of the Soviets, view with the Kremlin,
December 1931. Second round of the contest.
[Source: Naum Gabo 1992, p. 147]*

Lay-contribution "One sixth of the Earth": Concept for the Palace of the Soviets, December 1931. Second round of the contest. [Source: Soiuz sovetskikh arkhitektorov (ed.) 1933, p. 99]

and abroad. "Among the foreign projects", according to "Pravda" on 20 January 1932, "general attention is concentrated on the project of Le Corbusier, the most brilliant theoretician and practitioner of modern western architecture. The project presents a bold solution for the halls. Unacceptable in Le Corbusier's project is the fact that he handles the Palace of the Soviets as naked 'industrialism', as if it were a hall for conferences."[68]

Great attention was also paid to the entries by the lay architects. Concepts were entered by workers from throughout the Soviet Union, and even from abroad, but also by the representatives of different occupational groups, by school children, by the attendees of evening classes, by students of technical colleges, by artistically educated professionals, by Komsomols and by Party members.[69] The lay concepts often preferred simple symbolic forms to express the glory of socialism: buildings, for example, in the form of a tractor or in the form of machines, or buildings as a symbol of the worldwide Soviet, resting on five continents. Themes such as the industrial building site Soviet Union, one sixth of the Earth, the struggle of the working class, revolution, hammer and sickle, red star, the coat of arms of the Soviet Union, the letters USSR, the world globe, a speeding steam engine, a lighthouse etc. were suggested. Suggestions such as these strengthened the orientation toward the artistic emphasis of "victorious socialism" by means of powerful symbolic images. The influence of the lay concepts on the later decision of the Palace Building Council in favour of a sculptural, monumental solution, and even on the design activity of soviet architects in the 1930s generally,[70] should not be underestimated.

The urban development dimension still did not play a paramount role for many of the contest participants. The Palace of the Soviets was often regarded as a solitary structure and its relationship to the rest of the city was of no particular interest. This can also be seen in the documentation of the contest results by the Association of Soviet Architects.[71]

After the entries to the contest had been submitted the preparations for construction were accelerated. The jury started work. The chairman of the jury was the politician Gleb Krzhizhanovsky, and members included Anatoli Lunacharsky, Maxim Gorky and Konstantin Stanislavsky. In December 1931 the Cathedral of Christ the Saviour was demolished to make way for the huge new building. Shortly before the decision of the jury Vladimir Semenov, who was in charge of the work on the Moscow Master Plan, spoke out against modernist urban development and in favour of the critical appropriation of the historical legacy.[72] On 28 February 1932 the Palace Building Council presented its report and its instructions.[73] The three "highest awards" went exclusively to non-modern concepts: to the concepts of Ivan Zholtovsky, Boris Iofan and Hector O. Hamilton.[74]

Zholtovsky's entry presented an urban development concept that differed considerably from that of Iofan. Whereas Iofan interpreted the Palace as the point of departure for rough axes that penetrated into the surrounding area, Zholtovsky gave his Palace a fine urban framework that at the same time functioned as a shield and illustrated its separation from the historic city. Much to the surprise and indignation of the international professional community, the only foreigner to be honoured was an unknown US-American architect of English origin: Hector O. Hamilton. His concept was not further qualified from an urban

68 Quoted in Adkins 1992, p. 198.
69 Cf. Soiuz sovetskikh arkhitektorov (ed.) 1933, pp. 95–96.
    The occupational groups included: chefs, doctors, accountants, savings bank employees etc.
70 Borngräber 1987, p. 419.

71 Cf. Soiuz sovetskikh arkhitektorov (ed.) 1933, pp. 10–51.
72 Pistorius 1994, p. 160.
73 Postanovleniia Soveta stroitel'stva Dvortsa Sovetov 1933, p. 53–55.
74 Soiuz sovetskikh arkhitektorov (ed.) 1933, pp. 54, 131–132.

Ivan Zholtovsky and Georgi Gol'ts: Historical concept for the Palace of the Soviets with colosseum and tower, December 1931. Second round of the contest. [Oshchepkov (ed.) 1955, p. 60]

Boris Iofan: Concept for the Palace of the Soviets, model, December 1931. Second round of the contest. [Source: Mosca 1991, p. 101]

development point of view. As a whole the judgement of the jury on the results of the public contest was negative, however: "None of the concepts did justice to the greatness of our socialist epoch, which should be expressed in the Palace of the Soviets by monumentality, simplicity, coherence and beauty."[75]

The greater weight of the urban development dimension could no longer be ignored. With the entries by Zholtovsky and Iofan two urban development concepts were awarded prizes that fundamentally contradicted one another: the concept of separation from the city on the one hand and the concept of penetration of the city on the other; an urban development concept in the style of the Neo-Renaissance

and a concept in the style of Neo-Baroque. The decision on the preferred option was postponed. The third award-winning concept by Hamilton must be classified as a gesture of politeness towards the foreign participants. Subsequently, it did not play a central role.

The contest for the Palace of the Soviets was not yet over following the public phase in 1931–32. The Palace Building Council combined the announcement of the prizewinners on 28 February 1932 with a directive "On the organisation of the work for the final project of the Palace of the Soviets in the city of Moscow"[76]. The directive emphasised that the public contest had not led to the finding of a "definitive solution". The latitude for the subsequent work was limited: the Palace, according to the directive, should be a uniform

75 Cf. Mitteilungen der Internationalen Kongresse für Neues Bauen. In: die neue stadt 2/1932, p. 45, quoted in: Pistorius (ed.) 1992, p. 136.

76 Postanovleniia Soveta stroitel'stva Dvortsa Sovetov 1933, pp. 55–56.

*Hector O. Hamilton:
Concept for the
Palace of the Soviets,
December 1931.
Second round of
the contest.
[Naum Gabo 1992,
p. 130]*

complex with the main rooms all in one building. The Palace should soar upwards. Reminiscences of religious motives were to be avoided, however. The architectural design should pay attention to monumentality, simplicity and uniformity. The glory of the construction of socialism should find expression. A particular style was not explicitly prescribed. In the programme it was stated that "the merging of new forms with the best principles of traditional architecture should be aspired to."[77] The direction was therefore clear: a large building stretching upward was to be created that was technically on the cutting edge, with a design that represented a confrontation with the classical legacy. The Palace Building Council further suggested commissioning individual prizewinning architects with the subsequent work. A new phase of the contest thus began.

This final, once more closed, phase of the contest went through two rounds. The third round ran from March to July 1932, and the fourth from August 1932 to February 1933. In the third round twelve designs were commissioned[78], and in the fourth, five[79]. Foreign architects no longer played any role. The final phase of the contest did not produce anything fundamentally new. The star of this phase was Boris Iofan. His proposal for the fourth round was a building over 200 metres high that was topped by an 18 metres high statue of the "liberated proletarian". This was in line with the condition that the required rooms should be contained in one uniform building that stretched upward. This solution was juxtaposed to other, less convincing ones that emphasised the vertical element by a separate structure, a tower. In addition to this "special feature" the emotional character of the concept was emphasised.[80]

Iofan's urban planning concept also received great praise. The difficult problem of the relationship between the new Palace and the old Kremlin was well-solved. The uniform volume of the upwardly stretching Palace was contrasted with the horizontal complex of the Kremlin.[81] "The immense building", said Lunacharsky, "to judge by the preliminary draft, does not overwhelm the Kremlin despite its enormousness. It goes without saying that its immediate neighbourhood must be built with less monumental buildings, but in roughly the same style."[82] Precisely the spatially dominant reorganisation of the area surrounding the Palace of the Soviets that was characteristic of Iofan thus met with approval. The Palace with its squares formed the centre of a wide boulevard that began at Dzerzhinsky Square and led to the Gorky Central Park of Culture and Leisure. The boulevard, like the riverside esplanade, connected the Palace with Red Square. The huge building was thus not segregated from the centre of Moscow but was integrated into it. The still open question of the preferred urban development concept was thus decided to the disadvantage of Zholtovsky. Iofan, it was said, was designing a new centre, a "forum of the socialist capital". This included the Museum of the Arts, the Marx-Engels-Lenin Institute, the Museum of the Revolution, the Lenin Library, the STO building, the House of the Trades Unions, the Bolshoi Theatre, Red Square, Dzerzhinsky Square and the Lenin Prospekt. A monument for Karl Marx was foreseen on the Palace Square and the open spaces around the Palace were designed in the form of green areas with sculptures and fountains.[83]

With its directive of 10 May 1933 the Palace Building Council set the course for the "ultimate solution": Boris Iofan's concept was specified as the basis for the subsequent work. Iofan should take the best proposals by other architects into account. The possibility of integrating other architects into the work was introduced. The upper part of the Palace – this was the most far-reaching decision – should be topped with a monumental, 50 to 75 metres high sculpture of Lenin.[84]

This increased the ideological importance of the building. The decision by the Palace Building Council "to give precedence to an illustrative, tangible architecture, was not far removed from the concepts of the workers in the rounds of discussion on the Soviet Palace or from the lay entries in the public contest."[85] The embalmed dead Lenin next to the Kremlin Wall was to experience a stunning resurrection – as the crowning of, as the giver of meaning to, the Palace. Karl Marx, with his nearby monument, would have been forced to live a dwarf-like existence in Lenin's shadow. Lenin resurrected as a solitary giant enhanced above all his self-named successor: Stalin. The wish for Lenin as a

77 Cooke/Kazus 1991, p. 59.
78 Cf. Ter-Akopyan 1992, p. 188.
79 Cf. Ter-Akopyan 1992, p. 188.
80 Dvorets Sovetov 1/1933, p. 4.

81 Dvorets Sovetov 1/1933, p. 5.
82 Lunacharsky 1992, p. 151.
83 Cf. Dvorets Sovetov 1/1933, p. 8.
84 Cf. Postanovleniia Soveta stroitel'stva Dvortsa Sovetov 1933, p. 59.
85 Pistorius 1994, p. 165.

saviour figure was the bang of the drum introducing the excessive personality cult of the new dictator. The Stalin era had found its visually powerful symbol.

The architectural structure of the Palace was changed decisively with this decision: it mutated to a monumental plinth for a giant figure and thus became a giant sculpture. At least as important, however, were the consequences for urban development: whereas up to this point in time only the immediate surroundings of the Palace of the Soviets were to be rearranged, the decision for a gigantic Lenin figure implied the subordination of much larger areas. This change was made particularly clear by the dominant orientation of the huge building: in the first rounds of the contest the urban space in front of the Palace facing the Kremlin – if anywhere – was of interest; following the decision of May 1933 the urban space behind the Palace also became increasingly important.

The result was finally a building with a height of about 415 metres with a roughly 80 metres high statue of Lenin "surrounded by an enormous plain with marching grounds, triumphal arches and avenues for parades".[86] The building was to be higher than the highest building in the world at that time, the Empire State Building, completed in 1931. On 19 February 1934 the concept of Vladimir Gel'freikh, Vladimir Shchuko and Boris Iofan was finally accepted by the Palace Building Council.[87] The construction period for the Palace was determined as 1935 to 1942.[88]

In an article in the journal "Architecture of the USSR" in 1935 Boris Iofan explained the new urban dimensions of the Palace of the Soviets by referring to European models. The Palace itself with its squares and the adjacent Prospekt was declared to be the key project for the reconstruction of the Moscow centre and therefore the key project for the reconstruction of Moscow. The largest designed square in Europe, with an area of 110,000 sq.m. was to be extended in front of the Palace.[89] "Its purpose is not the separation from the city but the organic fusing of the Palace of the Soviets with the city landscape, with the life of the capital and with the people."[90] This was a clear rejection of an "exclusionary" solution such had been proposed by Zholtovsky, for

example. Since an immense building with a height of over 400 metres was now planned, the neighbouring city district had to be integrated by means of a corresponding increase in heights. Iofan suggested that high-rise buildings supporting the silhouette of the Palace should be planned with a great deal of tactfulness. Altogether 16 high-rise buildings[91] were to be constructed within the Garden Ring. "The tower of the Soviet Palace should play a role in the 20th century analogue to that played by the Ivan the Great Bell Tower in the 16th century at the centre of the church towers in historic Moscow."[92]

In view of this development the concept for the reconstruction of the city centre had quietly changed. A new centre was now to be created that freed itself in both function and design from the old centre around the Kremlin. This new centre was to become the "most beautiful place in socialist Moscow".[93] Instead of the original concept of a double centre Kremlin/Palace, de facto a dominant new centre was proposed which now assigned to the Kremlin only the role of a parade ground collateral to the Prospekt. The central area of Moscow thus lost its equilibrium: alongside the Palace of the Soviets the Kremlin would be dwarfed.

From a strategical point of view the contest was a masterpiece: it shifted attention in a fundamental way – towards Moscow, towards the centre, towards monumental architecture, towards a building assignment that went beyond the new towns with their industrial giants, towards an urban development that respected the historic structure in principle but nevertheless reinterpreted it in a radical, monumental way. In this respect the contest procedure for the Palace of the Soviets reflected the work on a Master Plan for Moscow as if under a magnifying glass. The coordination of the work on the Master Plan and that on the Palace of the Soviets was in the hands of a key figure in urban development in the Stalin era: Boris Iofan, who had been the head of the Planning Workshop No. 2 of the Mossovet since 1933.

Between 1934 and 1937 the project for the Palace of the Soviets was again revised. The statue of Lenin "grew" on paper to 100 metres and the total height of the Palace fluctuated between 419 and 474 metres.[94] A model of the Palace was proudly presented at the international exposition in Paris in 1937. Following the approval of the Master Plan in 1935 the demolition of entire districts had begun. It was intended not only to create the space needed for the surrounding squares, but also – in connection with the completion of the Boulevard Ring in the south – for the broad

86 Schlögel 1992, p. 179. By this point in time Western interest in the Palace of the Soviets had already died out. The Italian professional community was an exception: in March 1934 Marcello Piacentini, the perhaps most influential architect in Fascist Italy, published an article in the journal "Architettura" with the title: "Un grande avvenimento architettonico in Russia: Il Palazzo dei Sovieti a Mosca" (pp. 129–140). In it he writes: "neither the grandiosity nor the originality of the composition of Iofan's gigantic building can be disputed. It lacks in character, however: it is neither antique nor modern: it lacks style." Quoted in: Borngräber 1987, p. 421.
87 Cf. Borngräber 1987, p. 421.
88 Cf. Pistorius 1992, p. 138.
89 Cf. Iofan 10–11/1935, p. 25. Iofan referred to other European squares in this connection, for example the Piazza del Popolo in Rome (20,000 sq.m.), the Place d'Étoile in Paris (38,000 sq.m.), St. Peter's Square in Rome (57,000 sq.m.) and the Place de la Concorde in Paris (79,000 sq.m.).
90 Iofan 10–11/1935, p. 25.

91 Cf. Flierl 2000, p. 165. Flierl is referring to information from Aleksandr Riabushin.
92 Flierl 2000, p. 165.
93 Iofan 10–11/1935, pp. 25–28.
94 Cf. Borngräber 1987, p. 423.

*Boris Iofan:
On the realisation of
selected concepts for a
220 metres high Palace
of the Soviets, photo
of a model, February
1933. Fourth round
of the contest.
[Source: Dvorets
Sovetov 1/1933, p. 3]*

*Boris Iofan,
Vladimir Shchuko and
Vladimir Gel'freikh:
Revised concept for a
420 metres high Palace
of the Soviets, 1933.
[Source: URSS anni
'30–'50 1997, p. 131]*

approaches to the Palace building. Ultimately, "a territory of 1,000 hectares with important architectural monuments and a quarter of a million residents would have been affected"[95] by the planned redevelopment. At the same time the new "Palace of the Soviets Prospekt" was to be constructed with numerous buildings, particularly for social institutions. The demolitions concomitant to the development of the banks of the Moskva River and the subsequent

greening were to round off the "Gesamtkunstwerk", the Palace of the Soviets. On 4 May 1937, the excavation work finally began for the Palace that would never be built.[96]

---

95 Flierl 2000, p. 165. Bruno Flierl is referring to Isaak Ėigel', 1939–49 scientific secretary to the architectural and planning studios for the Palace of the Soviets and biographer of Boris Iofan.

96 In June 1941, after the beginning of the war, "all construction work had to be stopped. The steel skeleton was dismantled and used for defence purposes." In: Flierl 2000, p. 171. On the site of the Palace of the Soviets Khrushchev later built an open-air swimming pool that was opened in 1960. In 1993, the swimming pool was closed and a year later work began on the reconstruction of the Cathedral of Christ the Saviour. The outer reconstruction of the Cathedral was completed for the 850th anniversary of the founding of Moscow in 1997.

Red Square

The most important place in the historic centre of Moscow was Red Square with its political and social functions. Although the Palace of the Soviets with its surrounding squares was intended to form a new centre, the historic heart of Moscow – Red Square – continued to be rated the most important inner-city square in accordance with its past importance.[97] In this place, the new socialist society was to be represented not only by the maintaining of the existing historic buildings, but also by the appropriate design of the square and by new buildings. As the main city square within the historic centre, which was now almost exclusively occupied by Party and government institutions, it fulfilled above all the function of a place for parades and demonstrations.[98]

The Resurrection Gate[99] had already been demolished in 1931 in order to create sufficiently broad approaches to, and exits from, Red Square for demonstrations and parades. In addition, the Cathedral of Our Lady of Kazan and the old quarter behind St. Basil's Cathedral were demolished.[100] In preparation for the contest for the People's Commissariat for Heavy Industry (Narkomtiazhprom)[101] announced in 1934 and the connected redevelopment of Red Square, it was also proposed to demolish the Historical Museum and the department store (GUM). The planned new building was to represent a clear and widely visible symbol for the success of the Soviet Union regarding industrial policy.

Red Square with a view of the St. Basil's Cathedral, c. 1938.
[Source: Institut izobrazitel'noi statistiki 1938]

97   Cf. Moskva. 850 let II 1997, p. 104.
98   Cf. Moskva. 850 let II 1997, p. 104.
99   The Voskresenskie vorota (Resurrection Gate), the main entrance to Kitai-gorod, was built in 1638 and renewed and extended in 1680. It lay on the ceremonial route of the tsar to Red Square. The Gate was demolished in 1931 and rebuilt in 1995. Cf. Kiernan 1998, p. 42.
100   Cf. Moskva. 850 let II 1997, p. 105. The eighth, uncompleted high-rise building – in addition to the "seven sisters" – would be built at this location after the Second World War. Cf. Kiernan 1998, p. 172.
101   Cf. Aranovich, 10/1934, pp. 20–29; Dom Narodnogo komissariata tiazheloi promyshlennosti 6/1936, pp. 1–28; Cooke/Kazus 1991, p. 85.

View in the direction of Red Square before the reconstruction. The historic buildings between St. Basil's Cathedral and the Moskva River were torn down for the reconstruction. [Source: Sovetskaia arkhitektura 1917–1957 1957, no page number]

Aleksandr and Viktor Vesnin: Entry for the contest for the building of the People's Commissariat for Heavy Industry on Red Square, 1934. [Source: URSS anni '30–'50 1997, pp. 128–129]

An area of approximately nine hectares to the east of Red Square in Kitai-gorod was intended as the site for the new building for the People's Commissariat for Heavy Industry, with a planned building volume of almost one million cubic metres. It was an essential requirement of the participants in the closed contest that the building blend into the "environment of the world-famous historical and architectural monuments" on Red Square[102] and form a counterpart to the newly constructed Lenin Mausoleum on the opposite side of the Square. Through traffic should in principle be barred from Red Square. At the same time, the complicated organisation of mass demonstrations was to be ensured.[103]

The great majority of the concepts submitted proposed the demolition of St. Basil's Cathedral and the construction of high-rise buildings with more than 30 storeys.[104] Only in one variation of the proposal by Konstantin Mel'nikov was the maintenance not only of the Cathedral on Red Square foreseen, but also of the department store (GUM).

By 1935, a total of 19 projects were devised by major Soviet architects. None of the proposed projects was awarded a prize and adopted for the reconstruction of the square, however. Nevertheless, all the projects were regarded as important contributions and steps on the way to the reconstruction of the square because they had shown the importance of proportionality for Red Square and the necessity of taking into consideration the relationship between the size of the square and the height of the surrounding buildings.[105]

Following the extensive preparations for the development of the eastern side of Red Square it was admitted that the proposed dimensions of the building were incommensurate with the historical proportions of Red Square and its neighbouring buildings.[106] This was the officially named main reason for the abandonment of the planned site for the building of the People's Commissariat for Heavy Industry.[107] In a further round of the contest in 1936 "a new site was chosen: in nearby Zariad'e, below St. Basil's Cathedral directly on the bank of the Moskva. Again gigantic buildings were designed, even more massive than before [...], but with a much less modern architectural concept than in the first phase of the contest."[108] This round also produced no result. One major change to Red Square was made in the second half of the 1930s, finally, with the construction of the large New Moskvoretsky Bridge, which provided a better connection between the Square and the southern districts of the city.

102 Cf. Cooke/Kazus 1991, p. 85.
103 New Manege Square between Gorky Street and Red Square was used as a gathering area for the demonstrations, as the historical buildings there had been completely demolished.
104 Cf. Cooke/Kazus 1991, p. 85; Colton 1995, p. 326.
105 Cf. Aranovich 10–11/1935, p. 39.
106 Cf. the criticism of the construction in Aranovich 10–11/1935, pp. 37–43.
107 Cf. Aranovich 10–11/1935, p. 40.
108 Flierl 2000, p. 166.

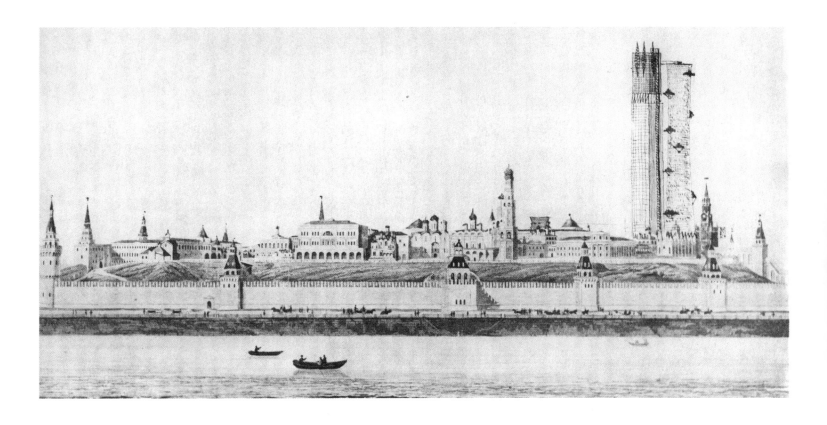

Ivan Leonidov: Entry
for the contest for
the building of the
People's Commissariat
for Heavy Industry on
Red Square, 1934.
[Source: URSS anni
'30–'50 1997, p. 138]

Ivan Fomin, Pavel Abrosimov and
Mikhail Minkus: Entry for the contest
for the building of the People's Commissariat
for Heavy Industry on Red Square, facade
facing Sverdlov Square, 1934.
[Source: Tyrannei des Schönen 1994, p. 120]

Arkadi Mordvinov: Entry for the contest for the building of the People's Commissariat for Heavy Industry, 1936. Photomontage with parade of athletes. [Source: Institut izobrazitel'noi statistiki 1938]

Boris Iofan and Aleksei Baransky: Project for the building of the People's Commissariat for Heavy Industry, 1936. [Source: Moskva. 850 let II 1997, p. 111]

Aleksei Shchusev, Patvakan Sardar'ian and Vyacheslav Kirillov: The Kremlin and Red Square with the newly built New Moskvoretsky Bridge, c. 1938. [Source: Institut izobrazitel'noi statistiki 1938]

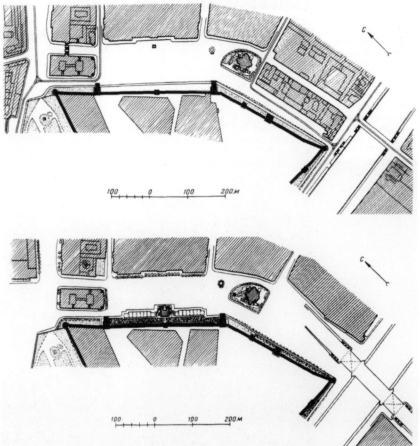

Red Square before (top) and after (bottom) the construction of the bridge and the reconstruction. [Source: Sovetskaia arkhitektura 1917–1957 1957, no page number]

Ivan Zholtovsky:
Residential building at
Mokhovaia Street 2,
built in 1934.
View with the
neighbouring
Old University.
[Source: Oshchepkov
1955, p. 63]

Hunters' Row and
New Manege Square

Directly adjoining Red Square are New Manege Square and the wide street called Okhotnyi Ryad (Hunters' Row). This square-like area played a key role in the emergence of the architectural style of the Stalin period. Numerous architectural monuments bordered on the square, such as the Moscow Manege and the Old Moscow University.

The New Manege Square was integrated into the new Palace of the Soviets Prospekt between Dzerzhinsky Square and Luzhniki. It was intended that after its redevelopment it would allow a direct view of the building of the Palace of the Soviets with the statue of Lenin. Until the demolition this historic site was characterised by market stalls and small shops, trading and commercial premises. Before the redevelopment Moiseevskaia Square with a small chapel lay in the prolongation of Okhotnyi Ryad.[109] The new, large square was needed above all to provide adequate gathering and waiting areas for the demonstrations and parades on Red Square. Most of the time, however, the New Manege Square was simply a huge, unused area of asphalt.

The construction of the residential building of the Mossovet on the northwestern border of the Square between the Old University and the Hotel National according to a design by Ivan Zholtovsky in 1934 – in line with the decisions in the

contest for the design of the Palace of the Soviets – represented a further rejection of modern architecture.

In addition, a further building was constructed in this area between 1935 and 1938 that was considered trendsetting for the redevelopment of the centre: the Hotel Moscow. Following a design by Aleksei Shchusev, this building was created as a hotel for the Moscow city soviet. In a central location and directly neighbouring on the centre of power in the Kremlin it rapidly developed into a prestige project, which also promoted the architectural turnaround. Furthermore, the decision to remove the existing historic structures in their entirety was also an expression of the disdain for the traditional, small-scale structures of the city and the will to transform its entire layout on a large scale that was also becoming apparent in the projects for the Palace of the Soviets with its squares and the extension of the Prospekt. Only the sections of this building project facing New Manege Square und Okhotnyi Ryad were completed by the beginning of the war.

109   Cf. Huber/ETH Zürich (ed.) 1995, p. 73.

The centre of Moscow
between New Manege
Square and Theatre
Square in front of
the Bolshoi Theatre –
situation c. 1930 (left)
and following the re-
development measures
1940 (right).
[Source: Istoriia
sovetskoi arkhitektury
1962, p. 113]

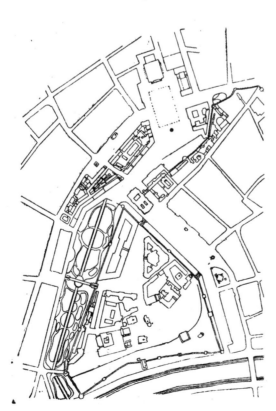

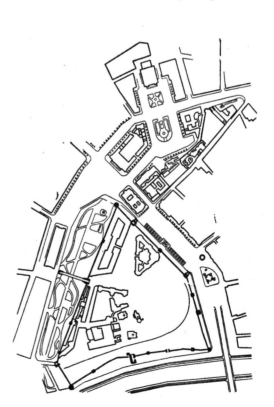

New Manege Square, and in the background the building of the Hotel Moscow, designed by Aleksei Shchusev, 1937. [Source: Institut izobrazitel'noi statistiki 1938]

The old Tverskaya (later Gorky Street) in its historical state with the planned new width drawn in. [Source: Gendel' 16/1940, p. 25]

Gorky Street

The redevelopment of Gorky Street was the most important project concerning a major arterial road within the historic centre of Moscow. The removal of the old, partly winding Tverskaya Street, which was renamed Gorky Street in 1932, was intended to enable the creation of "a uniform, urban ensemble that should, in addition, exhibit a festive-triumphal character"[110]. It was planned that the new boulevard should have a width of more than 60 metres. This meant that the old Tverskaya (later Gorky Street), which was between 19 and 25 metres wide, would have to be widened to the specified dimension primarily by means of numerous demolitions.[111] The existing subterranean technical infrastructure and the already completed Metro installations were not to be damaged by this, and the dense traffic and daily use of the street by countless people were to be only minimally disrupted.[112]

The entire area of Gorky Street between the Kremlin and the Belorussky railway station can roughly be divided into two parts with Pushkin Square as a hinge. On this square, the crossing point of Gorky Street with the Boulevard Ring, the arterial road changes its direction. Pushkin Square also marks the entrance into the old city. It was considered necessary to emphasise the change of direction there by the construction of dominant urban features.[113] The area

from Pushkin Square to Okhotnyi Ryad (Hunters' Row) constituted the most important and representative section of Gorky Street and a preliminary to the central point of the city – the Kremlin with its surrounding open spaces and the buildings opposite. In this section, which was subject to the highest design requirements and for which monumental architecture was demanded, all the buildings on both sides of the street completed by 1941 were built according to designs by the architect Arkadi Mordvinov, with the exception of the Telegraph Office[114] on the western side, which had already been built in 1927. This area of the old city with its many backstreets was always full of life. This urban character was to be maintained by the reconstruction. In

110   Suetin 4/1957, p. 14.
111   Cf. Gendel' 16/1940, p. 25; Abrosimov 4/1940, p. 38.
112   Cf. Pronin 11–14/1940, pp. 23–24.
113   Cf. Abrosimov 4/1940, p. 40.

114   The building of the Telegraph Office was constructed in 1925–1927 on the old Tverskaya according to a design by Ivan Rerberg and, following its construction, was extremely controversial, especially in the professional community.

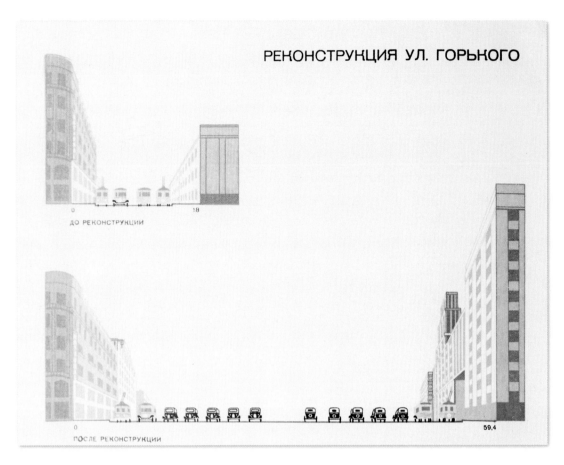

Depiction of the profile of the old and the new Gorky Street, 1938. [Source: Institut izobrazitel'noi statistiki 1938]

addition, the topology of the site, which sloped downward towards the city centre, had to be incorporated. The new buildings were staggered with regard to both depth and height, and were superimposed on the grid of small streets. The majority of the historic backstreets continued to exist, but they were only reachable via large archways and individual passageways and were thus no longer perceptible in the cityscape.

The historic development, which was characterised by three and four-storey buildings with a height of between 10 and 24 metres, protruded in this section to a total of more than 600 metres[115] over the stipulated "red lines" that marked the new road boundaries on the main Moscow arterial roads. However, since numerous monumental buildings were among those that stood at disposal, some of which had been officially classified as such only after the October Revolution and had been restored at considerable expense,[116] deliberations took place as to how these buildings could be preserved despite the widening of the street. As a result the relocation of the buildings rather than their demolition and reconstruction elsewhere was estimated to be the most time-saving and cost-effective option.[117] A special trust was founded in 1936 for this relocation. By 1940, it was able to gather initial experience with ten houses in the centre in the nearest section of Gorky Street.[118] In 1939, the building of the Mossovet was moved, and in 1940 several building relocations took place on the western side of the street between Pushkin Square and Mayakovsky Square.[119] In 1941, further buildings were moved in Gorky Street, some of them more than 50 metres.

Depending on the amount of space between the existing edge of the building and the newly established red lines, some of the new buildings were completed on the red lines behind the existing structures before the old buildings were torn down. Following the demolition the new dimensions of Gorky Street were perceptible – in the initial sections already in 1938.[120]

115 Cf. Pronin 11–14/1940, p. 24.
116 According to statements and materials provided by Elena Ovsiannikova, whose grandfather was Moscow's first monument conservator appointed by Lenin after the October Revolution.
117 It is interesting that studies at the time showed that the costs of relocation differed only slightly from those of demolition and reconstruction. It also made only a minimal difference to the expenditure involved whether the building was first rotated and then moved or both took place at the same time, but in two stages. The costs for the first variation were 2,187,100 rubles, and for the second 1,972,000 rubles. Cf. Gendel' 16/1940, p. 26.
118 Cf. Pronin 11–14/1940, pp. 23–24.
119 Cf. Pronin 11–14/1940, pp. 23–24.
120 Cf. Shkulev 17/1940, pp. 23–26.

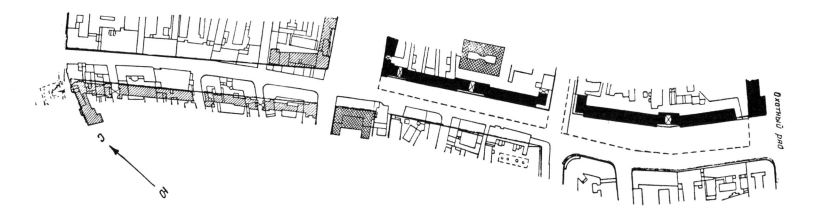

The redevelopment of Gorky Street vanquished the undesirable impression of a "medieval historical alleyway"[121].
The new street was not only one of the most important
urban arterial roads but also an object of prestige that had
been particularly highlighted in the propaganda. Whether,
and how, its residential use could be combined at all with
the functions of an arterial road (traffic, parades) was not
discussed. It was assumed that residential buildings could
also emanate monumentality, which was intended to be
demonstrated by the residential building by the architect
Andrei Burov,[122] which was described as "one of the first
really modern"[123] and monumental buildings in the corresponding section. The residential buildings nos. 4 and 6
(Blocks A and B) were also regarded as exemplary.[124] These
were constructed with standardised parts in 1937 to 1939
according to designs by Arkadi Mordvinov and were part
of the section between Okhotnyi Ryad (Hunters' Row) and
Pushkin Square that was already completed in 1940.[125]

Up until the beginning of the war the reconstruction of
Gorky Street was driven forward intensively. The activities
realised, in addition to the construction of new buildings
and the alteration of, and addition of storeys to, existing
buildings, also included the asphalting of the road surface[126] and the installation of new electric lights[127].

*Outline of the planned
new limits for building
development over the
historical layout of the
city in Gorky Street
in the section between
Okhotnyi Ryad
(Hunters' Row)
(right) and Pushkin
Square (left).
[Source: Pronin
11–14/1940, p. 2]*

*Moving of house
no. 24 in Gorky Street.
[Source: Institut
izobrazitel'noi
statistiki 1938]*

*Arkadi Mordvinov: Residential
buildings nos. 4 and 6 (Blocks A
and B) in Gorky Street, built
between 1937 and 1939.
[Source: Soiuz sovetskikh arkhitektorov SSSR (ed.) 1940, fig. 12]*

121 Shkulev 17/1940, p. 38.
122 Kozhin 2/1937, pp. 42–45.
123 Shkvarikov 1/1941, pp. 3–10.
124 Cf. Castillo 1994, p. 59.
125 Cf. Abrosimov 4/1940, pp. 42–43.
126 In 1936, c. 57,000 sq.m. of the road surface in Gorky Street were
     asphalted, in 1938 c. 33,000 sq.m. and in 1939 11,600 sq.m.
     Cf. Pronin 11–14/1940, pp. 20–21.
127 In 1936, more than 140 new street lamps were erected in Gorky Street
     and in 1939 a further 80. Cf. Pronin 11–14/1940, pp. 20–21.

Policy of Urban Renewal

In Moscow in the 1930s a new, independent variation of historic city centre redevelopment evolved. The handling of the historic centre and its transformation into a socialist centre was one of the most important themes of the Master Plan for Moscow. Its objective was to maintain the ring-radial system as a structural principle but at the same time to extend it within the framework of a radically new interpretation. This implied a completely new monumental, magnificent building development, a radical widening of the main roads and a reduction in the number of side-streets. The redevelopment of the arterial roads, squares and river banks was of paramount importance here. An essential condition for this was the construction of the Metro, which had long begun and which considerably improved the accessibility of the new city centre and therefore defined its centrality anew. The construction measures were framed by the lavish planning of green spaces and parks as well as by the Union-wide archetype of the Park of Culture and Leisure (from 1932 onwards Gorky Park).

Particularly the outdated, unwanted historic centre was the subject of planning efforts, in particular the new central point of the future centre, the location of the Palace of the Soviets, the spatial expression of the centralism of the Stalin era. The neo-baroque objective was the monumental new production of the image of the city by means of interventions in the places in the historic city with particularly powerful images: in the large main roads, in the most important squares, in the water fronts along the banks of the Moskva. The consistently applied principle of the dominance of urban construction over architecture, the concept of the ensemble as a building block in the plan for the city as a whole, is evident here. Dominance in this context does not mean the constant repetition of a few standard types, but the subordinating of the architecture, which can vary in the (facade) details – even of standardised elements – to the requirements of the overall design of a block of buildings, of a quarter, and in the final analysis of the entire city. The urban development conditions not only allowed a limited architectural flexibility, but even demanded it.

With the project of the Palace of the Soviets a highly centralist type of capital city historic centre reconstruction was developed that soon brought pressure to bear on the other two hegemonial dictatorships. Fascist Rome answered in a twofold manner: with the contest for the Palazzo del Littorio on the new Via dell'Impero between the Piazza Venezia and the Colosseum, and with the project of a huge colossus symbolising Fascism on the Monte Mario outside the historic centre. National socialist Berlin focused on a Great Hall on the bank of the River Spree. The building was to represent not only the capital but the entire state.

None of these gigantic buildings were realised. Nevertheless, their existence in plans had a decisive influence on urban development in the respective dictatorship. In Moscow itself directly after the war the construction of the seven high-rise buildings dedicated to Stalin followed the invisible dictate of the Palace of the Soviets.

In the core area of the former historic centre a kind of double centre was planned in which the Palace of the Soviets represented a new optical and symbolic focal point, but Red Square with the Kremlin was to continue to be the seat of power. Because of the new main settlement area in the southwest of Moscow it was planned to extend the central area further in that direction. Red Square was to be connected with the Palace of the Soviets via a representative axis which was embedded in the Palace of the Soviets Prospekt between Luzhniki in the southwest and Dzerzhinsky Square in the northeast. Envisaged was also a radical change in the silhouette of the city. From the very beginning, therefore, high-rise buildings – in addition to the Palace of the Soviets – were planned. Demolition work began even before the final concept for the Master Plan had been adopted, for example in preparation for the planned new construction or extension of the arterial roads and prospekts.

The urban renewal of historic centres in the socialist Soviet Union also meant city-building, i.e. the displacement of the old, small-scale, mixed use, of the poorer residents and of small craftsmen. For the new elite of the dictatorship – as in Rome, but more so than there – a new world was created with relatively good living quarters and workplaces in the new large buildings of central institutions. The large department store (GUM) on Red Square was endangered, but survived. At the same time space was created for the new means of transport: cars on the new main streets and the Metro under the ground. But Soviet city-building also meant the promotion of motor vehicle transport without private cars, and new buildings for the institutions of economic management without a private sector. And of course: state control of the land. The transformation of the historic centre took place under the motto: the reconstruction of Moscow.

The reconstruction of the city was therefore anything but cautious urban development. Even after the urban development turnaround the demolition of old buildings and the surmounting of small-scale construction were on the agenda. The destruction of the Cathedral of Christ the Saviour together with its surroundings made everyone dramatically aware of that. In the course of the implementation of the Master Plan – quite apart from the clearing of simple

Yuri Pimenov: The new Moscow, 1937. New buildings tower over, and even dwarf, the old ones. In the background the STO building (seat of the workers' and defence council) soars up potently. On the street the motor car, a symbol of progress, is dominant – in the foreground with a modern communist woman at the wheel.
[Source: Tarchanow/Kawtaradse 1992, image 79]

structures – more than 400 historically valuable buildings were destroyed according to official figures, including the Kitai-gorod wall.[128] The recognition of the historic ring-radial structure certainly did not mean the conservation of the historical layout of the city but, rather, its enormous extension. The dimension of the planned ensembles had nothing in common with the traditional structures and the existing ensembles. In detail they were a very contradictory innovation of urban development in the Stalin era. The leap in dimensions between the new palaces and the traditional buildings as well as between the new boulevards and the old alleyways led to a radically redeveloped city with completely new kinds of space and sequences of spaces. Measures such as adding storeys and moving historic buildings served the work on the new image of the city. The new city replaced the old or at least placed it in the shadows. The Palace of the Soviets served here as the baton for the leap in dimension.

Triumphal presentation of the planned new, light inner-city silhouette of Moscow compared to the old, dismal silhouette marked by church towers, c. 1952. The drawing pays homage to the eight planned and seven built new high-rise buildings, and besides them it continues to pay homage to the phantom building of the Palace of the Soviets, which towers over them all, and with these "stupendous buildings", according to the accompanying text, at the same time to the "great architect of communism, J. V. Stalin". [Source: Jugend und Technik 2/1954, pp. 6–7]

128   Cf. Moskva. 850 let II 1997, p. 112.

References

Abrosimov, Pavel: Ulitsa Gor'kogo [Gorky Street].
In: Arkhitektura SSSR [Architecture of the USSR]
4/1940, pp. 38–43

Adkins, Helen/Gabo, Naum: Die internationale
Beteiligung am Wettbewerb zum Palast der Sowjets.
In: Naum Gabo 1992, pp. 197–201

Aranovich, David: Arkhitekturnaia rekonstruktsiia centra
Moskvy (Konkurs proektov doma Narkomtiazhproma)
[Architectural reconstruction of the centre of Moscow
(Contest for designs for the Narkomtiazhprom building)].
In: Stroitel'stvo Moskvy [Moscow's building industry]
10/1934, pp. 20–29

Aranovich, David: Rekonstruktsiia moskovskikh
ploshchadei [The reconstruction of Moscow's squares].
In: Arkhitektura SSSR [Architecture of the USSR]
10–11/1935, pp. 37–43

Atarov, Nikolai: Dvorets Sovetov [Palace of the Soviets].
Moscow 1940

"Die Axt hat geblüht …". Europäische Konflikte der
30er Jahre in Erinnerung an die frühe Avantgarde. Jürgen
Harten/Hans-Werner Schmidt/Marie Luise Syring (eds.).
Düsseldorf 1987

Bodenschatz, Harald: Stadterneuerung Moskau – vom
Arbat nach Teplyi Stan. In: Bodenschatz/Hannemann/
Welch Guerra (eds.) 1992, pp. 36–56

Bodenschatz, Harald/Flierl, Thomas (eds.): Von Adenauer
zu Stalin. Der Einfluss des traditionellen deutschen Städtebaus in der Sowjetunion um 1935. Berlin 2016

Bodenschatz, Harald/Hannemann, Christine/Welch
Guerra, Max (eds.): Stadterneuerung in Moskau.
Perspektiven für eine Großsiedlung der 70er Jahre.
TU Berlin. Berlin 1992

Bodenschatz, Harald/Post, Christiane (eds.): Städtebau
im Schatten Stalins. Die internationale Suche nach der
sozialistischen Stadt in der Sowjetunion 1929–1935.
Berlin 2003; Russian edition: Bodenshatts, Kharal'd/Post,
Kristiane (sost.): Gradostroitel'stvo v teni Stalina. Mir v
poiskakh sotsialisticheskogo goroda v SSSR 1929–1935.
St. Petersburg 2015

Borngräber, Christian: Der Sowjetpalast im Zentrum
von Moskau. Chronologie der sieben Entwurfsphasen bis
zum Baubeginn am Ende der 30er Jahre. In: "Die Axt hat
geblüht …" 1987, pp. 417–425

Bunin, Andrei/Kruglova, Mariia: Arkhitekturnaia
kompozitsiia gorodov [Architectural composition of the
towns]. Moscow 1940

Castillo, Greg: Gorki Street and the Design of the Stalin
Revolution. In: Celik/Favro/Ingersoll 1994, pp. 57–69

Celik, Zeynep/Favro, Diane/Ingersoll, Richard: Streets.
Critical Perspectives on Public Space. London 1994

Chlewnjuk, Oleg W.: Das Politbüro. Mechanismen der
politischen Macht in der Sowjetunion der dreißiger Jahre.
Hamburg 1998

Chmelnizki, Dmitrij: Iwan Scholtowski. Architekt des
sowjetischen Palladianismus. Berlin 2015

Colton, Timothy J.: Moscow. Governing the Socialist
Metropolis. Cambridge, Mass./London 1995

Cooke, Catherine/Kazus, Igor: Sowjetische Architektur-
wettbewerbe 1924–1936. Basel 1991

Deutsche Bauakademie (ed.): Dreissig Jahre sowjetische
Architektur in der RSFSR. Leipzig 1950

Dom Narodnogo komissariata tiazheloi promyshlennosti
[Building of the People's Commissariat for Heavy
Industry]. In: Arkhitektura SSSR [Architecture of the
USSR] 6/1936, pp. 1–28

Dvorets Sovetov [Palace of the Soviets]. In: Arkhitektura
SSSR [Architecture of the USSR] 1/1933, pp. 3–10

Flierl, Bruno: Hundert Jahre Hochhäuser. Hochhaus
und Stadt im 20. Jahrhundert. Berlin 2000

Gendel', Ėmmanuil: Peredvizhka deviati zdanii po ulitse
Gor'kogo [Moving of nine buildings in Gorky Street].
In: Stroitel'stvo Moskvy [Moscow's building industry]
16/1940, pp. 25–28

General'nyi plan rekonstruktsii goroda Moskvy.
1. Postanovleniia i materialy [Master Building Plan for
the reconstruction of the city of Moscow. 1. Decisions
and materials]. Moscow 1936

Gorzka, Gabriele: Arbeiterkultur in der Sowjetunion.
Industriearbeiter-Klubs 1917–1929. Ein Beitrag zur
sowjetischen Kulturgeschichte. Berlin 1990

Graf, Oskar Maria: Reise nach Sowjetrußland 1934.
Berlin 1977

Hegemann, Werner: City Planning Housing. A Graphic
Review of Civic Art 1922–1937. Vol. III. New York 1938

Hildermeier, Manfred: Geschichte der Sowjetunion 1917–1991. Entstehung und Niedergang des ersten sozialistischen Staates. München 1998

Huber, Werner: Hauptstadt Moskau. Ein Reiseführer durch das Baugeschehen der russischen Metropole von Stalin über Chruschtschow und Breschnew bis heute. Zürich 1998

Huber, Werner/ETH Zürich (eds.): Moskau – Die Hauptstadt der UdSSR. Zürich 1995

Institut izobrazitel'noi statistiki sovetskogo stroitel'stva i khoziaistva TsUNKhU Gosplana SSSR [Pictorial statistical institute of the Soviet building industry and the economy CUNChU Gosplan of the USSR] (ed.): Moskva rekonstrui-ruetsia. Al'bom diagramm, toposkhem i fotografii po rekon-struktsii gor. Moskvy [Moscow is being reconstructed. Album with diagrams, topographical sketches and photographs of the reconstruction of the city of Moscow]. Moscow 1938

Istoriia sovetskoi arkhitektury 1917–1958 [History of Soviet architecture 1917–1958]. Moscow 1962

Iofan, Boris: Ploshchad' i prospekt Dvortsa Sovetov [Square and prospekt of the Palace of the Soviets]. In: Arkhitektura SSSR [Architecture of the USSR] 10–11/1935, pp. 25–28

Jugend und Technik 2/1954

Kaganovich, L. M.: Za sotsialisticheskuiu rekonstruktsiiu Moskvy i gorodov SSSR. Pererab. stenogramma doklada na iiun'skom plenume CK VKP(b) [For the socialist recon-struction of Moscow and the cities of the USSR. Revised stenograph of the report to the June Plenum of the CC of the VKP(b)]. Moscow/Leningrad 1931

Kaganovich, L. M.: Socialist Reconstruction of Moscow and other Cities in the U.S.S.R. New York 1931

Kaganovich, L. M.: Die sozialistische Rekonstruktion Moskaus und anderer Städte der UdSSR. Hamburg/Berlin, undated (c. 1931–32)

Kaganovich, L. M.: Moskovskie bol'sheviki v bor'be za pobedu piatiletki. Doklad o rabote MK i MGK na III Mosk. obl. i II gor. konferentsiiach VKP(b) 23 janv. 1932 g. [The Moscow Bolsheviks in the struggle for the success of the five-year plan. Report on the activities of the MK and MGK at the Third Moscow Area Conference and the Second Moscow City Conference of the VKP(b) of 23 January 1932]. Moscow 1932

Kaganovich, L. M.: Die sozialistische Rekonstruktion Moskaus und anderer Städte der UdSSR. Hamburg/Berlin, undated (c. 1931–32)

Kaganovich, L. M.: Die Moskauer Bolschewiki im Kampf um den Sieg des Fünfjahrplans. Moscow 1932

Kaganovich, L. M.: Der Bau der Untergrundbahn und der Stadtplan Moskaus. Rede auf der Plenartagung des Moskauer Sowjets unter Teilnahme der Stoßarbeiter des U-Bahnbaus und der Moskauer Betriebe. 16. Juli 1934. Moscow/Leningrad 1934

Kazus, Igor: Stalin und der Palast der Sowjets. In: Tyrannei des Schönen 1994, pp. 51–54

Kazus, Igor: Da Tatlin a Iofan. Il fenomeno concorsuale nella storia del Palazzo dei Soviet. In: URSS anni '30–'50 1997, pp. 79–90

Khazanova, Vigdariia (ed.): Iz istorii sovetskoi arkhitek-tury 1917–1925 gg. Dokumenty i materialy [From the history of Soviet architecture 1917–1925. Documents and materials]. Moscow 1963

Kiernan, Maria: Moskau. Köln1998

Knoch, Peter: Architekturführer Moskau. Ed. by Philipp Meuser. Berlin 2011

Kosenkova, Juliia (ed.): Sovetskoe gradostroitel'stvo 1917–1941 [Soviet urban development 1917–1941]. 2 Vols. Moscow 2018

Kozhin, Sergei: Zhiloi dom Narkomlesa na ulitse Gor'kogo [The Narkomles residence on Gorky Street]. In: Arkhitektura SSSR [Architecture of the USSR] 2/1937, pp. 42–45

Lenin, V. I.: Ausgewählte Werke in drei Bänden. Vol. II. Berlin 1967

Lunacharsky, A. V.: Sotsialisticheskii arkhitekturnyi monument [The socialist architectural monument]. In: Stroitel'stvo Moskvy [Moscow's building industry] 5–6/1933, pp. 3–10, documented in: Pistorius (ed.) 1992, pp. 144–151

Meuser, Philipp/Martovitskaya, Anne: Hidden Urbanism. Architecture and Design of the Moscow Metro 1935– 2015. Berlin 2016

Mosca. Capitale dell'utopia. Wissenschaftliche Leitung: Vieri Quilici. Milan 1991

Moskva v cifrach [Moscow in numbers]. Moscow 1934

Moskva. Ėntsiklopediia [Moscow. Encyclopaedia]. Ed. by S. O. Shmidt. Moscow 1997

Moskva. 850 let [Moscow. 850 years]. Ed. by
V. A. Vinogradov et al. Vol. II. Moscow 1997

Naum Gabo und der Wettbewerb zum Palast der Sowjets,
Moskau 1931–1933. Ed. by Berlinische Galerie. Berlin 1992

Neutatz, Dietmar: Die Moskauer Metro. Von den
ersten Plänen bis zur Großbaustelle des Stalinismus
(1897–1935). Köln/Weimar/Wien 2001

Oshchepkov, Grigori (ed.): I. V. Zholtovsky. Prospekty
i postroiki [I. V. Zholtovsky. Prospekts and Buildings].
Moscow 1955

Pamiatniki arkhitektury Moskvy. Kreml' – Kitai-gorod –
Central'nye ploshchadi [Moscow's architectural monu-
ments. The Kremlin – Kitai-gorod – central squares].
Ed. by M. V. Posochin et al. Moscow 1983

Pamiatniki arkhitektury Moskvy. Belyi gorod
[Moscow's architectural monuments. White City].
Ed. by G. V. Makarevich et al. Moscow 1989a

Pamiatniki arkhitektury Moskvy. Zemlyanoi gorod
[Moscow's architectural monuments. Earthern City].
Ed. by M. V. Posochin et al. Moscow 1989b

Pistorius, Elke: Der Wettbewerb um den Sowjetpalast.
In: Pistorius (ed.) 1992, pp. 132–138

Pistorius, Elke: Der Wettbewerb um den Sowjetpalast.
In: Gorzka (ed.) 1994, pp. 153–167

Pistorius, Elke (ed.): Der Architektenstreit nach der
Revolution. Zeitgenössische Texte Rußland 1920–1932.
Basel/Berlin/Boston 1992

Post, Christiane: Arbeiterklubs als neue Bauaufgabe der
sowjetischen Avantgarde. Berlin 2004

Postanovleniia Soveta stroitel'stva Dvortsa Sovetov pri
Presidiume TsIK SSSR [Resolutions of the Building Council of the Palace of the Soviets at the Executive Committee
of the CIK of the USSR]. In: Soiuz sovetskikh arkhitektorov (ed.) 1933, pp. 53–55

Programma proektirovaniia Dvortsa Sovetov SSSR
v Moskve [The programme for the project of the Palace of
the Soviets of the USSR in Moscow] (September 1931). In:
Soiuz sovetskikh arkhitektorov (ed.) 1933, pp. 123–129

Pronin, Vasili: Itogi rekonstruktsii Moskvy za 5 let
[Results of the reconstruction of Moscow in the last
5 years]. In: Stroitel'stvo Moskvy [Moscow's building
industry] 11–14/1940, pp. 20–24

Schlögel, Karl: Der Schatten des imaginären Turms.
In: Naum Gabo 1992, pp. 177–184

Sidorow, Alexys A.: Moskau. Berlin 1928

Shkulev, A. P.: Vzryvnye raboty po snosu domov na
ulitse Gor'kogo [Detonation work for the demolition
of the houses on Gorky Street]. In: Stroitel'stvo Moskvy
[Moscow's building industry] 17/1940, pp. 23–26

Shkvarikov, Vyacheslav: Itogi konkursa na luchshii zhiloi
dom [Results of the contest for the best apartment block].
In: Stroitel'stvo Moskvy [Moscow's building industry]
1/1941, pp. 3–10

Soiuz sovetskikh arkhitektorov (ed.): Dvorets Sovetov.
Vsesoiuznyi konkurs 1932 g. [Association of Soviet archi-
tects (ed.): Palace of the Soviets. All-Union contest 1932].
Moscow 1933

Soiuz sovetskikh arkhitektorov SSSR (ed.): Rekonstruktsiia
Moskvy [Association of Soviet Architects of the USSR
(ed.): The reconstruction of Moscow]. Moscow 1940

Sovetskaia arkhitektura 1917–1957 [Soviet architecture
1917–1957]. Moscow 1957

Suetin, S.: Na glavnoi ulitse stolitsy [On the main street of the
capital]. In: Arkhitektura i stroitel'stvo Moskvy [Moscow's
architecture and building industry] 4/1957, pp. 12–14

Tarchanow, Alexej/Kawtaradse, Sergej: Stalinistische
Architektur. München 1992

Ter-Akopyan, Karine: Projektierung und Errichtung des
Palastes der Sowjets in Moskau. Ein historischer Abriß.
In: Naum Gabo 1992, pp. 185–196

Tyrannei des Schönen. Architektur der Stalin-Zeit.
Ed. by Peter Noever. München/New York 1994

Über die städtische Wirtschaft Moskaus und die Entwicklung der städtischen Wirtschaft in der UdSSR. Resolution
zum Bericht des Genossen Kaganowitsch, angenommen
vom Plenum des ZK der KPdSU am 15. Juli 1931. In:
Kaganovich (c. 1931/32), pp. 126–146

URSS anni '30–'50. Paesaggi dell'utopia staliniana.
Ed. by Alessandro De Magistris. Milan 1997

Weiskopf, Franz Carl: Umsteigen ins 21. Jahrhundert.
Berlin 1959

Winkler, Klaus-Jürgen: Der Architekt Hannes Meyer.
Anschauungen und Werk. Berlin 1989

Moscow: The Centre of the Soviet Union
For centuries the Kremlin formed the heart of the historic centre of Moscow.
That did not change after the October Revolution of 1917. On the contrary:
the relocation of the capital city from Petrograd (St. Petersburg) to Moscow in
1918 meant that the Kremlin became the seat of command of the Bolshevik
dictatorship. In the following decades several important ecclesiastical
buildings within the Kremlin walls were demolished. The famous Lenin
Mausoleum was built in front of the Kremlin Wall on Red Square in 1924
based on a design by Aleksei Shchusev. At first it was relatively small and built
of wood; later it was enlarged in oak and finally rebuilt in dark red granite
in 1930. The embalmed corpse of the leader of the revolution, who died on
21 January 1924, has been on public display there ever since – with a few
rare exceptions. The Mausoleum is an exceptional construction, appearing
to subordinate itself to the Kremlin but in the final analysis dominating it
due to its central urban location on Red Square. Behind the Mausoleum is a
cemetery of honour for other Soviet leaders, including the grave, with bust, of
Stalin, who died in 1953 and whose corpse lay in state next to Lenin's in the
Mausoleum from 1953 to 1961. Since 1990, Red Square and the Kremlin are
a UNESCO World Heritage Site. The Lenin Mausoleum is thereby recognised
as an unusual example of Soviet monumental architecture.
[Photo: Harald Bodenschatz, 2015]

Moscow: Resurrection I
Red Square today is closed to the north by the Resurrection Gate, which stands next to the Historical Museum (on the left of the photo). In front of the Gate on the side facing the city is the small but famous Iversky Chapel with an icon of the Mother of God, an important Moscow shrine. The original of the icon is kept in the Historical Museum, and a copy in the reconstructed chapel. This was not always the case. The Gate has in fact been resurrected. It used to be the main entrance to Kitai-gorod, but it was also the point of entry for the tsars on their way to Red Square. In 1931, it was torn down in order to provide space for large military demonstrations. It was reconstructed in 1995/1996. Immediately next to the Resurrection Gate stands the Cathedral of Our Lady of Kazan, which was torn down in 1936 and rebuilt in 1993. The resurrected Gate, like the Cathedral of Christ the Saviour and the Cathedral of Our Lady of Kazan, is an indication of the new, important role of the Orthodox Church in Russian urban development following the demise of the Soviet Union.
[Photo: Harald Bodenschatz, 2015]

Moscow: Resurrection II
The reconstruction of the Cathedral of Christ the Saviour to the southwest of the Kremlin on the bank of the Moskva River was, and is, of the greatest symbolic importance. The mighty central building, which was originally inaugurated in 1883 – the highest building in Moscow at that time – was demolished in 1931 in order to make room for the most important project of Stalin's dictatorship in the centre of Moscow, the four times higher Palace of the Soviets. Although the Palace was never built, it functioned as an imaginary baton, determining urban development over an extensive area during Stalin's dictatorship. The seven high-rise buildings that were constructed in the inner city immediately following the Second World War also took their reference from it. Excavation activities began on the site of the demolished Cathedral in 1937. Following the invasion of the Soviet Union by National Socialist Germany in the summer of 1941, all building activities ceased. After the death of Stalin, Khrushchev built an open-air swimming pool on the abandoned building site, which was opened in 1960. In 1993 the pool was closed and two years later the work on the reconstruction of the Cathedral began with the financial support of the state. In 2000, the 103 metres high Cathedral was inaugurated anew. The central ecclesiastical building of the Russian Orthodox Church thus stood once again in the centre of Moscow – a reversal of the urban development of Stalin's dictatorship – with regard to architecture, town planning and social policy – that is visible for all to see.
[Photo: Sergey Detukov, 2019]

Moscow: The Old City Moved to the Second Row
One of the most spectacular projects concerning the old city during Stalin's dictatorship was the moving of historic buildings to behind the new buildings of the widened main roads. This technique was regarded at the time as less expensive than demolition followed by reconstruction. The most important field of experiments for the relocations was the project of widening Gorky Street. By 1940, experience could be gathered there with ten houses in the section of the street nearest to the city centre. Following the relocation, the old buildings disappeared behind the self-asserting new buildings but remained a little visible from the street through large entrance gates – like this magnificent, well-maintained building in neo-Russian style now standing in the courtyard. Until 1932, Gorky Street was called Tverskaya Street and since 1990 it again has that name – another form of dealing with the urban development of the dictatorship.
[Photo: Harald Bodenschatz, 2015]

The Urban Renewal of Historic Centres in Hitler's Germany: Berlin*

Harald Bodenschatz

During the national socialist dictatorship (1933–1945) urban development was an important policy field, a means of control and at the same time a means of communication of the new relationships of power, the evocation of a heroic past, the promise of a magnificent future and a demonstrative sign of a racist social policy that excluded, and would soon destroy, entire groups of the population. Urban development was not only talked about, it was drawn and modelled, put on display in exhibitions and, finally, it was also realised, although in a different way to that often portrayed in the postwar period. Our picture of national socialist urban development is defined primarily by the propaganda of the dictatorship, which was increasingly canonised from the end of the 1930s onward. Then, and now, the grand plans for restructuring were, and are, repeatedly emphasised, first and foremost in Berlin, then in Munich, in Nuremberg, concerning the Gauforum in Weimar, the autobahns and their bridges. Other building projects that made an impact on everyday life remain in the shade: housing construction above all, but also urban redevelopment.

Particularly the early years of national socialist rule were characterised in many German towns and cities by extensive urban redevelopment measures in the historic centres that were visible to everyone and underlined the energy of the new regime. Among the major examples were Braunschweig[1], Frankfurt am Main[2], Hamburg[3], Kassel[4] and Cologne[5]. Weimar was a remarkable special case.[6] Reconstruction plans had often already been drawn up during the Weimar Republic but could not be implemented due to inadequate municipal funds and legal instruments. That changed conspicuously with the assumption of power in 1933: the local authorities lost their autonomy but at the same time were given new freedom of action. Following the at first extremely modest funds for urban renewal in 1933 under the job creation programme, a programme for the reconstruction of historic centres was begun at the national level in 1934 under the control of the Ministry of Labour, the first programme of

List of the cities in which measures under the programme for the redevelopment of historic centres were carried on in 1933–1943, compiled by Folckert Lüken-Isberner, 1991. [Source: Lüken-Isberner 1991, p. 37]

* This text is an updated, modified and expanded version of earlier deliberations: Bodenschatz 1987; 2009; 2014; 2016; 2018; Bodenschatz/Engstfeld/Seifert 1995; Bodenschatz/Goebel 2010; Bodenschatz (ed.) 2010. The author wishes to thank Benedikt Goebel for comments, criticism and advice on illustrations.

1   On Braunschweig cf. Petz 1987, pp. 47–66. The publications by Ursula von Petz can be regarded as pioneer work on the redevelopment of historic centres in the period of the national socialist dictatorship. On the redevelopment of Berlin's historic centre cf. the fundamental works by Schäche 1991, pp. 153–202, and Goebel 2003, pp. 221–267.
2   On Frankfurt am Main cf. Petz 1987, pp. 95–115; Cunitz 1996.
3   On Hamburg cf. Schubert 1986, pp. 62–83.
4   On Kassel cf. Schulz 1983; Petz 1987, pp. 116–134; Lüken-Isberner 2016.
5   On Cologne cf. Petz 1987, pp. 135–156.
6   On Weimar cf. Bodenschatz 2016, pp. 19–31. Folckert Lüken-Isberner was a member of a working group led by Christian Kopetzki in Kassel which published comprehensive studies on urban renewal under the national socialist dictatorship already in the late 1980s. Cf. Neuer-Miebach/Kopetzki (eds.) 1988. Together with Ursula von Petz' doctoral thesis from 1987, "Stadtsanierung im Dritten Reich dargestellt an ausgewählten Beispielen" [Selected Examples of Urban Renewal in the Third Reich], in Dortmund at the end of the 1980s the foundations for this subject were already established, and they should be brought to mind again today.

Braunschweig: Example of the gutting of a block in the historic centre, 1939. [Source: Flesche 1939, p. 21]

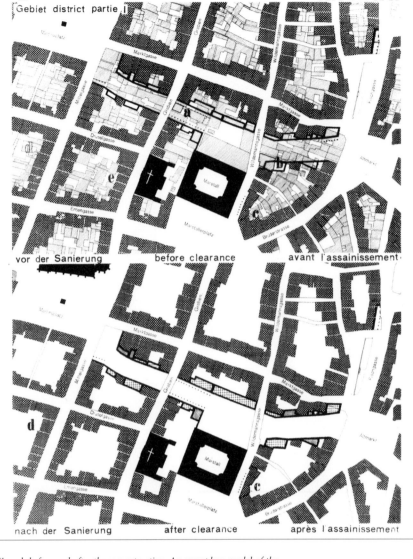

Hamburg: Gängeviertel before and after redevelopment, 1935. Here, again, block-gutting was planned as well as street widening and the creation of squares that are reminiscent of the method of "thinning out" propagated by Gustavo Giovannoni. [Source: Scheck 1995, p. 118]

Kassel: before and after the reconstruction. An exemplary model of the combination of a street breakthrough with the gutting of a block, presented in the documentation "Elendsviertelsanierung" [slum clearance] of the Internationaler Verband für Wohnungswesen [International Housing Association], 1935. [Source: Internationaler Verband für Wohnungswesen (ed.) 1935, p. 36]

its kind in Germany.[7] It was not exactly generously funded with 15 m. Reichsmark. Nevertheless, 41 towns had recourse to it, especially small and medium-sized towns. Projects for the redevelopment of historic centres were not only implemented under the urban renewal programme, however.

The redevelopment of historic centres was of great importance primarily in the early years of the national socialist dictatorship. From 1937 onward this area of work was overshadowed both financially and in the propaganda by the plans for the "Führer Cities" and the urban development projects in connection with rearmament, and it forfeited political weight. Even in Berlin's 700th anniversary

celebrations, the historic centre no longer played a large role, neither as a setting nor as a theme. The efforts to establish a national law on the urban renewal of the historic centres, in which the aspect of air-raid protection was of increasing importance,[8] were no longer seriously pursued after 1935.[9] It was not until the strategic bombing by the Allied air forces began in 1942 that the historic centres moved back onto the agenda – under the aspect of reconstruction. Already on 13.11.1941 the Reich Ministry of Labour published a circular on "air-raid damage and the recovery of historic centres", which called on the municipalities to carry out reconstruction "from the perspective of the urban

7   On this cf. Lüken-Isberner 1991, pp. 23–43.

8   Lehweß/Winter 1935.
9   Scheck 1995, p. 116.

Potsdam: Example of "Entschandelung" [removal of "disfigurement"]. Original text: "The ugly tower, which is particularly objectionable in the landscape with regard to the high location of the imperial war archives, has been stripped of its superficialities. For the extension only the depth of the building, the roof profile and the type of roofing have been retained from the old building." [Source: Lindner/Böckler 1939, p. 265]

renewal of the historic centres". Air-raid protection, in turn, was to be given special consideration. In these final years of the national socialist dictatorship numerous compounds for forced labourers, prisoners of war and concentration camp prisoners were set up in the historic centres, and forced labour was also employed in redevelopment areas.[10]

No other historic centre of a German city was so comprehensively replanned during the national socialist dictatorship as that of Berlin, and in no other historic centre was the reconstruction started on such a large scale. Most of the measures in the capital of the Reich were not completely new but had already been prepared in the period of the Weimar Republic. But what exactly was meant by Berlin's historic centre? As a rule, in Berlin that part of the city was defined as the historic centre, even in the period of the national socialist dictatorship, which had its origins in the Middle Ages, i.e. the area of the twin cities Berlin and Cölln. For dealing with the historic centre in Berlin the directly neighbouring areas were of decisive importance, the periphery of the old town, such as Friedrichswerder and the Museumsinsel, but also the surroundings of Alexanderplatz and the former Bülowplatz.

Nowadays when national socialist urban development in Berlin is evoked, pictures of the new centre along the north-south axis are conjured up, while the historic centre is ignored. The future heart of the capital of Germany, and of the entire German Reich, was to be built from scratch to the west of the existing city centre. That was in fact unique: no other dictatorship planned its new centre outside of the existing centre of the capital, only the German dictatorship. The city centre did not offer enough space and it did not contain any buildings, streets or squares that the new rulers regarded as internationally presentable, not even the Palace, not even the grand boulevard Unter den Linden. Due to the fact that attention so far has been paid almost exclusively to the north-south axis, the plans and activities of the national socialist period in the area of the historic centre have

Frankfurt am Main: Example of the gutting of a block in the historic centre, praised as "ideal", 1939. [Source: Lindner/Böckler 1939, p. 267]

Cologne: "Improvement measures", 1939. [Source: Lindner/Böckler 1939, p. 269]

The future centre of the national socialist capital of the Reich was intended to lie beyond the historic centre, in the central area of a monumental north-south axis. On the plan the proposed users of the planned new buildings are drawn in. [Source: Schusev State Museum of Architecture, Moscow]

remained relatively unknown until the present day. This is entirely inappropriate as the historic centre was to experience a radical push for change in the national socialist era – following the reconstruction phases of the Baroque era, the Schinkel era and the imperial era, came a fourth thrust, which now questioned the very structure of the historic centre but came to a standstill halfway, however.

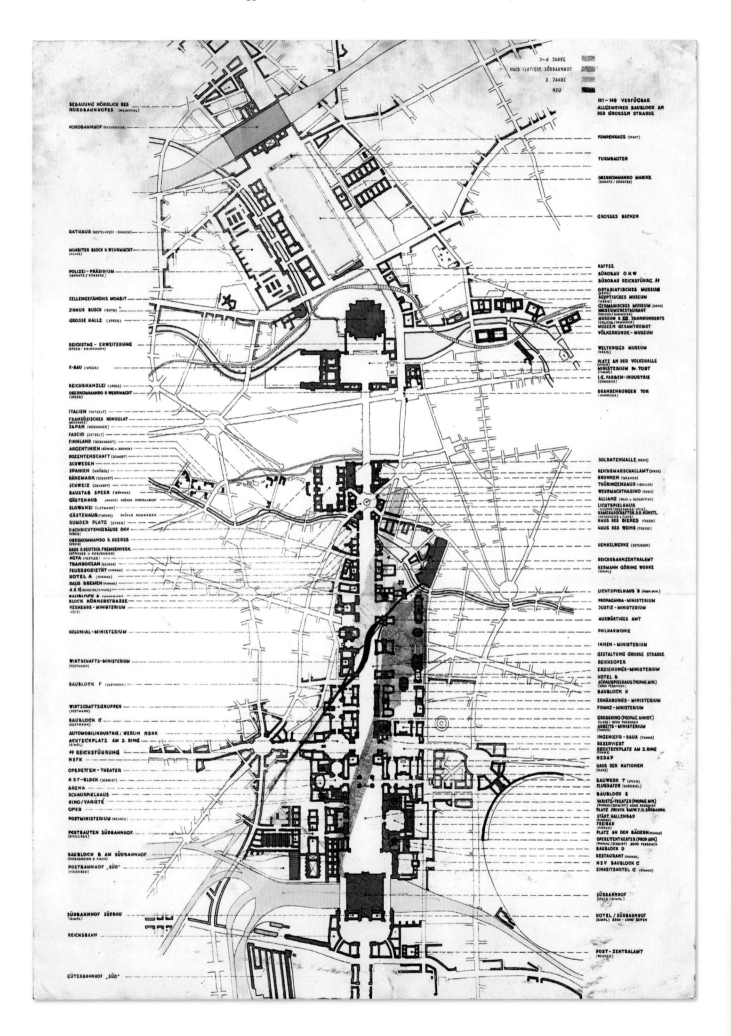

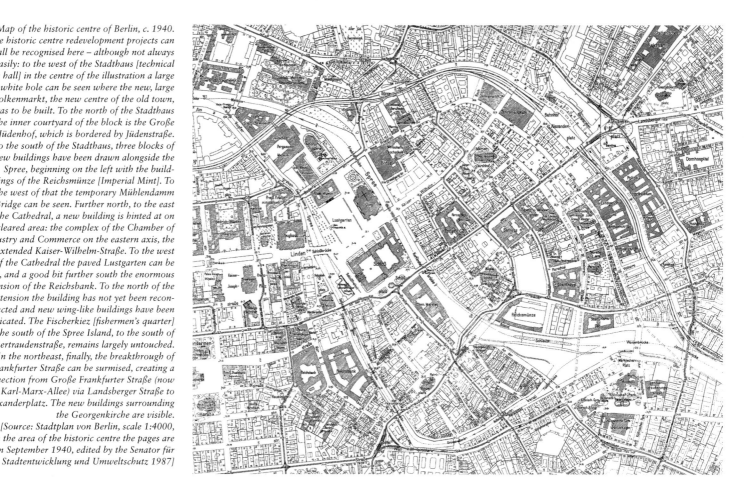

Map of the historic centre of Berlin, c. 1940. The historic centre redevelopment projects can all be recognised here – although not always easily: to the west of the Stadthaus [technical city hall] in the centre of the illustration a large white hole can be seen where the new, large Molkenmarkt, the new centre of the old town, was to be built. To the north of the Stadthaus in the inner courtyard of the block is the Große Jüdenhof, which is bordered by Jüdenstraße. To the south of the Stadthaus, three blocks of new buildings have been drawn alongside the Spree, beginning on the left with the build- ings of the Reichsmünze [Imperial Mint]. To the west of that the temporary Mühlendamm Bridge can be seen. Further north, to the east of the Cathedral, a new building is hinted at on a cleared area: the complex of the Chamber of Industry and Commerce on the eastern axis, the extended Kaiser-Wilhelm-Straße. To the west of the Cathedral the paved Lustgarten can be seen, and a good bit further south the enormous extension of the Reichsbank. To the north of the extension the building has not yet been recon- structed and new wing-like buildings have been indicated. The Fischerkiez [fishermen's quarter] in the south of the Spree Island, to the south of Gertraudenstraße, remains largely untouched. In the northeast, finally, the breakthrough of Frankfurter Straße can be surmised, creating a connection from Große Frankfurter Straße (now Karl-Marx-Allee) via Landsberger Straße to Alexanderplatz. The new buildings surrounding the Georgenkirche are visible. [Source: Stadtplan von Berlin, scale 1:4000, in the area of the historic centre the pages are from September 1940, edited by the Senator für Stadtentwicklung und Umweltschutz 1987]

Plans for the Historic Centre of Berlin towards the End of the Weimar Republic

For the Berlin politicians and planners of the late Weimar Republic there was no doubt as to the necessity of a radical reconstruction of the historic centre, even for those with a Social Democratic leaning. Martin Wagner, the famous director of urban development in the Berlin of the Weimar Republic, summarised his experiences in the USA in 1929 in the foreword to his book "Städtebauliche Probleme in amerikanischen Städten und ihre Rückwirkung auf den deutschen Städtebau" [Urban development problems in American cities and their impact on German urban devel- opment] as follows: "It is futile for us to rebel against the development of the automobile as a means of mass trans- portation. Liberation from spatial and temporal confine- ment lies in the nature of modern man. The concentra- tion of millions of city residents in the narrow spaces of work and housing demands expansion, demands freedom from confinement. And this individual liberation out into the plains, into the outdoors, to physical regeneration can only be achieved by automobiles. America is the classical country of cities. The city residents have achieved their individual freedom from place and time by means of the automobile. [...] The German urban planner, however,

must be full of care and anxiety when he sees this triumphal flow of automobiles through his towns and cities. They are not prepared for such a flaring up of traffic. They must be reconstructed. [...] Berlin is on the best way to growing into the American traffic revolution."[11]

With this perspective the classical street breakthrough and street extension gained a new meaning, especially in Berlin's historic centre. The Prussian Minister for Social Welfare from 1921 to 1933, Heinrich Hirtsiefer, a politician from the Centre Party with Christian-social roots, spoke in this connection of "traffic misery". "The rapid and strong de- velopment of automobile traffic has made the transforma- tion and restructuring of our road network one of the most pressing problems of the present."[12] The transformation of the road system to facilitate the flow of traffic would, ac- cording to Berlin's Mayor Gustav Böß, accelerate the for- mation of a "business city": "The more traffic increases,

11 Wagner 1929b, p. 5.
12 Hirtsiefer 1929, p. 452.

the more will this stimulate business. The earlier Berlin begins to tackle these tasks, the easier and cheaper will be the solution. We must not shy away from tearing down and destroying, even if the objects affected have an emotional value."[13] The plea for demolition in favour of road traffic found its emotional climax in a statement by Martin Wagner in 1929: "Fear and awe of the old makes us weak, it paralyses and kills. [...] A people that does not build, does not live, it dies. Germany and Berlin want to, and must, live. We want to live in the way that Frederick the Great let Berlin live through his buildings. He tore down the old in order to erect something new in its place."[14]

The reason for this evocation of the new at the cost of the old was the experience made with the shifting of the business city towards the west: "The development pull in the inner city is [...] from east to west. The main business areas, which originally encompassed only the historic centre to the right of the Spree, have spread over Unter den Linden, Friedrichstraße, Leipziger and Wilhelmstraße to Potsdamer Platz and its surroundings. This development will continue. The area next to the Zoologischer Garten will become a part – even though of a special nature – of the business city."[15] In particular the eastern Kurfürstendamm had developed into a main shopping street. The move of the business city towards the west pushed the historic centre ever further aside. The attempts since 1926/27 of the two city councillors, Ernst Reuter and Martin Wagner, together with the town planner Martin Mächler,[16] to reconstruct the southern historic centre to facilitate traffic must be seen against this background.

If Old Berlin was regarded as behind the times, this was all the more true of the Fischerkiez. The formation of a business city had not yet displaced the residents here. In 1925 an impressive number of residents were still counted: 3,698 persons. Up to 480 residents lived on one hectare; that was the highest density of population in the centre. Here there was a plethora of small and very small plots, of small, narrow, and in some cases low, houses, and here there were still exceptionally narrow alleyways. The residents of this area were as a rule very poor and the living conditions were correspondingly wretched. It can be assumed that these were the worst living conditions in the whole of Berlin.

In a democracy legitimation was required for the radical transformation of the historic centre. This was to be secured by means of "scientific" assessments. For this purpose a survey was commissioned in 1930 from the Verein für

Wohnungsreform [Association for Housing Reform] with the support of the "City Committee" and the "Berliner Verkehrs-A.-G." (BVG) [Berlin Transport Company] and assisted by Martin Mächler. The expert report "Die Wohnungsverhältnisse der Berliner Altstadt" [The housing situation in the historic centre of Berlin], compiled under the direction of Bruno Schwan and published in 1932, demonstrated the misery of the housing on individual plots *in situ*. "House for house, residence for residence", the survey states, the reports speak "in certain streets of vermin, damp, the smell of rot, decay, of well-worn, dark stairways, crumbling plasterwork, so that one is gripped by horror."[17] The conclusion was clear: the tearing down of the slums, to use the terminology of the survey, was not only justified but from a social point of view necessary. The question of what was to happen to the residents, however, was discussed only marginally. The legitimation of the demolition strategy from a construction perspective was less complicated. The built environment in the southern historic centre, so it was argued, had no architectural value whatsoever. The romanticisation of the historic centre was castigated as an aberration. "Some may perhaps regret that the presently existing romantic built environment of the inner city is to be replaced by a new business city. But in the long run it will be impossible to save Berlin's historic centre either as a residential town or as a museum. The cityscape that will one day emerge here after the residential and manufactory district has been relocated will be unromantic and poor in tradition, but it will be more hygienic and economically more rational."[18] These were the summarising words in 1931 of Hermann Ehlgötz, Professor at the Technical University of Berlin and the author of a report on the subsoil of Berlin's historic centre, which was also intended to legitimise its wholesale redevelopment.

The contest for the reconstruction of the southern historic centre that was under consideration for 1930 did not take place due to the political and economic problems of the late Weimar Republic. In March 1931 the Berlin city parliament refused to vote for the motion on the invitation to tender. But Martin Wagner did not give up. In his essay on the subject of "The new Berlin" in 1932 he mounted a picture that showed Berlin and its districts. Above the map a magnifying glass is hovering, enlarging a part of the city plan: the area of the southern Spree Island, the Fischerkiez. Martin Wagner added the following: "The city of a new world metropolis on the basis of the limitation of space to live and limitations to property ownership as in the Middle Ages! It is impossible for a capital city of the Reich, a machine city and a world city, to develop in this spider's web of borders that are tailored to the small 'citizen' but not to 'society', and to the 'pedestrian' but not to the 'machine'!"[19]

13 Böß 1929, p. 119.
14 Wagner 1929, p. 130.
15 Böß 1929, p. 115.
16 At that time Martin Mächler represented the City Council formed in 1926, a coalition of Berlin businessmen with the objective of countering the decline of the historic centre.

17 Schwan 1932, p. 13.
18 Ehlgötz 1931, p. 128.
19 Wagner 1932.

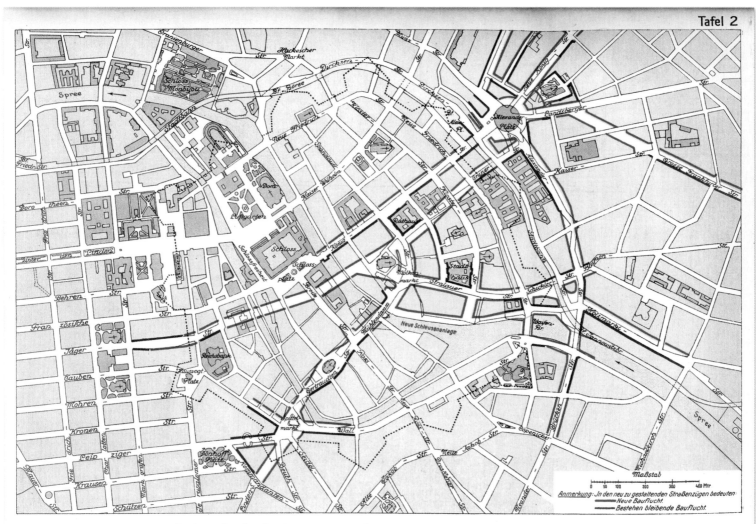

Tafel 2

Geplante Straßendurchlegungen und Straßenverbreiterungen in der Jnnenstadt.

Nach der Vorlage des Magistrats vom 18. April 1930 an die Stadtverordneten

*"Planned street breakthroughs and widening of
streets in the inner city", 18.04.1930. In this draft
by the municipal administration for the city councillors the widespread demolition of the southern
historic centre was envisaged.*
[Source: Wittig 1931, Table 2]

*Martin Wagner, View with a magnifying glass of the
urban layout of the southern Spree Island. The medieval urban structure, according to Wagner, was not
appropriate for the city of a new world metropolis.*
[Source: Wagner 1932, Fig. 17]

The Reconstruction of Berlin's Southern Historic Centre after 1933

Following the accession to political power of the NSDAP in 1933 the protagonists of the Weimar Republic took the plans that had failed in 1931 back out of the drawer. A key role was played here by the "Deutsche Bauzeitung" [German Building Journal] that was still published by Martin Mächler. In 1934 a whole series of articles was published in it reminding readers of the plans of the Weimar Republic. The provisional mayor of the district Berlin-Mitte, Wilhelm Lach, attacked the inability of the Weimar Republic to redevelop Berlin's historic centre in the January issue: The centre of Berlin, according to Lach, "is substantially the most important and most valuable part of the capital of the Reich; this has been completely underrated in recent years. The inner city has been allowed to become bloodless and insubstantial. The emigration of trades was tolerated and nothing was done to stop the move towards the west that had become fashionable. Nothing was done to realise the idea that had existed for years that the inner city should be deconcentrated. The Stadthaus [technical city hall] has derelict hovels as neighbours, the desolate condition of which cannot be surpassed, such as e.g. the houses between the Stadthaus and the Spree on Stralauer Straße. In the Fischerkiez [...] entire housing blocks are only fit for demolition."[20]

The article by the district mayor was immediately followed by a comprehensive presentation of the results of the expertise by the Deutscher Verein für Wohnungsreform on living conditions in the historic centre of Berlin in 1932. This report is preceded by the following words: "The question of the redevelopment of Berlin's historic centre naturally comprises not only the improvement of living conditions but is to the same degree, if not even to a greater degree, the improvement of the economy as a whole, of Berlin trade and of traffic. A glance at the accompanying plan of the inner city from a bird's eye view with its maze of narrow streets, its plots of land nested within one another, the fragmentation of which does not allow an economic utilisation from a modern perspective, shows this without further explanation."[21]

In the following month a longer article was published: "The urban renewal of the Berlin 'city'", signed by a Dr. Sandow. The state of the historic centre was again lamented: "How is the city to allow the most modern life currents of the city dweller to flow, if it is itself in its entire form so undynamic that it cannot even meet the increased requirements of metropolis dwellers with regard to buildings or to traffic? The city is caught up in a spider's web of tiny property boundaries, making every widening of a street and every expansion of a business property dependent on chance or on the good mood and the good or bad will of the neighbours."[22] In order to overcome this situation, a "state commissar for the urban renewal of the city of Berlin", a "*F u e h r e r* of the city of Berlin", was needed. His task was clearly defined: "The residential districts of the poor and the poorest with their decimated spending power *h a m p e r* the development of the city and must be removed by the radical destruction of the wretched residential districts."[23] Hiding behind the pseudonym Dr. Sandow was Dr. Martin Wagner, who was forced to vacate his position as chief city planner on 13 March 1933 because he was a Social Democrat.[24]

The attempt by Martin Mächler and Martin Wagner to bring the plans of the Weimar Republic back into play under the new political conditions failed, however – at least in the desired form. The City Council, characterised by Jewish businessmen and industrialists, which Martin Mächler represented, had still referred to itself in January 1934 as a bulwark against "communism" and prepared a memorandum on the development of a "German business city", was dissolved in March 1934.[25] Mächler was forced to relinquish his editorship of the "Deutsche Bauzeitung" in 1935. As a Swiss citizen, however, he remained in Germany. Martin Wagner, on the other hand, left Germany in 1935. The redevelopment of the historic centre was not forgotten, however. On the contrary.

A key project that had already been prepared in the Weimar Republic – in connection with the extension of the Mühlendamm lock – was the redevelopment of Mühlendamm, which connected the southern Old-Cölln with the southern Old Berlin and was regarded as a bottleneck for east-west traffic. Mühlendamm, which had been redeveloped in the imperial era, was torn down with all its buildings and replaced by an emergency bridge in 1938. The wholesale redevelopment of southern Old Berlin was prepared in connection with this.[26] The redevelopment comprised two – connected – urban development project areas: one was that around the Molkenmarkt, the oldest square in Berlin, and the other was the Rolandufer next to the Spree. While a new, representative square was planned for the Molkenmarkt, the old buildings on the bank of the Spree were to be replaced by completely new ones. In particular, the

---

20   Lach 1934, p. 25.
21   Eiselen 1934, p. 26–36.

22   Wagner [Dr. Sandow] 1934, p. 142.
23   Wagner [Dr. Sandow] 1934, p. 144.
24   Cf. Scarpa 1986, p. 148.
25   Sonderbericht 1934.
26   On this cf. Schäche 1991, pp. 170–202.

Plan for the "Mühlendamm site", Department of Town Planning
(Felix Unglaube), 1936/37. Large areas of the southern historic centre with their small, old houses were planned for demolition. The
expanse of the new Molkenmarkt can be seen in the middle to the
left of the Stadthaus. To the north of the new square the extension
of the Rathaus is perceptible, to the north of the Stadthaus is the
new building of the Municipal Feuersozietät [Fire insurance], which
borders on the Großer Jüdenhof to the south. The planned new
Mühlendamm bridge is visible on the left, in the Spree the future
lock is indicated and alongside the Spree are the three new planned
blocks on the northern Rolandufer. On the Fischerkiez to the south
the planned Public Health Department has been outlined.
[Source: Landesarchiv Berlin, C Rep. 110-01 (Maps), No. 22]

*Mühlendamm with temporary bridge, 1940. The
building of the Sparkasse [Savings bank] in the form
of a castle, the old Mühlendamm lock and the Palais
Ephraim were torn down in 1935–1937.
[Source: Berlin Mitte Archiv, No. 7511]*

famous-infamous Krögel was to give way to demolition, a
poor people's alleyway that was wrongly equated with the
old town per se. The layout of the historic centre there was
to be maintained in principle but be considerably simplified.
Three administrations were the major participants in the
large-scale project: the Reich Waterways Administration
(Mühlendamm lock and bridge), the Prussian State Building Administration (The Mint[27]) and the Berlin Municipal
Administration (municipal administration building).[28]

A start had already been made on the redevelopment of
the southern historic centre in 1934. In 1935 an extensive
plan by Richard Ermisch already existed. Whereas to begin
with new, improved housing was envisaged, another option soon came into the foreground: a huge administration
centre, a particular form of catching up on the formation
of a business city on the territory of Old Berlin.[29] Its centrepiece was an extension to the Rathaus [city hall] that had
actually been planned before the First World War. It was
intended to augment the Rotes Rathaus [red city hall] and
the Stadthaus, which had been built in 1902–1911 according to plans by Ludwig Hoffmann, by a third Rathaus. The
Stadthaus and the planned new building, together with a
new house for the city president, provided the framework
for a large parade-ground, the new Molkenmarkt, also
known as the Old Town Forum, that was to replace the
modest, old Molkenmarkt. This would have meant that
the historic heart of medieval Berlin, denounced as an "ir-
regular, ineffective square",[30] would have been eliminated.
A large, architecturally designed forecourt in front of the

new Rathaus was, however, already envisaged by Ludwig
Hoffmann before the First World War.[31]

Administrative buildings were also envisaged for the new
blocks along the Rolandufer. Next to the House of the City
President the western block was to include the Reichsmünze.
A historic building, the Palais Schwerin, was included –
moved by a few metres – in the new building complex.[32] For
the two blocks that were to follow in the east further city
administrative buildings were planned. The overall planning
for the reconstruction of the southern historic centre came
from the City Head of Planning Benno Kühn[33] and his colleague, Building Officer Döscher.[34] Following the extensive
wholesale clearing of buildings along the Rolandufer, however, only the western and eastern of the three blocks on the
Spree were actually built. The eastern (partial) block was
built according to plans by Richard Ermisch in 1937–1939,
and the Reichsmünze according to plans by Fritz Keibel and
Arthur Reck in 1936–1942. With these buildings a radical
change in function in the southern historic centre was put
into effect – to the benefit of the public authorities.

The reorganisation of the quarter around the Nikolaikirche
[St. Nicholas's Church] was also envisaged as a special part
of the reconstruction of the southern historic centre. The initiative for this came from the Prussian State Civil Engineering
Administration.[35] Today's neo-medieval, free re-creation of
the Nikolai Quarter, a product of GDR urban development
of the 1980s, was therefore – like many other projects – not
a purely GDR invention: "The present character of the buildings around the Church should be maintained at all costs and
around them a type of Old Berlin open-air museum should
be created in which valuable old buildings existing here are
saved and, in addition, good, old houses that are forced elsewhere to give way to the recovery of the historic centre, can
rise up again here and thus be preserved for posterity – a
quiet corner from long forgotten times."[36] The Ephraim-
palais had already been demolished in 1936 in favour of
the car-friendly widening of the street from Mühlendamm
to Molkenmarkt, with the intention of rebuilding it later "in
an identical fashion – moved by a few metres".[37] Berlin had
to wait half a century, however, for this to happen – in 1987.

Nevertheless, in the southern historic centre there was one –
though modest – preservative redevelopment measure: the
restoration of seven houses of the Großer Jüdenhof in 1936
to 1938. This publicly accessible inner courtyard was in the

---

27 The Reichsmünze (Mint) was responsible for minting coins. It required a
   new building because the old Mint building had been forced to give way
   to the building of the Reichsbank somewhat further west.
28 Landesdenkmalamt Berlin 2003, p. 158–159.
29 On the administration buildings cf. also Verwaltungsbericht der
   Hochbauverwaltung 1937, 31–34.
30 Kühn 1936, p. 712.

31 Cf. Schäche 1991, p. 170–171.
32 Landesdenkmalamt Berlin 2003, p. 159.
33 Benno Kühn assumed the position of City Head of Planning on 13 March
   1933 and died on 16 September 1936. Verwaltungsbericht der Hochbauverwaltung 1937, p. 7. On the political and administrative management of
   Berlin city planning cf. Goebel 2003, p. 221–224.
34 Schäche 1991, p. 170–172.
35 Goebel 2003, p. 225.
36 Kühn 1936, p. 712.
37 Kühn 1936, p. 712.

*Wholesale clearing on the Rolandufer, c. 1936.
[Source: Bundesarchiv, Bild 183-R97900/without specification]*

*Model of the area between the Molkenmarkt and the Spree, 1937.
[Source: Landesdenkmalamt Berlin 2003, p. 159]*

*Model for the reconstruction of the Nikolaiviertel, 1939. Historic buildings that had been demolished in other parts of the historic centre were to be reconstructed in the Nikolaiviertel.
[Source: Stahn 1991, p. 32]*

*The eastern side of the Großer Jüdenhof after the reconstruction, April 1939. The apparently historic building on the far right is a new building.
[Source: Verein für die Geschichte Berlins, photo by Heinrich Lichte – Landesarchiv Berlin, F Rep. 290, No. 61-3928]*

immediate neighbourhood of the Molkenmarkt. It was to be "preserved at the request of the City President, Dr. Lippert, as the last example of the old Berlin inner courtyards."[38]

A "Guide to Berlin" published on the occasion of the Olympic Games already informed visitors to the city in 1936 about all these measures: "The so-called '*Old Berlin*', often sung about and regarded romantically, but in reality a dismal, squalid place of poverty, which defied description as far as the sanitation of its housing was concerned, has been torn down. Dark, narrow alleyways, half collapsed, crumbling house facades

with buckled windows fell, while bright housing blocks arose. Large-scale projects, longing for implementation after spending decades on the desks of architects, were begun."[39] Only the area of the southern Spree Island, the Fischerkiez, the rehabilitation of which the protagonists of the reconstruction of the historic centre in the Weimar Republic, Martin Wagner and Martin Mächler, had still energetically advocated even after 1933, was spared from eradication. The demolition was certainly planned – partially by Richard Ermisch in 1935 and comprehensively by Fritz Keibel and Arthur Reck in 1938.[40]

---

38 Statement by one of the participating architects in 1938, quoted in: Goebel 2003, p. 246.

39 Trurnit 1936, pp. 37–38.

40 Cf. the plan by Fritz Keibel and Arthur Reck from 1938, documented in: Architekten- und Ingenieur-Verein zu Berlin e. V. (ed.) 2009, p. 173.

Projects on the Periphery of the Historic Centre

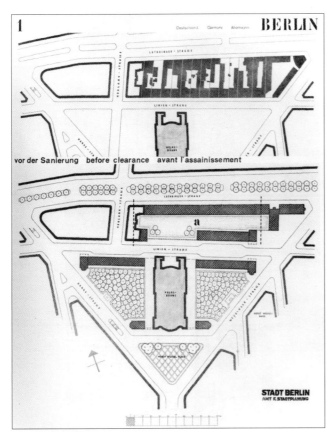

The redevelopment of the southern area of Old Berlin was "the largest building project in the context of historic centre urban renewal"[41] in the national socialist epoch. In the early years of the dictatorship, however, redevelopment projects on the periphery of the historic centres – not only in Berlin – were also important, above all in the north (former Bülowplatz), east (behind Alexanderplatz) and west (southern Friedrichswerder, Lustgarten).

Bülowplatz had already been created before the First World War within the framework of an extensive wholesale clearance project. The objective at that time was the removal of socially and structurally undesirable residential quarters, the so-called "barn alleys". A large theatre was built on the new triangular square, the *Volksbühne*, which became internationally famous in the Weimar Republic – as a domain of left-wing theatre, especially under the direction of Erwin Piscator. Directly on this square was another important building: the headquarters of the German Communist Party (KPD) and its party organ, the "Red Flag" ("*Rote Fahne*"). This square, like no other place, was a platform for left-wingers in Germany, particularly the Communists, and the workplace of the KPD Chairman, Ernst Thälmann. It was, in addition, a residential area for Eastern European Jews. These characteristics were the reason why the dictatorship wanted to change this place in order to make a cult site for national socialism out of the stronghold of communists. Bülowplatz became Horst-Wessel-Platz, the KPD House became Horst-Wessel-House, and a Horst-Wessel monument was erected in front of the Volksbühne.[42] At the same time

Horst-Wessel-Platz before and after the reconstruction, presented in the documentation "Elendsviertelsanierung" [slum clearance] of the Internationaler Verband für Wohnungswesen, 1935. [Source: Internationaler Verband für Wohnungswesen (ed.) 1935, p. 10]

Horst-Wessel-Platz on German Police Day, 1937. [Source: Bundesarchiv, Bild 183-C00678/ without specification]

---

41 Kühn 1936, p. 711.

42 Horst Wessel, a Sturmführer of the SA, was wounded by a communist in 1930 and later died of his injuries. He was then declared a "martyr" of the national socialist movement. He was also the author of the Horst-Wessel-Lied, anthem of the NSDAP and during the dictatorship part of the national anthem. Cf. Horst Wessel 1907–1930.

Alexanderplatz with the Georgenkirche and the breakthrough of Frankfurter Straße, c. 1933. In the front we can see the Alexanderplatz railway station and behind it the new buildings by Peter Behrens. Behind the oval area of the square is a large cleared area bounded to the left by the Georgenkirche. To the right of the church, on the other side of Landsberger Straße, the breakthrough of Frankfurter Straße can be seen. Modest residential buildings were constructed in Landesberger Straße in 1936–1939. Today only the buildings by Peter Behrens remind us of this vanished district. [Source: Collection Harald Bodenschatz]

the square was redesigned. Within the framework of historic centre reconstruction the residential buildings to the north of the theatre were torn down to create room for the new buildings with 220 apartments that still stand there today. The old buildings disturbed the new rulers because they had belonged primarily to Jewish owners and their residents were often also of Jewish descent. "The reconstruction thus also represented the first comprehensive and systematic eviction of a Jewish population from its residential district in Berlin *after* 30 January 1933. This also pertained to the existing Jewish shops and social organisations [...]." The new buildings were to be let to "old combatants ... who have acquired merit in the national socialist movement."[43]

The "Guide to Berlin" published on the occasion of the Olympic Games stated: "*Bülowplatz*! The centrepiece of this place that is known and feared in all parts of the city is *Karl-Liebknecht-Haus*. The origin of Bolshevism's orders to murder. The heart of the *Communist Party* in Germany. Around this house is a circle of ugly, dark tenements filled with the foulest subhumanity from the whole of Germany. [...] And today the square bears [...] the name of the national socialist freedom fighter, Horst Wessel, who fell for the victory of his ideas in the struggle for Berlin. [...] The transformation of Horst-Wessel-Platz is symbolic for the entire reconstruction of Berlin."[44] After the war Horst-Wessel-Platz was first renamed Liebknecht-Platz, then Luxemburg-Platz and in 1969 Rosa-Luxemburg-Platz.[45] In contrast to some other places of importance in the national socialist dictatorship there is a lot of information and artistic activity there. Nevertheless, today the square is known only to insiders.

That the contemporary Karl-Marx-Allee leads directly to Alexanderplatz appears completely natural to today's observer. This connection was, however, only created one step at a time, starting on the occasion of the construction of the underground railway from 1926 to 1928 with a street breakthrough named Frankfurter Straße, which led from Große Frankfurter Straße to Landsberger Straße and then took a slight bend in the direction of Alexanderplatz. This project was part of the grand plan for the redevelopment of the southern historic centre promoted by Martin Wagner and Martin Mächler. The development of the extensively cleared urban area did not take place until during the dictatorship, however. Within the framework of the reconstruction of the historic city centre, between 1936 and 1939 very basic new buildings were constructed there with a total of 415 apartments. The construction work was done largely on behalf of the Berlin municipal authorities.[46]

Rally on 1 May 1936 at the Altes Museum in the paved Lustgarten. [Source: Bundesarchiv, B 145-P022065 / without specification]

In the south of Friedrichswerder, which lay to the west of the historic centre, in contrast, the emphasis was on demonstrating superiority. After long deliberations, the first large-scale building of the dictatorship, the new Reichsbank building, was constructed there in 1934–1940.[47] The design for the huge new building complex was to be determined in a limited contest announced in February 1933, in which Walter Gropius and Mies van der Rohe participated. None of the contest participants was given the commission, however. Instead it went to Reichsbank Building Director Heinrich Wolff. In order to create the space needed for the new building complex an entire historic district with allegedly "obsolete slums"[48] was eradicated in 1933/34. In the commemorative publication for the celebration of the laying of the foundation stone on 5 May 1934 it is stated: "Unfortunately it could not be avoided that several houses which were important artistically and for cultural history had to be sacrificed for the greater good."[49] A welcome result of the redevelopment of southern Friedrichswerder was the extension of Jägerstraße to Schlossplatz, which was very desirable from the point of view of traffic policy.[50] The huge, austere building of the Reichsbank was finished in 1940, but did not enter into the propaganda machine of national socialist urban development. The other new buildings envisaged by the Amt für Stadtplanung [Urban Planning Department] were never realised.

43 Haben 2017, p. 199. The quoted parts of the last sentence stem from the then State Commissioner of the Reich Capital, Julius Lippert.
44 Trurnit 1936, p. 35–37.
45 Karl Liebknecht and Rosa Luxemburg were the leaders of the Spartakusbund, a predecessor of the German Communist Party. They were murdered by volunteer corps soldiers in 1919.
46 Cf. Kühn 1936, p. 711; Haben 2017, pp. 286–289.

47 Cf. Schäche 1991, pp. 154–169.
48 Kühn 1936, p. 711.
49 Festschrift 1934, p. 15.
50 Goebel 2003, p. 231.

Like Königsplatz in Munich, the Lustgarten to the north of the Berlin Palace was also paved in the early years of the national socialist dictatorship and transformed into a parade ground according to plans by Conrad Dammeier in 1935 to 1936. The equestrian statue of Friedrich Wilhelm III and the granite basin of the fountain were moved to the edge of the square so that the flight of steps to the Altes Museum could more easily be used as a grandstand. The square was also used for the celebrations during the Olympic Games. After the war the square continued to be used for rallies and the paving was not changed. It was only following the reunification of Berlin that the square was again given a green surface.

The eastern side of the extension building of the Reichsbank neat to the Spree, 1937. The building of the Mint that can be seen on the right was still to be demolished. Its cornice had already been salvaged so that it could be incorporated into the new building of the Reichsmünze near the Molkenmarkt. [Source: Monatshefte für Baukunst und Städtebau 9/1937, p. 289]

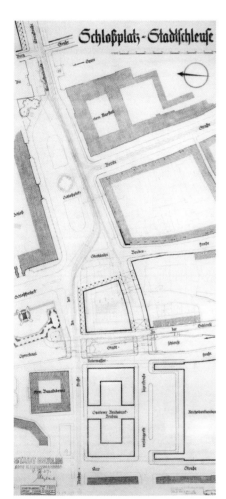

Plan for the redevelopment of the area between Werderscher Markt and Schlossplatz with the extended Jägerstraße, Amt für Stadtplanung, 1937/38. Was not implemented in this form. [Source: Landesarchiv Berlin, C Rep. 110-01 (maps), No. 23]

Construction site for the extension building of the Reichsbank on the cleared area, southern Friedrichswerder, c. 1934. [Source: Monatshefte für Baukunst und Städtebau 9/1937, p. 289]

"Die Reichsbank im Stadtbild" [The Reichsbank in the cityscape] – a huge new complex that transcends the scale of the historic centre. The planned northern building – to the left in the picture – was not built. Right at the front – partially cut off – the old Reichsbank can be seen. [Source: Monatshefte für Baukunst und Städtebau 9/1937, p. 292]

A Second Phase of Historic Centre Redevelopment

Sketch of the redevelopment of the east axis in the area of the historic centre, status 1939. It shows clearly that large buildings are planned along the axis and that the rest of the historic centre, including the projects there, are of no interest whatsoever and are not even included in the sketch. [Source: Reichhardt/ Schäche 1998, p. 72]

Master Plan, Albert Speer, 1942, Excerpt showing the central section of the eastern axis running through the historic centre. [Source: Landesarchiv Berlin, A Pr. Br. Rep. 107 (maps), No. 227]

Draft for the new building of the Chamber of Industry and Commerce on the east axis, c. 1938. [Source: Bundesarchiv, R 4606/3611, fol. 22]

Building site of the new building of the Chamber of Industry and Commerce, July 1939. [Source: Landesarchiv Berlin, F Rep. 290, No. 61-2752]

With the nomination of a General Building Inspector (Albert Speer) for the capital of the Reich in 1937, a national government authority with special powers and excellent financial resources that was subordinate only to the Reich Chancellor, the conditions for urban development in Berlin changed fundamentally. The municipal Amt für Stadtplanung lost its importance and became de facto an auxiliary body to the General Building Inspector. The master planning for the "Reichshauptstadt" that now determined and outshone everything else placed the former historic centre redevelopment on the side-lines and aimed at a comprehensive reorganisation of the centre of the capital of the Reich. Its starting-point was the proclaimed enormous need for new, large city buildings, for which there were no suitable building sites in the existing centre of Berlin: "The idea of expanding one of the existing large streets for this purpose was considered, carefully examined and rejected. One of the first practical examples already shows that even the widest and most spacious street in Berlin, the street named 'Unter den Linden', could no longer be considered for certain new buildings because it would not be able to cope with the resulting additional traffic [...] It is completely clear that in this case Friedrichstraße or Leipziger Straße, for example,

would be much less suitable for the further construction of large buildings that draw traffic since today's normal traffic there already leads to considerable traffic jams. It follows from this that for the construction of the necessary large new buildings a new street must be built which can cope not only with the traffic of the present time but also with the significantly greater amount of traffic expected in the future."[51]

51 Speer 1938.

The plans for the redevelopment of Berlin under the direction of Albert Speer, specifically for the first section of the east axis, marked a second phase of historic centre redevelopment that did not start until the planning for the southern historic centre and the periphery of the "old town" had long been completed. The concept drawn up by Albert Speer aimed at complementing or, rather, replacing the business city with its east-west direction by a new centre along the middle section of a monumental north-south axis. This proposal had already been formulated by Martin Mächler two decades earlier and would have moved the focal point of the city even further west. The historic centre would have been degraded to a secondary appendage the east axis. Along the east axis monumental buildings were envisaged,[52]

including a new building for the Berlin Chamber of Industry and Commerce according to a design by Paul Schwebes and Rudolf Ullrich, as well as a Telephone Audit Office, the Berlin Inland Revenue Department and a municipal art gallery.[53] This would have resulted in an extremely dissonant cityscape in the historic centre: in the south an austere administrative centre in the form of an imitation of an "old town", in the north a cold boulevard without any reference to the southern part and which would have destroyed the structure of the historic centre. In contrast, with a view to the further route of the east axis on the other side of the historic centre, Horst-Wessel-Platz was shown respect and was explicitly to be spared.[54]

52   On the planning history of the east axis in the historic centre
     cf. Goebel 2003, pp. 233–235.

53   Cf. Reichhardt/Schäche 1998, pp. 71–75; Goebel 2003, pp. 235–242.
54   Goebel 2003, p. 234.

"Geraubte Mitte" [Stolen centre], 2013: The map, which is part of the exhibition of the same name in the Stadtmuseum Berlin designed by Benedikt Goebel and Lutz Mauersberger, shows in red the properties in the historic centre that were stolen between 1933 and 1945, the owners of which had been of Jewish descent. [Source: Benedikt Goebel/Lutz Mauersberger]

The monumental plans for the north-south axis planned by Albert Speer were never implemented. That was also true of the projects for the east axis on the territory of the historic centre. The end buildings in Kaiser-Wilhelm-Straße near the Stadtschloss and the old buildings that were in the way of the Chamber of Industry and Commerce had already been demolished. The construction of new buildings in their place had already begun in 1939.[55] The preparations for the redesign of the centre of the capital of the Reich were not visible at first glance and were overlooked for decades: Albert Speer developed a brutal machinery of violence in order

to get hold of a large number of properties in the historic centre that were needed for the implementation of the plans. The eviction of citizens of Jewish descent from their homes was introduced early on in order to requisition replacement homes for Germans who had had to give up their own homes to make way for the building of the axes.[56] In addition, property owners of Jewish descent were expropriated. Two hundred and twenty-five Jewish properties in Berlin's city core were stolen during the national socialist dictatorship by a variety of methods. It is only recently that light has been shed on these occurrences within the framework of the exhibition "Geraubte Mitte" [Stolen centre] (2013).[57]

55 In the GDR epoch at first a barracks was built on the site, then the Palace Hotel, which was inaugurated in 1979. The hotel then had to give way to the DomAquarée, which went into operation in 2001 – a German construction story. Cf. Goebel 2003, p. 238.

56 On this cf. Willems 2002.
57 Geraubte Mitte 2013. Cf. also Goebel 2003, pp. 260–267.

Policy of Urban Renewal

The importance of the redevelopment of historic centres for the national socialist dictatorship has been underestimated up to the present day. Because of the negative fascination evoked by the plans of the second half of the national socialist epoch, particularly the plans that were not implemented for a new centre of the capital of the Reich to the west of the historic centre, the plans and their implementation for the "old towns" have been overshadowed. In many cities, however, the redevelopment of the historic centre was a means of stabilising the national socialist dictatorship. It could follow up on plans from the Weimar Republic and with the measures implemented visibly demonstrate the energy and superiority of the new regime.

An evaluation conducted by the Deutsche Gesellschaft für Wohnungswesen [German Housing Association] in 1940 differentiated between the following types of reconstruction: deconcentration, demolition and rebuilding, deconcentration and demolition with new building, and reconstruction of a special kind.[58] In practice there were two main variations: radical wholesale clearance in favour of completely new building, often involving changes in the layout of the city ("demolition and rebuilding") and limited demolition, affecting primarily the interior of a block while maintaining the perimeter ("deconcentration"). The second variation became known as the policy of gutting, which was applied in historically important "old towns" with building structures going back to the Middle Ages. The radical variation was applied especially, as in other dictatorships, in the capital. The two variations were often combined ("deconcentration and demolition with new building").

The programme for the redevelopment of historic centres under the national socialist dictatorship included every aspect that this field of urban construction had produced up to that point: the car-friendly improvement of traffic conditions, the elimination of slums together with the eviction of the undesired, poorer residents and mundane businesses, the promotion of a residence-free business city and new monumental buildings on amalgamated plots of land in the cities, the emphasis on historical greatness by accentuating architectural testimonies and the creation of neohistorical buildings as well as the embellishment of the cityscape via the dismantling of unwelcome architectural elements[59].

The accentuation was new: the evocation of the German Middle Ages[60] – for example in Braunschweig, where Henry the Lion was celebrated as the protagonist of the colonisation of the East, but also in Frankfurt am Main, Nuremberg and Kassel; the planning of huge buildings and large squares, e.g. in Munich and Berlin, in the latter case along the east axis and on the Molkenmarkt, with the Reichsbank on Friedrichswerder and the paved Lustgarten on the northern Spree Island; the creation of cult locations for the movement, e.g. the Feldherrnhalle in Munich and Horst-Wessel-Platz in Berlin. The racist or political ostracism of selected social strata, together with the robbery of – primarily – Jewish property, was also new. New, in addition, was the particular emphasis on air-raid protection, which served urban development as an additional

59 Cf. for example Lindner/Böckler 1939, p. 251. Measures against "disfigurements" in historic centres are meant here, i.e. structural details such as stucco, windows and doors, roofs, timber framing, shop fittings and advertising. Ibid. pp. 137–144.
60 The German Middle Ages were an important point of reference as the German town was essentially considered to have medieval origins: "The greater number of our German towns were founded in the Middle Ages." Lindner/Böckler 1939, p. 123.

58 Harlander 1995, p. 109.

argument for deconcentration. Remarkable in this context is the deconcentration concept of block-gutting, which was applied in many small and medium-sized towns. Its objective was the maintenance of the historic buildings on the perimeter of the block while the buildings in the interior of the block, which were regarded as worthless and had often only been built in the course of the 19th century, were demolished.[61] This was associated with a particular German form of the redevelopment of historic centres that was programmatically similar to the Italian form of "*diradamento*" (thinning out).

New was also the development of an instrument that enabled the redevelopment of historic centres throughout the Reich: a corresponding programme and the at least informal clarification of criteria for the selection of the areas to be redeveloped. In addition to that there was the great weight of financial considerations and the clarification of procedural issues. New in this form was also the generalised cultural devaluation of that which was typologically destined for demolition by the use of derogatory words as "outdated", "ugly", "crumbling", "gloomy", "dark", "hovels", "slum area" or "tenement houses" (Mietkasernen). The criteria that were developed programmatically expanded the setting for urban redevelopment considerably – to the inner-city buildings from the imperial epoch.[62] This was also true of the later plans for reconstruction.[63] Thus the foundations were laid for a systematic urban redevelopment after the Second World War. It proved impossible, however, to pass a law on the urban renewal of historic centres, as was often demanded.

The final phase of the dictatorship was marked by the destruction of numerous historic centres in Germany. In Berlin not much was left of the buildings in the historic centre following the bombings of the Second World War. The planners of the national socialist dictatorship already concerned themselves during this period with the question of reconstruction. The "zero hour" at the end of the war was in many ways fiction with regard to the redevelopment of historic centres. In Berlin as in other prominent cities the period of planning for their redesigning was over, but the plans for the redevelopment of the historic centres were continued and the actors often remained at the wheel: in Berlin, for example, Richard Ermisch, who presented major plans for the reconstruction of the historic centre after 1945. The contempt for Berlin's historic centre that had been cemented over a period of decades was also continued, but now under a completely different sign, with a view to the socialist centre, which was to be an expression of the overcoming of the past national socialist dictatorship.

---

61 "These are all the later ingredients that now step by step are made to fall victim to the reconstruction of the historic centres." Lindner/Böckler 1939, p. 124.
62 Cf. Bodenschatz 1987, pp. 114–134.
63 Cf. for example Der Reichskommissar. Der Beauftragte für die Gestaltung der Wohngebiete (ed.) 1944.

References:

Architekten- und Ingenieur-Verein zu Berlin e. V. (ed.): Berlin und seine Bauten. Teil I – Städtebau. Berlin 2009

Berlins vergessene Mitte. Stadtkern 1840–2010. Stiftung Stadtmuseum Berlin. Exhibition documentation. Berlin 2010

Bodenschatz, Harald: Platz frei für das neue Berlin! Geschichte der Stadterneuerung in der "größten Mietskasernenstadt der Welt". Berlin 1987

Bodenschatz, Harald: Alt-Berlin, Marienviertel, Rathausforum … Geschichte und Zukunft eines umstrittenen Stadtraums [Old Berlin, Marien district, Rathausforum … History and future of a disputed city area]. In: Forum Wohnen und Stadtentwicklung 5/2009, pp. 249–254

Bodenschatz, Harald: Die Berliner Mitte – Produkt zweier Diktaturen. In: Merkur. Deutsche Zeitschrift für europäisches Denken 10/2014, pp. 903–909

Bodenschatz, Harald: Berlin Mitte: Bühne der Toleranz. In: Baukammer Berlin 3/2015, pp. 82–84

Bodenschatz, Harald: Weimar. Modellstadt der Moderne? Ambivalenzen des Städtebaus im 20. Jahrhundert. Weimar 2016

Bodenschatz, Harald: Berlin Mitte: The product of two dictatorships. In: Hökerberg, Håkan (ed.): Architecture as propaganda in twentieth-century totalitarian regimes. History and heritage. Florence 2018, pp. 167–184

Bodenschatz, Harald/Engstfeld, Hans-Joachim/Seifert, Carsten: Berlin auf der Suche nach dem verlorenen Zentrum. Hamburg 1995

Bodenschatz, Harald/Goebel, Benedikt: Berlin – Stadt ohne Altstadt. In Nentwig, Franziska/Bartmann, Dominik (eds.): Berlins vergessene Mitte. Stadtkern 1840–2010. Stiftung Stadtmuseum Berlin. Berlin 2010, pp. 16–36

Bodenschatz, Harald (ed.): Renaissance der Mitte. Zentrumsumbau in London und Berlin. Berlin 2005

Böß, Gustav: Berlin von heute. Berlin 1929

Braunschweig. Illustrierte Zeitung 28 March 1935

Cunitz, Olaf: Stadtsanierung in Frankfurt am Main 1933–1945. Magister thesis at the Johann Wolfgang Goethe University, submitted 1996. Revised version.

Ehlgötz, Hermann: Der Untergrund der Berliner Altstadt als Grundlage der städtebaulichen Gestaltung. In: Deutsche Bauzeitung 77–78/1931, supplement "Stadt und Siedlung" No. 14, pp. 121–128

Eiselen, Fritz: Wohnungsverhältnisse der Berliner Altstadt. In: Deutsche Bauzeitung 2/1934, pp. 26–28

Festschrift zur Feier der Grundsteinlegung für den Erweiterungsbau der Reichshauptbank. Berlin, 5 May 1934

Flesche, Hermann: Braunschweigs Altstadtsanierung. Braunschweig 1939

Frank, Erich: Wege zur Altstadtsanierung. In: Zentralblatt der Bauverwaltung 39/1934, pp. 572–576

Geraubte Mitte. Die "Arisierung" des jüdischen Grundeigentums im Berliner Stadtkern 1933–1945. Benedikt Goebel and Lutz Mauersberger. Catalogue. Berlin 2013

Goebel, Benedikt: Der Umbau Alt-Berlins zum modernen Stadtzentrum. Planungs-, Bau- und Besitzgeschichte des historischen Berliner Stadtkerns im 19. und 20. Jahrhundert. Berlin 2003

Haben, Michael: Berliner Wohnungsbau 1933–1945. Mehrfamilienhäuser, Wohnanlagen und Siedlungsvorhaben. Berlin 2017

Harlander, Tilman: Zwischen Heimstätte und Wohnmaschine. Wohnungsbau und Wohnungspolitik in der Zeit des Nationalsozialismus. Basel 1995

Hirtsiefer, Heinrich: Die Wohnungswirtschaft in Preußen. Eberswalde 1929

Hoefer, Friedbert: Die Bauten der Altstadtsanierung in Weimar. In: Moderne Bauformen. Monatshefte für Architektur und Raumkunst 12/1941, pp. 513–538

Horst Wessel 1907–1930, www.dhm.de/lemo/biografie/horst-wessel [16.01.2021]

Internationaler Verband für Wohnungswesen [International Housing Association] (ed.): Beseitigung von Elendsvierteln und Verfallswohnungen. Vol. 2: Pläne [Slum Clearance and Reconditioning of Insanitary Dwellings. Vol. 2: Plans.] Stuttgart 1935

Ketter, Alfred: Technik der Altstadtsanierung [The method of historic centre redevelopment]. Bad Liebenwerda/Berlin 1935

Kühn, Benno: Das Gesicht des neuen Berlin. In: Städtebau. Zeitschrift der Deutschen Akademie für Städtebau, Reichs- und Landesplanung, February 1936, pp. 17–23

Kühn, Benno: Die Altstadtgesundung. In: Zeitschrift des Vereins deutscher Ingenieure 23/1936, pp. 710–713

Lach, Wilhelm: Die nächsten Aufgaben der Erneuerung der Berliner Innenstadt. In: Deutsche Bauzeitung 2/1934, pp. 25–26

Landesdenkmalamt Berlin: Denkmale in Berlin. Bezirk Mitte, Ortsteil Mitte. Petersberg 2003

Lehweß, Walter/Winter, Fritz: Die Möglichkeiten städtebaulicher Maßnahmen zum Schutze von Wohnsiedlungen gegen Angriffe aus der Luft. Auf Veranlassung der Deutschen Akademie für Städtebau, Reichs- und Landesplanung und der Deutschen Gesellschaft für Bauwesen. Berlin 1935. Documented in: Geist, Johann Friedrich/Kürvers, Klaus: Das Berliner Mietshaus 1945–1989. Munich 1989, p. 58

Leyden, Friedrich: Groß-Berlin. Geographie der Weltstadt. Breslau 1933

Lindner, Werner/Böckler, Erich: Die Stadt. Ihre Pflege und Gestaltung. Munich 1939

Lüken-Isberner, Folckert: Das Programm der (Alt-)Stadtsanierung im Nationalsozialismus. In: Lüken-Isberner (ed.) 1991, pp. 23–43

Lüken-Isberner, Folckert: Große Pläne für Kassel 1919 bis 1949. Projekte zu Stadtentwicklung und Städtebau. Marburg 2016

Lüken-Isberner, Folckert (ed.): Stadt und Raum 1933–1949. Beiträge zur planungs- und stadtbaugeschichtlichen Forschung II. Kassel 1991

Neuer-Miebach, Therese/Kopetzki, Christian (eds.): Stadterneuerung als Teil großstädtischer Entwicklungspolitik in der Weimarer Republik und im Nationalsozialismus. Teil A und B. Kassel 1988

Paquet, Alfons: Und Berlin? Abbruch und Aufbau der Reichshauptstadt. Frankfurt am Main 1934

Petz, Ursula von: Stadtsanierung im Dritten Reich dargestellt an ausgewählten Beispielen. Dortmund 1987

Reichhardt, Hans J./Schäche, Wolfgang: Von Berlin nach Germania. Über die Zerstörungen der "Reichshauptstadt" durch Albert Speers Neugestaltungsplanungen. Berlin 1998

Der Reichskommissar. Der Beauftragte für die Gestaltung der Wohngebiete (ed.): Wiederaufbau zerstörter Städte. Untersuchung eines Baublocks in Berlin-Charlottenburg. Galvanistraße/Guerickestraße/Röntgenstraße/Charlottenburger Ufer. Berlin 1944

Scarpa, Ludovica: Martin Wagner und Berlin. Architektur und Städtebau in der Weimarer Republik. Braunschweig/Wiesbaden 1986

Schäche, Wolfgang: Architektur und Städtebau in Berlin zwischen 1933 und 1945 – Planen und Bauen unter der Ägide der Stadtverwaltung. Berlin 1991

Scheck, Thomas: Denkmalpflege und Diktatur. Die Erhaltung von Bau- und Kunstdenkmälern in Schleswig-Holstein und im Deutschen Reich zur Zeit des Nationalsozialismus. Berlin 1995

Schubert, Dirk: Gesundung der Städte. Stadtsanierung in Hamburg 1933–1945. In: Böse, Michael et al.: … ein neues Hamburg entsteht … Hamburg 1986, pp. 62–83

Schulz, Hartmut: Altstadtsanierung in Kassel. Stadtumbau und erhaltende Erneuerung vor dem Zweiten Weltkrieg. Kassel 1983

Schwan, Bruno: Die Wohnungsverhältnisse der Berliner Altstadt. Berlin 1932

Schwan, Bruno (ed.): Städtebau und Wohnungswesen der Welt. Berlin 1935

Der Senator für Stadtentwicklung und Umweltschutz (ed.): Die städtebauliche Entwicklung Berlins seit 1650 in Karten. Erläuterungsheft. Berlin 1987, Excerpt of topographical maps c. 1940

Sonderbericht. Um den Berliner City-Ausschuss? 15.01.1934. In: Balg, Ilse (ed.): Martin Mächler – Weltstadt Berlin. Schriften und Materialien. Berlin 1986, pp. 363–364

Speer, Albert: Wie Berlin umgebaut wird. Der Wortlaut des Berichtes von Generalbauinspektor Professor Speer – Grundsätze für die Neugestaltung Berlins. In: Berliner Morgenpost 28.01.1938, First supplement

Stahn, Günter: Das Nikolaiviertel. Berlin 1991

Trurnit, Hansgeorg (ed.): Das neue Berlin. Stadt der Olympischen Spiele. Berlin 1936

Verwaltungsbericht der Hochbauverwaltung (einschl. Ziegelwerke der Stadt Berlin in Gransee) für die Zeit vom 1. April 1932 bis 31. März 1936. Berlin 1937

Wagner, Martin: Zur kommenden Umbildung Berlins. Die Notwendigkeit einer planmäßigen Führung. In: Die Bauwelt 29/1927, pp. 707–709

Wagner, Martin: Verkehr und Tradition. In: Das neue Berlin 7/1929, pp. 129–130

Wagner, Martin: Behörden als Städtebauer. In: Das neue Berlin 11/1929, pp. 230–232

Wagner, Martin: Städtebauliche Probleme in amerikanischen Städten und ihre Rückwirkung auf den deutschen Städtebau. Berlin 1929b

Wagner, Martin: Das Neue Berlin. Teil II. Synthese. Berlin 1932 (unpublished typescript, Architekturmuseum der TU Berlin)

Wagner, Martin [under the alias Dr. Sandow]: Die Sanierung der Berliner "City". In: Deutsche Bauzeitung 8/1934, pp. 142–146

Willems, Susanne: Der entsiedelte Jude. Albert Speers Wohnungsmarktpolitik für den Berliner Hauptstadtbau. Berlin 2002

Paul Wittig, Paul: Das Verkehrswesen der Stadt Berlin und seine Vorgeschichte. Der öffentliche Verkehr von 1870 bis zur Gegenwart. Privatdruck. Berlin 1931

Wölz, Otto: Die Altstadt-Sanierung. Ein Vorschlag zur rechtlichen Regelung der Althaus- und Altstadt-Erneuerung. In: Zentralblatt der Bauverwaltung 39/1934, pp. 569–572

Berlin: The Lost Molkenmarkt

Hardly anybody in Berlin now knows where Molkenplatz lies, never mind the fact that this square used to be the central point of the oldest part of Berlin. To-day it is covered by a huge traffic wasteland that, with multiple-lane roadways and even more parking spaces, pays homage exclusively to the automobile. During the national socialist dictatorship the buildings at the Molkenmarkt were torn down on a large scale to create a huge square – called the "old town forum" – in front of the Stadthaus [technical city hall]. The entire non-place has been dominated since the late 1960s by Grunerstraße, an expressway that was created in the GDR era, which ploughs through the former historic centre and tears it apart. Certainly, there are some spectacular buildings here, above all the Stadthaus, designed by Ludwig Hoffmann and finished in 1911, an imposing building with a tower, part of which can be seen in the photo. Next to it on the right the new building complex of the company headquarters of the Berliner Wasserbetriebe [Berlin Waterworks] from 1999 puts on a mighty show of splendour. Less enormous, but all the more remarkable, is the neocubist facade to its right from 2000, designed by the architect Christoph Langhof. On the far right of the photo we can see the Palais Schwerin, a stately home that was originally built around 1700 and which was torn down, leaving only the facade, in the course of the reconstruction in the 1930s. Behind the Palais further new buildings from the national socialist epoch can be seen that are part of the Reichsmünze building complex and were part of the reconstruction of the Rolandufer. Molkenmarkt is among the most inhospitable squares in the historic centre despite desperate attempts to make the area to the east of Grunerstraße more pleasant with a little greenery. This photo, like the following three, was taken from the tower of the Rotes Rathaus [city hall], the heart of the former, not very expansive, territory of Old Berlin.
[Photo: Harald Bodenschatz, 2010]

Berlin: Nikolaiviertel, 2nd Edition
In the view from the Rathaus tower towards the southwest, an exceptional city quarter immediately catches one's eye: the Nikolaiviertel, one of the oldest districts in the city, which was newly built in the 1980s in the course of the preparations for Berlin's 750th anniversary celebrations. Previous to that, there were hardly any still existing buildings and even the church was badly damaged. If the new buildings are examined more closely it can be seen that – in addition to numerous prefabricated buildings that roughly attempt to remind us of the scale of the historic centre – there are also reconstructed historic buildings, including the Ephraim Palais, which had been demolished in the 1930s and was rebuilt from 1985 to 1987. The fact that the Nikolaiviertel, which is often ridiculed by intellectuals but is very much loved by visitors, and which was freely designed in a neomedieval manner by Günter Stahn, was not an invention of GDR politics, has almost been forgotten today. Within the framework of the redevelopment of the historic centre in the 1930s it had already been considered, in fact planned, to establish a sort of open-air museum there, in which buildings that had been torn down, or which would have to be torn down, in other parts of the historic centre should be resurrected. Politicians and experts in the GDR were aware of the plans from the 1930s but they wanted something else. The new Nikolaiviertel was to be reminiscent of the urban development of the vanished Old Berlin. At the left edge of the picture, behind the Nikolaiviertel, are several three-storey buildings which form the building complex of the Reichsmünze, built from 1936 to 1942. A new cultural quarter is presently planned there. Behind those buildings we can see the high-rise buildings of the Fischerinsel, a complex planned in the 1960s, for which the quite numerous remaining buildings of the Fischerkiez were demolished. In contrast to the plans of the late 1920s, exclusively residential buildings were erected there.
[Photo: Harald Bodenschatz, 2010]

Berlin: The Lost East Axis
*Looking from the Rathaus tower towards the west, it is impossible to
imagine that the western part of Old Berlin once stood here. The wide street
to the right of the picture is the – historic – Spandauer Straße, but without
peripheral buildings and extremely widened. The park on the left was previously densely built. The traces of the national socialist redevelopment of the
historic centre have also disappeared. To the far left, next to the Cathedral,
we can just see the green Lustgarten, which replaced the parade ground that
was paved over in the era of the national socialist dictatorship. On the other,
right-hand side of the Cathedral stands the mighty DomAquarée, which was
finished in 2004. In the 1930s this was the construction site for the building
of the Chamber of Industry and Commerce, a monumental building that was
intended to mark the beginning of the planned east-west axis in the historic
centre. The DomAquarée is divided in the middle by a passageway that is
intended to be reminiscent of a historic street in the old town. The prominent East Berlin Palast Hotel, which was opened in 1979, stood here until it
was demolished in 2001. The history of demolition on this site began in the
1880s, and is a testimonial to the many hard breaks in the redevelopment of
Berlin's historic centre, but it is invisible because it has been forgotten and it
will not be remembered.*
[Photo: Harald Bodenschatz, 2010]

Berlin: The Lost Großer Jüdenhof

*The view from the Rathaus tower over the Berlin inner city along the Spree
towards the southeast is dominated by Ludwig Hoffmann's Stadthaus,
opened in1911, in the foreground to the right. In front of or, rather, next to
the Stadthaus stands the somewhat stiff and bulky building of the Städtische
Feuersozietät [municipal fire insurance] that was constructed according to
plans by Franz Arnous from 1936 to 1938 as part of the redevelopment of
the historic centre, its premises on the Molkenmarkt having been demolished.
After the war it served the East Berlin municipal administration as a "New
Stadthaus", and today it is occupied by a registry office. The area also shows
another redevelopment measure in the historic centre, however: the large white
delivery van standing in front of the New Stadthaus is parked on the site of
the Großer Jüdenhof, which was also reconstructed in 1936 to 1938, nothing
of which remains, however. The Großer Jüdenhof, in the light of more recent
excavations, was an 18th century, Christian, lower-middle-class residential
courtyard. Its name stems from its position on Jüdenstraße. In the 1930s it was
to be maintained as "the last medieval residential courtyard". The buildings,
which were badly damaged in the war, were demolished in 1968. The courtyard
became a parking lot – and has remained so until the present day. The site is
to be redesigned in the near future. In what way the design will pay fitting
testimony to the historic Großer Jüdenhof has not yet been decided.
[Photo: Harald Bodenschatz, 2010]*

The Urban Renewal of Historic Centres in Salazar's Portugal

Christian von Oppen

Not only dictatorships, but primarily these, like to relate their programmes and their actions to the glorified history of their country. This was also true of Portugal. The reference to the country's great history was created by exhibitions, monuments and the demonstrative display of structural testimonies.

For the Portuguese dictatorship the historical facts were clear: Portugal is the oldest European nation and Portugal founded Europe's first global colonial empire. One of the oldest of Portugal's heroes is King Afonso I (1109–1185), who went down as the founder of Portugal (*Afonso o Fundador*) in the country's history. The heroes of the era of conquests were above all Henry the Navigator (1394–1460), the fourth son of the Portuguese King John I (1357–1433) and secular administrator of the Military Order of Christ that resided in Tomar; Vasco da Gama (1469–1524), who discovered the sea route to India; and the national poet of that period, Luís Vaz de Camões (1525–1580), who handled Vasco da Gama's expedition to India in his principal work "*Os Lusíadas*". The heroic history of these first four centuries of Portugal is evoked by numerous towns, castles and monuments which were restored or newly created in the epoch of the *Estado Novo*. New State – Salazar's dictatorship was called by that name as of 1933, and Franco's dictatorship later followed this example.

The *Estado Novo* developed a programme that was intended not only to commemorate the "greatness" of Portugal throughout the country but also to redevelop the country with "a great past" through a policy of modernisation, because Portugal was backward, agrarian, hardly urbanised, with many illiterate inhabitants, technically and scientifically not up to date, trapped in old preindustrial conditions. The *Estado Novo* developed a complete arsenal of instruments and institutions to overcome these conditions in a controlled form. Urban development played an important role in this context, even though the emergence of this modern policy and profession in Portugal remained far behind the leading nations in this field such as the United Kingdom, Germany and France, but also behind Italy and Spain. Visible testimonials to the specific modernisation policy of the *Estado Novo* can be found throughout the country, even in the historic centres. But modernisation also meant the demolition of historic buildings and, above all, the displacement of undesired residents. In the focus of the urban development policy, including the policy of the redevelopment of historic centres, was the capital, Lisbon.

Lisbon: Centre of the Empire

The policy of unredeemed promises of the First Republic induced the columnist of the daily newspaper "*Diário de Notícias*", Ribeiro Christino, to write an article in the mid-1910s on the shortcomings of urban development in Lisbon. Under the title "Various 'building sites of the Church of Santa Engrácia'..."[1] he summarised Lisbon's most urgent problems. In his view these included the redevelopment of the city centre. For the oldest district, the Alfama, he demanded the remediation of the unhygienic situation without changing the medieval character of the district, without destroying the quarter through demolition. For St. George's Castle, which dominates Lisbon, on the contrary, he urged the dismantling of the extensions to the barracks in order to make the royal "alcoves" from the 14th century visible again.[2] The many plans for the redevelopment of the Baixa, the lower town, had proved to be nothing but "hot air".[3] The plans for the redevelopment of the historic centre should therefore be implemented at last.[4] The general discontent with the inaction of the First Republic, which Ribeiro Christino had summarised so succinctly that he was able to publish his columns as a book in 1923, accelerated the Portuguese dictatorship's programme of redevelopment of the historic centre in Lisbon.

The poor accessibility of the city centre, in particular of the quarters that escaped the huge sea- and earthquake of 1755, was already a major urban development issue during the First Republic,[5] but it remained largely without consequence due to the political instability. The expansion of traffic infrastructure in the districts of the centre therefore presented itself as a suitable project for demonstrating the dictatorship's ability to act.[6] Connected with this was the hope that the historic quarters would appreciate in value. A further major impulse for the redevelopment of the centre was, finally, the commemorative ambitions of the dictatorship, which left profound marks, above all on the castle hill.

Excavation of St. George's Castle (1938–1940)

A few months after the appointment of the engineer and professor, Duarte Pacheco, as mayor of Lisbon and shortly before his renewed nomination as Minster of Public Works and Transport in Salazar's cabinet, the Portuguese dictator officially announced the preparations for the "Exhibition of the Portuguese World" (*Exposição do Mundo Português*) that was planned for 1940.[7] In the announcement he evoked the importance of St. George's Castle (*Castelo São Jorge*) in Lisbon as a monument to national independence. As a sacred acropolis that held sway over the urban cityscape of Lisbon, and ideally over the entire country, the Castle was to be developed into a national pilgrimage site for all patriots.[8]

At the end of August 1938 an administrative regulation placed St. George's Castle under the auspices of the General Directorate for National Buildings and Building Monuments[9]. The latter was commissioned by the state to present the illustrious castle and its military character to Lisbon and the entire country by the anniversary celebrations in 1940.[10] According to the regulation, the castle was "the probably greatest and most noble testimony to our glorious national heritage", and therefore deserved undisputed appreciation, freedom from "detrimental annexes" and the liberation of its "majestic beauty".[11]

The Castle thus became the key building for the Portuguese dictatorship's great propaganda show in remembrance of the historical importance of Portugal. Under the management of the General Directorate for National Buildings and Building Monuments the unpretentious remains of the Castle were uncovered from 1938 onwards by the comprehensive removal of the many layers of building that had been deposited there in its more than 800 year old history.

---

7   The "Exhibition of the Portuguese World" (*Exposição do Mundo Português*), which was presented from 23rd June to 2nd December 1940, was the largest exhibition of the Salazar dictatorship. At the same time it was a gigantic urban development project. This was the 800th anniversary of Portugal's independence and the 300th anniversary of the regaining of independence from foreign rule by Spain, according to the proclamation of the dictatorship. The exhibition in Belém, a district in Lisbon, formed the centre of the nationwide anniversary celebrations.

8   Salazar 1939, p. 4.

9   The General Directorate for National Buildings and Building Monuments (*Direcção-Geral dos Edifícios e Monumentos Nacionais*, DGEMN) was the most important operative arm of the Ministry of Public Works and Transport. Its remit covered the management of all the major urban building blocks: the planning and implementation of social housing estates, the reconstruction and maintenance of historic buildings and ensembles, and the construction of schools, post offices, museums, prisons and state hostels.

10 Ministério das Obras Públicas 1941, p. 5.

11 Ministério das Obras Públicas 1941, p. 5.

---

1   The article "Diversas 'Obras de Santa Engrácia'..." from "*Diário de Notícias*" was again published in 1923 in the small anthology "*Estética Citadina*" by Ribeiro Christino. Cf. Christino 1923, pp. 210–213. The Church of Santa Engrácia mentioned in the title, the construction of which was begun at the end of the 16th century and, following many disruptions, finally ground to a halt at the beginning of the 18th century, became an allegory in Lisbon for protracted public building operations. The church was completed, converted to the National Pantheon, in 1966, towards the end of the rule of António Salazar.

2   Christino 1923, p. 211.

3   Christino 1923, p. 211.

4   Christino 1923, pp. 211–212.

5   Cf. Mangorrinha 2007, p. 119.

6   Oppen 2013, p. 265.

St. George's Castle before the reconstruction for the anniversary celebrations in 1940, photo by José Pedro Pinheiro Corrêa, c. 1934. [Source: Ministério das Obras Publicas 1941, pictorial appendix following p. 40]

St. George's Castle after the reconstruction for the anniversary celebrations in 1940, photo by Marques de Abreu, c. 1941. [Source: Ministério das Obras Publicas 1941, pictorial appendix following p. 40]

<< The historic district of Encosta do Castelo during the wholesale redevelopment of the surroundings of St. George's Castle, photo by Marques de Abreu, before 1940. [Source: Ministério das Obras Publicas 1941, pictorial appendix following p. 40]

The reconstruction that followed was not a search for the original building. It was intended to visualise the idea of a historical truth, the *História Única*[12]: according to the official interpretation, the political and cultural rise of Portugal began in 1140 with the expulsion of the Moors and the founding of the empire, and with it the development of the true Portuguese architectonics.[13] Free of any stylistic overlapping, the phantasy product of the *Estado Novo* conveyed the picture of a fortified medieval castle and was intended to keep the memory alive of the heroic victory over the Moors and the birth of Portugal.

The urban development mise en scéne of St. George's Castle as the acropolis of the nation was aimed at a long-range effect. In order for it to be visible from as many places in the city as possible a green belt was laid out around the castle at the cost of one of the oldest districts in Lisbon. The expropriation of the densely populated historic quarter Encosta do Castelo was implemented with the aid of regulations from 1932[14] and 1938[15]. The Castle, which previously was structurally integrated into the city, distanced itself sharply from the surrounding buildings following the wholesale reconstruction due to the exposed defensive walls and ditches. The wholesale reconstruction often did without providing new facades for the buildings that remained, so that visitors to the Castle today can still look into the unadorned backyards of the remains of the district of Encosta do Castelo when they look down on Lisbon from the castle hill.

Nevertheless, the reconstruction of St. George's Castle, which was completed with more than a year's delay in the spring of 1942,[16] must be rated a success from the point of view of the dictatorship. The apparently medieval building became, as was intended, the key project of the urban cityscape development policy for the anniversary celebrations in Lisbon's historic centre. Due to its prominent location it could be seen from many places in the city. New buildings could therefore be placed in direct line of sight of the Castle and thus be connected to the desired history.[17]

The historic district of Encosta do Castelo after the wholesale redevelopment of the surroundings of St. George's Castle, photo by Marques de Abreu, before 1941. The photo shows the same place as the previous picture. [Source: Ministério das Obras Publicas 1941, pictorial appendix following p. 40]

Plans for the Area between the Lower Town and the Avenida Almirante Reis

With the growing importance of the radial road Avenida Almirante Reis the pressure also increased to improve its connection to the historic centre. The historic district of Mouraria stood in the way of such a project, however, i.e. that part of the lower town that had survived the earthquake of 1755 almost without damage and was characterised in the first half of the 20th century by decay, overcrowding, bars and street prostitution.[18] At the beginning of 1934 planning was already far enough advanced for the demolition of the central indoor market on the Praça da Figueira to be decided. The market, the concession for which ended in May 1935,[19] was to give way to a representative city square into which the Avenida Almirante Reis was to open.[20]

The idea of a sequence of representative squares between the lower town and the radial road Avenida Almirante Reis assumed an ever more tangible shape following the commissioning of Étienne de Groër with the development of a master plan. Altogether two squares were intended, the Praça da Figueira and a new, elongated square, the Praça Martim Moniz, which would in future be renamed Praça

---

12 Pereira 1997, p. 100.
13 Sokol 1957, p. 52.
14 Decree 21875 of 18.11.1932 on the transfer to the State of sole organisational sovereignty within the protection zone of a monument.
15 Legal decree 28468 of 15.02.1938 on the extension of the classification category as *monumento nacional* to gardens, parks, landscapes, forests, but also to individual plants and animals.
16 O bairro das Minhocas 1927, p. 5.

17 Cf. Oppen 2015, pp. 111–112.
18 Mangorrinha 2009, p. 162.
19 Araújo 1949, p. 26.
20 Martins 2004, p. 147.

de Dom João I. The position of the new square resulted from the crossing point of the Avenida Almirante Reis with a road for bypassing the city centre that was envisaged in the master plan. The envisaged name, Praça de Dom João I, and the design of the new square were entirely subordinated to the official understanding of national history. Dom João I (King John I) is revered in Portuguese history as defender of the fatherland because he succeeded in repelling Spain's attempts, at the end of the 14th century, to bring Portugal under the Spanish crown with the aid of the superior strength of its troops.[21]

Faria da Costa's first drafts for the new square were made in 1944. They show how the image programme of *História Única* was to be translated into Lisbon's urban development programme: a larger than life statue of King John I, surrounded by contemporary architecture, dominates the square. The foundation on which the new Lisbon was to be built was Portugal's glorious past, which began with King Afonso I and is omnipresent in the cityscape thanks to the Castle. The remembrance programme stylised the historical figure of King John I into a hero whose decisive action for the nation was intended to serve the Portuguese people as an example.

For the planned Praça de Dom João I new office buildings, hotels, department stores and a venue for special events were envisaged, the design of which was to be fitting for the requirements of the capital city of an empire.[22] At the end of the 1940s demolition work for the new double square was

21 Cf. Castelo-Branco 1960, pp. 5–18.
22 Mesquita 1950, pp. 12–13.

Proposed facades for the redesign of the Praça da Figueira, 1949.
[Source: Martins 2004, p. 148]

begun parallel to the planning. Since no new housing was planned for the reconstruction in the area of the Mouraria the residents had to be evacuated to the new social housing estates. These were to be built in the urban expansion zone of Alvalade, the Bairro do Caramão da Ajuda and the barracks estate Quinta das Furnas.[23] However, most of the housing in the Bairro de Alvalade and all of the housing in the Bairro do Caramão were reserved for particular population groups, so that de facto only the barracks estate of Quinta das Furnas was available to the majority of the former residents of Mouraria as alternative housing.

The eye of the needle between the Praça da Figueira and the Praça de Dom João I was the Rua da Palma, a street typical of the lower town. This small, narrow street presented a variety of buildings, such as simple town houses, palaces, theatres, cinemas and churches.[24] Faria da Costa planned the complete demolition of these buildings in order to widen the street to 40 metres. In line with the requirements of de Groër to transform the lower town into a centre purely for commerce and administration[25] da Costa's plan no longer envisaged residential use of the buildings that were to be constructed concomitant to the new street.[26]

The demolition of the central indoor market on the Praça da Figueira created an unexpected problem: the exposed buildings on the newly created square now revealed their modest, undecorated facades that had never been meant to border a city square.[27] In order to remedy this flaw, the redevelopment plan proposed that the Praça da Figueira be bordered on three sides by narrow new buildings that would provide a fitting framework for this important square.

Martim Moniz Square in the lower town, drawing by João Faria da Costa, 1944. [Source: Lisboa Futura 1948, p. 31]

TRECHO DOS NOVOS BLOCOS COMERCIAIS NO EXTREMO SUL DA RUA DA PALMA

View over the planned Praça de Dom João I to St. George's Castle, drawing by João Faria da Costa, 1944. On the right is the planned huge statue in honour of King John I. [Source: Lisboa Futura 1948, p. 31]

TRECHO DA PRAÇA E ENTRADA DO TÚNEL DE LIGAÇÃO DIRECTA, RUA DA PALMA-CAMPO DAS CEBOLAS

23 Mesquita 1950, p. 13.
24 Fernandes José M. 2017, p. 82.
25 Tostões 2008, p. 209.
26 Cf. Mesquita 1950, pp. 12–13.
27 Tostões 2008, p. 213.

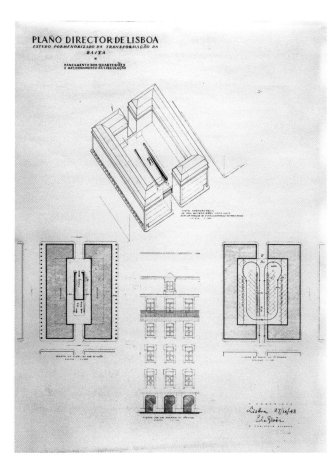

Detailed study for the redevelopment plan for the Baixa, Étienne de Groër, 1948. De Groër wanted to make two blocks in the Baixa into one by demolishing one long side of each block, thus solving the problems of light and the lack of parking space without changing the character of the Baixa.
[Source: Câmara Municipal de Lisboa (ed.) 2008, pictorial appendix (CD)]

The radical reconstruction of the Praça da Figueira did not only meet with agreement. In the city magazine "*Revista Municipal*" the publicist Noberto de Araújo printed an obituary for the central indoor market that stood on the Praça da Figueira. Araújo disputed that the new market halls, which were to replace the central indoor market, had a soul. Although they were hygienic, with a clear architectural form and worthy of a capital city such as Lisbon, they were all the same, without personality, without the nobility of a genuine market. They did not speak the language of the common people. In Araújo's view, Lisbon had lost all that with the demolition.[28]

Plans for the Baixa

For the central area of the lower town, that part of the Baixa that had been reconstructed following the sea- and earthquake in 1755 in a strictly orthogonal pattern according to uniform building regulations, Étienne de Groër[29] personally developed a contribution to the redevelopment plan. It was his desire to satisfy the traffic-related and health requirements prevailing at the time without destroying the specific urban character of the Baixa. The urban planner saw the main problem in the density of the centre. He therefore proposed that pairs of the narrow housing blocks should be amalgamated. The long sides of the two blocks facing one another would have had to be demolished for this. The road between the blocks would lose its function and become part of an inner courtyard. The inner courtyards would provide light and air for the surrounding buildings as well as parking spaces for 40 cars. With the parking spaces in the inner courtyards de Groër wished to free the remaining streets in the Baixa from stationary vehicles. The pavements on the streets were to be moved behind arcades that were still to be created in order to gain more room for motor vehicle traffic.[30]

Master Plan for the Historic Centre

The various subprojects for the centre which João Guilherme Faria da Costa, who had accompanied Étienne de Groër's work on the master building plan since 1946, had developed within the framework of the master plan, culminated in a comprehensive reconstruction project for Lisbon's lower town (*Plano de Remodelação da Baixa*).[31] The focal points of the concept, which was completed in 1949, were the improvement of traffic flow and the redevelopment of the overpopulated quarters of the historic centre.[32] The concept was based on the redevelopment strategies of the First Republic, which envisaged a wholesale reconstruction in the periphery of the lower town in favour of an improvement of traffic flow.

29   Étienne de Groër (1882–1952), architect and town planner of Polish-Russian descent, was the most influential foreign urban planning expert in Salazar's Portugal. From 1938 to 1940 and from 1946 to 1948 de Groër worked as a town planner in the town planning office in Lisbon. He drew up the regional plan for the connection between Lisbon, Estoril and Cascais, the *Plano de Urbanização da Costa do Sol*. In addition he drew up the master plan for Lisbon in 1948 and was responsible for many other urban development plans in Portugal, including the plans for Abrantes, Almada, Beja, Braga, Coimbra, Évora and Sintra, and also for Luanda, the capital of Angola.
30   Lôbo 1995, p. 96.
31   Tostões 2008, p. 212.
32   Mangorrinha 1999, p. 222.

28   Araújo 1949, p. 26.

Faria da Costa's concept for the relief of the centre envisaged three tunnels.[33] The first was to lead from the estuary bank between the Praça do Comércio and the Cais do Sodré station below the upper town (Bairro Alto) to the Praça dos Restauradores at the end of the Avenida da Liberdade. It was joined here by the second tunnel, which connected the Praça dos Restauradores with the new square into which the Avenida Almirante Reis opened, the Praça de Dom João I (Praça Martim Moniz). The third was to complete the semicircle from the Praça de Dom João I through the castle hill back to the Tejo and the Santa Apolónia station. In this system the two squares Praça dos Restauradores and Praça de Dom João I as well as the two stations Cais do Sodré and Santa Apolónia were the most important crossover points from the historic centre to the rest of the city.

Closely connected with the bypassing of the centre was the planned new underground railway line. The first plans for an underground railway were made in 1944. The underground railway tunnel was to run parallel to the motor vehicle tunnel from Cais do Sodré station to the Praça dos Restauradores at the end of the Avenida da Liberdade. The architect Carlos Rebelo de Andrade, together with the engineer, Carles Buïgas, designed a system of tunnels, lifts, shopping areas, exhibition halls and subterranean squares with fountains and plants. In addition to the drawings of the tunnel installations, Andrade's plans also included proposals for the incorporation of the tunnel entrances into the facades of the existing buildings.[34] The axis was to terminate in a head-end structure with a mighty overdimensional avant-corps. The construction of the underground railway finally began in 1955, and the first run followed in 1959. The first line connected the northern periphery of the lower town with the inland city quarters but did not play any role for the actual centre. It was not until 1963 that the line was extended to Rossio Square and the extension to Cais do Sodré station would not be built for decades.[35]

Demolitions for Traffic and Portugal's Greatness

The redevelopment of the historic centre was a key activity of the dictatorship in Lisbon. Its results were contradictory and without any real coherence, but in some areas they still determine our picture of the historic centre today. The redevelopment of the historic centre in the Portuguese capital meant primarily demolition, wholesale reconstruction. It was mainly parts of the oldest quarter of the city on the castle hill and at its foot, which had not been destroyed by the earthquake of 1755, which fell victim to the axe, particularly in the late 1930s and 1940s. Today's observer hardly notices this loss. The vacant area around the reconstructed St. George's Castle seems almost natural, like the Castle itself, and the considerable destruction in Alfama is no longer perceptible. The destruction in Mouraria in the area of the Praça Martim Moniz continue to be much more noticeable today – the square has still not found its natural form and its relationship to the rest of the amputated quarter is weak. The heart of the lower town, the regular layout from the period of the reconstruction following the earthquake of 1755, was largely spared by the redevelopment of the historic centre. The same is true of the presently much loved upper town (Bairro Alto).

Both the area around the Praça Martim Moniz and the area to the west of the Praça do Comércio were intended to provide above all an improvement in the traffic connection of the centre to the rest of the city. However, in the final analysis the traffic situation in the centre was hardly changed at all during the dictatorship. The bypassing of the centre for motor vehicles was too expensive because of the necessary tunnels, and the underground station Cais do Sodré was not inaugurated until 1998. Much more successful was the redevelopment of the historic centre motivated by the commemorative policy of the *Estado Novo*: the reconstructed St. George's Castle served during the dictatorship to evoke the historical greatness of Portugal and after the fall of the dictatorship it was integrated into tourism marketing without further ado.

33 Mesquita 1950, p. 6.
34 Almeida 2017, pp. 30–31.
35 Um pouco de história, no date.

*Presentation plan for the redevelopment of the centre, João Faria
da Costa, 1950. The not quite northward oriented plan is aligned
to the orthogonal street system of the lower town that was
reconstructed following the sea- and earthquake. In the middle
of the lower edge of the plan is the Praça do Comércio, which the
planned buildings on the bank of the estuary for the extension
of the state administration centre adjoin on the west side. At the
northern end of the orthogonally patterned layout of the streets in
the lower town, the bright Praça da Figueira with its simple square
shape stands out from the plan background. The north corner of
the square forms the junction to the planned row of buildings on
the new Praça de Dom João I and the Rua da Plama.
[Source: Mesquita 1950, following p. 8]*

Évora: "Museum City" *

The city of Évora played a special role in the policy of the urban renewal of historic centres and the preservation of historic monuments during the Portuguese dictatorship.[36] Its history offered hardly any points of reference for the official policy of remembrance. The only measure that was implemented within the framework of the great propaganda show of the *Estado Novo* was the reconstruction of the Chapel of St. Michael. It was to stand on the spot where the first Christian church was built after the expulsion of the Moors.[37] It was thus, according to the ruling interpretation, a structural testimony to the Christianisation accomplishment of the Portuguese people and its heroes, with whom the Portuguese dictatorship associated its claim to power. Due to its modest size, however, the chapel was not suited to provide the background for the procession that was organised in Évora in the summer of 1940.[38] The historic centre of Évora was therefore – in contrast to those of Lisbon, Porto and Guimarães – not reconstructed into a backdrop with a special message. Instead, the procession took place in the double square of Largo do Conde Vila Flor and Largo Márquez de Marialva in the shade of Évora's Roman Temple of Diana.

Redevelopment of the Historic Centre before the Dictatorship

In the middle of the 19th century, a period of growing interest in antiquity in Europe, the remains of Évora's Roman Temple of Diana[39], which had in the course of the centuries been merged with the Palace of the Inquisition (*Palácio da Inquisição*), were re-excavated. In order to improve its urban surroundings the City Council decided to demolish the Palace, leaving only a small part standing and creating a town park to the north of the temple. In 1863 the Passeio de Diana was inaugurated as Évora's first public park.[40]

The installation of the public park (Passeio Público) on the site of the former royal palace of Dom Manuel was also begun in 1863. The site was transferred into the possession of the municipality in 1834, which had erected a military

Évora, Tourist guide, cover picture by Daniel R. Sanches, before 1949. The picture shows the fountain on the market square of Évora, the Praça do Geraldo. Behind the fountain is St. Anton's Church. [Source: Comissão Municipal de Turismo de Évora (ed.) 1949, p. 1]

camp in the half-ruined buildings that had in the meantime been used as a monastery.[41] The palace annexes and the remains of the gardens from the Middle Ages and the Renaissance were destroyed for the public park. The actual palace, which was in danger of collapsing, continued to be used as a camp.[42] A decree by the city authorities of Évora, however, laid down that the Palace of Dom Manuel was to be restored and utilised for a purpose that was fitting of the monument.

A storm in the winter of 1881 caused large parts of the Palace to collapse.[43] Following the accident it was decided to reconstruct only a small residue of the ruins and to use this as a museum. The thus partially reconstructed palace, now called the Galeria das Damas, was developed into an exhibition building, the main front of which was formed by a facade of the former palace. The facades added on the sides and back of the building paid little attention to the front facade. Although their design in iron and glass was in keeping with contemporary concepts of a modern exhibition building,[44] it met with decided rejection on the part of the citizens.[45] The remaining parts of the collapsed palace were sold in 1892.

36 On Évora's historic centre cf. Clemente/Vieira 2013; on the redevelopment of Évora's historic centre cf. above all Câmara Municipal de Évora (ed.) 2001.

37 Fernandes, Maria 2007, p. 149.

38 Revista dos Centenários 5/1939, p. 13.

39 The Diana Temple is the most important surviving building of Roman antiquity in Portugal. It is not at all certain, however, that the temple was dedicated to the goddess Diana.

40 Rodrigues/Matos 2007, p. 137.

* Évora is frequently called a "museum city" (Cidade Museu). Cf. for example the poster Tradition et Pittoresque. Évora. Portugal. Une ville musée. ed. DNI 1949. In: Fundação Calouste Gulbenkian (ed.) 1982, p. 93.

41 Comissão Municipal de Turismo de Évora (ed.) 1949, p. 88.

42 Branco/Gordalina/Marques 2002.

43 Branco/Gordalina/Marques 2002.

44 Rodrigues/Matos 2007, p. 140.

45 Rodrigues/Matos 2007, p. 141.

The theatre of Évora (*Teatro Garcia de Resende*) was erected between 1881 and 1890, and in front of it a further public park was created.[46] The architecture of the theatre also failed to find approval. With the disappearance and sale of further important structural monuments such as parts of the historic city wall and the demolition of the arcades in Évora's main square the resistance to the local authorities' lack of appreciation of the structural heritage grew. The result was the founding of the initiative *Grupo Pró-Évora* for the preservation of the cityscape in 1919. The aim of the initiative was to have as many buildings as possible that were valuable from the point of view of architectural history or art recognised as national monuments.[47] In the early years following its foundation the group concerned itself with the salvation of individual monuments and the creation of a museum in order to eradicate the basis for the transfer of art objects to the museums in Lisbon.[48]

The redevelopment of Évora's historic centre in the early decades of the 20th century took place in this sphere of tension between conversion into a middle-class city with theatres, parks and museums, and the attempt to preserve as large a part as possible of the building heritage. During this period the city had hardly grown beyond the fortifications of the 14th century.[49]

Plans for the Historic Centre during the Dictatorship

When in 1934 the statutory requirement for master plans for all Portuguese towns and cities of the mother country and the bordering islands was announced,[50] the planning office of the city of Évora did not have the necessary staff to carry out the required tasks.[51] The city therefore set up a commission under the direction of the town planning office to develop a master plan. In addition to the town planning office and the municipal health authority, the state Directorate for National Building and Building Monuments was represented in the commission. In May 1937 the commission's draft for the master plan was agreed unanimously by the town council.[52]

Together with the draft a new building regulation for Évora was also passed, in the formulation of which the *Grupo Pró-Évora* was involved.[53] The structure of the building regulation follows that of Lisbon, which was formulated under the direction of Étienne de Groër, the town planner

Évora, Galeria das Damas with the unpopular facades from the 19th century after the reconstruction, photo c. 1890. [Source: Rodrigues/ Matos 2007]

of Polish-Russian descent who was educated in France.[54] In the foreword to the building regulation the unique architectural and historical heritage of the city is invoked and the effective protection of its historic buildings demanded in order to enable Évora to be upgraded as a tourist city. For this purpose it is absolutely necessary, the foreword continues, to establish disciplinary measures to enable intervention in the anarchic excesses of the private building industry in support of the attractiveness of the city.[55]

The building regulation divided the city into three zones: the historic centre, the ring road around the historic centre with its adjacent buildings and the remaining areas outside of the city walls. For the historic centre and the ring road it required that all buildings should have a clearly urban character. New buildings, extensions and renovation were not to contradict the general aesthetic impression of the historic centre.[56] A further chapter of the building regulation explained what conditions had to be fulfilled in order not to contradict the general impression. Thus, both for the historic centre and for the area of the historic centre ring road the building of block perimeters was envisaged. In order to preserve the harmonic overall image of the city, the design of the facades of new buildings had to be coordinated with the surrounding buildings. The maximum height of the eaves was defined as 20 metres.[57] Changes to the facades of historic buildings could only be made in agreement with the building authority. This was particularly the case for the construction of shops and their advertising. In addition the building regulation specified that only white was permissible as the colour for the facades.[58]

46   Bandeira 2007, p. 76.
47   David/Rodrigues 2001, p. 66.
48   Cf. Rodrigues 2001, pp. 417–418.
49   Património e Cidade 2007, p. 199.
50   Statutory decree 24802 of 21.12.1934 on the drafting of master building plans.
51   Barbosa 2001, p. 94.
52   Barbosa 2001, p. 95.
53   Rodrigues 2001, p. 423.

54   Um Regulamento Exemplar e um Plano Inexperimente 2001, p. 91.
55   Câmara Municipal de Évora (ed.) 1937, p. 4.
56   Câmara Municipal de Évora (ed.) 1937, p. 8.
57   Câmara Municipal de Évora (ed.) 1937, p. 34.
58   Câmara Municipal de Évora (ed.) 1937, p. 36.

In 1942 Étienne de Groër was commissioned by the city council on the personal recommendation of the Minster of Public Works and Transport, Duarte Pacheco, to develop a concept for Évora's master plan.[59] The town planning expert presented his concept in the same year.[60] Right at the beginning de Groër notes that the entire building activity is concentrated on the area inside the city walls. Évora's layout, as he formulates it, is organised like a spider's web, in the centre of which lies Geraldo Square. The top of the town is dominated by the cathedral which, together with the Diana Temple and the museum, forms the acropolis of Évora. This ensemble and the town silhouette were, in his view, considerably disturbed by a water tower from 1931 that stood directly next to the cathedral and the temple. Otherwise, in de Groër's judgement, Évora had been able to preserve its antique beauty. In this context he praised the building regulation of 1937 and its contribution to the preservation of the city's architectural heritage.[61]

The trade and business centre as well as the administration centre in de Groër's plan were located in the historic centre. The existing housing there should be preserved for wealthier strata of the population. In the narrow alleyways studios and handicraft workshops should be located systematically. The architectural character of the city within the city walls should be preserved in its entirety. In order to do so the modest style and the simple colours of the historic buildings should be preserved and the small number of necessary new buildings should conform to them.[62]

Étienne de Groër's completed draft was approved by all the city's levels of decision-making in 1945.[63] Two years later, in 1947, despite the wish of the municipal authorities that the draft be elaborated into an approvable and binding plan, the agreement of the Ministry of Public Works and Transport was denied.[64] The reason remains obscure.[65]

Projects for the Redevelopment of the Historic Centre during the Dictatorship

Following the refusal of ministerial approval, the municipal authorities continued to be guided by Étienne de Groër's draft plan, which for years to come provided a guideline, in addition to the building regulation of 1937, for measures within the city walls.[66] That there was no break in the municipal urban redevelopment policy can also be attributed to the initiative *Grupo Pró-Évora*, which had brought its ideas for the preservation of the historic centre into the draft planning.[67] In the following decades the main themes of de Groër's draft plan were continually implemented: the exposure and greening of the city wall, the open layout of squares and town parks, the upgrading of infrastructural facilities.

One of the first measures of urban redevelopment during the *Estado Novo* was the redesigning of the Praça Joaquim António de Aguiar. Together with the preparations for the master plan Étienne de Groër developed a concept in 1942 for the theatre square, which was implemented in 1944 to 1947 by the General Directorate for National Buildings and Building Monuments. A long extended green area framed in stonework was created that was intended to convey the differences in height on the square. The Garcia de Resende Theatre, which was inaugurated in 1890 and dominated the square, the design of which was controversial, was given a new facade in 1969 in a neo-Renaissance form.

The first sketches for the exposure of Évora's historic city wall were drawn in 1944 under the direction of the General Directorate for National Buildings and Building Monuments.[68] At the same time the work began on the segments of the wall, which only proceeded slowly, however. The state of the surviving wall segments was good but the demolition of the adjoining buildings delayed the completion of the entire project until into the 1980s.[69] The work on the city wall was connected with the creation of small accompanying parks. In those areas in which the parks reached up to the city wall, the coping of the wall was utilised as a further pathway or integrated into the park with stone recesses that could be used as seats. One of the first parks was created between 1953 and 1955. The small triangular square Largo dos Colegiais lies directly to the east of the tourism centre, in the shadow of the cathedral and the Diana Temple.

59 Os instrumentos fundamentais de protecção e requalificação 2011, p. 9.
60 Cf. Groër 1942.
61 Cf. Groër 1942, pp. 12–15.
62 Groër 1942, p. 34.
63 Fernandes, Maria 2007, p. 152.
64 Monteiro/Tereno/Tomé 2014, p. 625.
65 Simplício 2007, p. 328.

66 Fernandes, Maria 2007, p. 153.
67 Rodrigues 2001, p. 423.
68 Fernandes, Maria 2007, p. 151.
69 Fernandes, Maria 2007, p. 152.

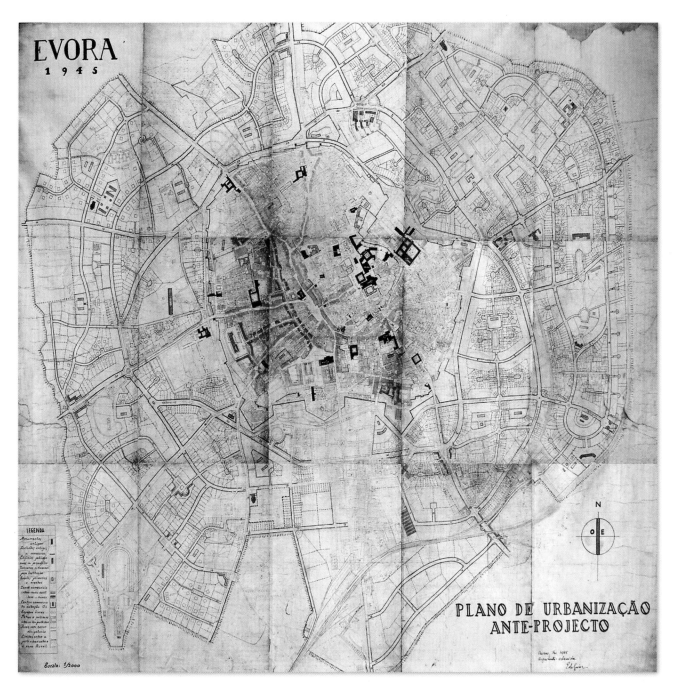

Évora, Preliminary draft of the master plan, Étienne de Groër, 1945. The guideline for the historic centre had three aims: the complete protection of the historic monuments, which are highlighted in black in the plan, the preservation of the residential quarters and the distribution of retail trade, the preferred sites for which are shown in the plan in red. Retail trade, which de Groër organised along the major access roads, was divided into trade of local importance (dark red) and trade of interregional importance (pale red). He thus organised the historic centre into a tourism centre between the Cathedral and the Diana Temple, an interregional business centre with Geraldo Square in the middle, and an area for local retail trade, the anchor of which was the indoor market on the western periphery of the city walls. [Source: Groër 1942]

A large playground was also built in the 1950s below the public park (Passeio Publico). Thus, in the course of the decades of the Portuguese dictatorship a string of small parks, decorative squares and playgrounds was created that transformed the city wall and fortifications into a green belt between the historic centre and the new town.

The exhibition hall *Galeria das Damas* was badly damaged by a fire in 1916. The General Directorate for National Buildings and Building Monuments did not take responsibility for the building, which was in danger of collapsing, until 1943.[70] It removed the facades from the late 19th century,

which had been the object of criticism from the very beginning, and created all the fronts according to the model of a facade fragment surviving from the building's period of origin. The reconstruction of the *Galeria das Damas* to a venue for special events meant the upgrading of the Passeio Público and therefore of the green belt next to the city wall. The green corridor and the picturesque design of the fortifications formed a major component in the tourist marketing of Évora's historical heritage during the Portuguese dictatorship. Part of its attractiveness is the romantic display of medieval building fragments, which reveals its inspiration from the teachings of the French architect Viollet-le-Duc.[71]

70 Cf. Branco/Gordalina/Marques 2002.

71 Cf. Comissão Municipal de Turismo de Évora (ed.) 1949, pp. 88–89.

Évora, town plan by Daniel R. Sanches, 1949. The plan shows the area of the historic centre within the city walls. The most important tourist attractions are highlighted. The public park (Passeio Público) in the bottom right-hand corner of the picture can be easily recognised by the green area and the clearly illustrated pathways.
[Source: Comissão Municipal de Turismo de Évora (ed.) 1949, following p. 2]

Évora, Praça Joaquim António de Aguiar, photo by David Freitas, 1947. This large square was redesigned in the years 1944 to 1947. In the background stands the Garcia de Resende Theatre with the facade from 1890, which was altered considerably in 1969. [Source: Câmara Municipal de Évora (ed.) 2001, p. 126]

Évora, the not yet completed decorative square Buraco dos Colegiais next to the excavated city wall, photo by David Freitas, c. 1955. [Source: Câmara Municipal de Évora (ed.) 2001, p. 113]

Évora, Part of the city wall, photo c. 1950. This part survived due to the initiative of the Grupo Pró-Évora. [Source: Évora mosaico 10/2011, p. 8]

Évora, Galeria das Damas with the "historic" facades reconstructed during the dictatorship, photo before 1949. [Source: Comissão Municipal de Turismo de Évora (ed.) 1949, p. 86]

In parallel to the reconstruction of the *Galeria das Damas* the city planning office conducted several studies on the improvement of the cityscape. Following de Groër's ideas on the tourism centre, a study was conducted on the redesign of the oldest city park, the Passeio de Diana. The study contained two drawings: the first showed the existing situation between the Passeio de Diana and the city quarter below the northern retaining wall. The second was intended to demonstrate how the place could look without the fortifications that had until then been necessary because of the differences in height in the terrain. It was quite obvious that the authors wanted to improve the spatial effect. The demolition of the water tower was recommended, as de Groër had proposed. The water tower was not demolished, however, nor was the site altered, so that the spatial impression of the first drawing has survived until the present day.

A further study deals with Évora's main square, the Praça do Geraldo. The neo-baroque building of the Bank of Portugal, which had dominated the southern end of the square since 1909, was perceived immediately after its completion as a break in the harmony of the square as a whole. In the 1950s various perspective sketches were made for the possible redesign of the facade. Apparently none of the concepts was convincing.

In the mid-1960s the municipal administration, together with the Bank of Portugal, made a second attempt to redesign the perceived as unfitting facade from 1909. The new facade was to be similar to that of the building preceding the Bank but was not to copy it. The Gothic window frames that were stored in the regional museum were to be incorporated into the new facade design. It was hoped, generally, that the redesigning would cause the building to blend more pleasingly into the facade ensemble of the Praça do Geraldo.[72] Apparently the facade study by the commissioned architect, Cassiano Branco, found just as little favour as the proposals made ten years earlier, with the result that the Bank has remained in place unaltered until the present.

In contrast to the Bank of Portugal, the department store *Armazéns do Chiado* that was finished in the same year as the Bank with a facade that also met with rejection, was replaced by a new building in 1955. The influential bank *Montepio Geral* had bought the department store. Several studies examined which facade construction would fit most harmoniously into the ensemble. The decision was made in favour of a facade that was not directly influenced by the neighbouring building, the Bank of Alentejo, but by the more modest buildings, which as a rule had two or three window axes and a further three storeys above the higher arcade storey. In fact the Bank building fits into the facade alignment so well that most visitors to the Praça do Geraldo today will not notice that it is a new building from the period of the Salazar dictatorship.

Évora's Head Post Office, which was completed in 1948,[73] is the most bombastic new building in the historic centre. The greater part of the old Salvador monastery in the historic centre was forced to give way to it.[74] Only the chapel and the mighty observation tower (*mirante*) of the monastery survive. In spite of its massive size the new Main Post

72 Vai ser reintegrado no ambiente arquitectónico geral um vetusto edifício de Évora 03.11.1965, p. 13.
73 As Obras do Estado Novo 2001, p. 111.
74 Os instrumentos fundamentais de protecção e requalificação 2011, pp. 9–10.

Évora, the tourism centre, two sketches c. 1950. Top: the state at that time with the unpopular water tower from 1931; bottom: the planned state without supporting wall and without the water tower, but with the Diana Temple visible and with an even more decorative garden in front. [Source: Câmara Municipal de Évora (ed.) 2001, p. 124]

Office can only be seen from a few places in the city because it was cleverly integrated into the existing built environment. The large building complex is comprised of several components, each of which interacts with its neighbours. The east facade, which can be seen from afar over the long, strung-out green area, rises like a bulwark crowned with a tower, while the part of the building facing towards the newly constructed Rua de Olivença submits somewhat modestly to the Town Hall opposite. The old chapel and the observation tower of the monastery form a sort of screen if one looks from the Town Hall square in the direction of the Main Post Office. So that the central Post Office building can be reached and used as easily as possible it is detached on all four sides. To achieve this, on its southeast side the Rua de Olivença forms a breakthrough, which opens up the building via its arcades to the Praça de Sertório, the Rathaus square of Évora.

Parallel to the construction of the Head Post Office numerous smaller projects on secular buildings were conducted in order to improve the cityscape under the management of the state's General Directorate for National Buildings and Building Monuments on the basis of a selective photographic documentation of the existing built environment and distinctive structural components. The spectrum extended from illusionistic paintings to facade extensions and the addition of extra storeys. In order to create the impression of a balanced, symmetrical facade windows or lattices were painted on the facades. Sometimes spolia were used that had been salvaged in the course of demolition work.[75] The reconstruction of simple housing was not based on construction research but followed the idea of a harmonic cityscape, such as was already aspired to by the Building Regulation of 1937.[76]

Like the Head Post Office, the new, massive cultural centre (*Salão Central*) is hardly perceptible in the public space of the historic centre. It was erected in the immediate vicinity of Évora's tourism centre according to plans by the Portuguese architect Keil do Amaral.[77] With the construction of the Post Office and the cultural centre in the historic centre the municipality followed the recommendations on the functional modernisation of the historic centre which Étienne de Groër had made in 1942 in his draft for the master plan.[78]

In German architectural journals of the 1930s to 1970s there are hardly any reports about Portugal. The contribution "Von einer Studienreise nach Portugal" [From a study

Évora, Praça do Geraldo, View of the Bank of Portugal built in 1909, with the unpopular facade (top) and the proposal for a new facade (bottom), photo and drawing c. 1950.
[Source: Câmara Municipal de Évora (ed.) 2001, p. 121]

Évora, facades of the eastern buildings on the Praça do Geraldo, photo c. 1944. The department store Armazéns do Chiado from 1909, like the Bank of Portugal, was perceived immediately after its construction as an intrusion in the square Praça do Geraldo as a whole.
[Source: Arquivo Direção-Geral do Património Cultural]

Évora, Praça do Geraldo, Facade study by Cassiano Branco for the Bank of Portugal, photomontage 1965.
[Source: Arquivo Municipal de Lisboa]

75 Cf. The photographic documentation on Évora in the archive of the (former) General Directorate for National Buildings and Building Monuments in the SIPA (*Sistema de Informação para o Património Arquitetónico*).
76 Câmara Municipal de Évora (ed.) 1937, p. 36.
77 A Construção de Equipamentos 2001, p. 137.
78 Groër 1942, pp. 33–34.

Évora, Praça do Geraldo, Facade studies by Cassiano Branco for the new building of the Bank Montepio Geral, c. 1950.
[Source: Câmara Municipal de Évora (ed.) 2001, p. 122]

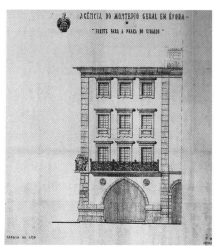

Évora, site plan for the new Head Post Office, drawing c. 1947. The outline of the Head Post Office is marked by a thick black line that detaches itself from the rest of the plan by a slightly reddish highlight. Small arrows indicate the different entrances to the building. To the left of the Post Office the remains of the Salvator monastery are shown in grey. Above the monastery the demolition of residential buildings for the breakthrough of the Rua Menino Jesus is indicated in yellow. The street to the southeast of the Main Post Office, the Rua de Olivença, was created by this building project. The Town Hall – cut off by the lower middle edge of the picture – received a new north-west facade.
[Source: Câmara Municipal de Évora (ed.) 2001, p. 117]

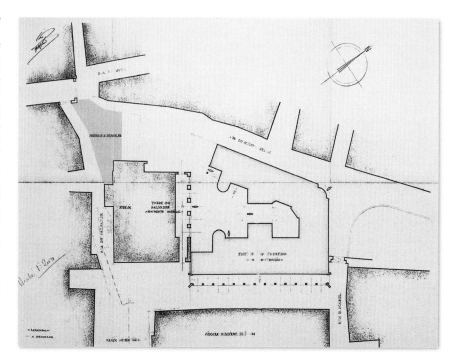

Évora, Rua de Olivença, photos c. 1950. In the course of the new construction of the Main Post Office Évora's Town Hall was extended. The extension annex closes off the Rua de Olivença on its southeast side (top). The facade front vis-à-vis was formed by a two-storey wing of the Main Post Office building (bottom).
[Source: Arquivo Direção-Geral do Património Cultural]

Évora, Eastern facade of the mighty Head Post Office, photo c. 1950. In the foreground are the greened water tanks from 1932.
[Source: Câmara Municipal de Évora (ed.) 2001, p. 86]

trip to Portugal] by Annemarie Jauss from 1931 is one of the few exceptions. Following her round trip the author came to the conclusion that "Evora [...] [can be] considered the most enchanting town in the South of Portugal."[79] As evidence for this statement she includes a photograph of Largo das Portas, in the centre right of which, hidden by a fountain, the unadorned outer walls of the *Palácio do Farrobo* are visible. The palace was demolished in the 1960s in the last great intrusion into the historic centre. On its foundation walls today stands the Palace of Justice, built there following the demolition. In addition, a small group of medieval buildings were forced to give way to the enlargement of the square in front of the Palace of Justice.[80]

Unlike the Head Post Office and the Salão Central, the Palace of Justice was not closely integrated into the historic built environment surrounding it, but was built to be visible. It formed a hinge between a double square and a small green decorative square. The architect of the Palace of Justice, Carlos Ramos, skilfully used the three different spaces for three different entrances to his building. The decorative square forms a kind of rear entrance from which one can get into the Palace of Justice directly via a stairway and a connecting enclosed bridge without having to cross the street. The second entrance is reached from the northern half of the double square Largo das Portas de Moura. The visitor is welcomed here by a two-storey-high portal that is supported by four massive pillars. The third entrance is open towards the southern part of the double square via a cloister-like atrium.[81] The expansive building complex of the Palace of Justice completed in 1963 does not appear particularly monumental and is not intrusive or disruptive due to its structure that skilfully relates to its surroundings.

Model for the Redevelopment of Historic Centres Spread over Several Decades

Due to the refusal in 1947 of a ministerial authorisation for the elaboration of Étienne de Groër's draft for a master plan the city of Évora implemented its projects in a planning vacuum for many years. Only in 1958 was a commission for a new draft plan granted, this time an Étienne de Groër's son, Nikita. Apart from the radically car-friendly proposal to build an express ring road around the historic centre of Évora immediately outside the city wall, Nikita's plan was not very different from his father's.[82] In his first sketches the city within the city walls is a *carte blanche*.

Évora, southern view of the city silhouette, photo 1949. In front of the cathedral is the Salão Central, a cultural centre with a theatre/ cinema auditorium for an audience of 548 persons. The huge dimension of the building is only perceptible from a distance. [Source: Arquivo Direção-Geral do Património Cultural]

Évora, view over the Largo das Portas de Moura to the cathedral, photo by Annemarie Jauss, 1931. [Source: Jauss 1931, p. 239]

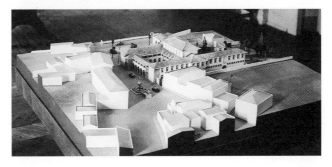

Évora, model of the new Palace of Justice, Carlos Ramos, photo by David Freitas, c. 1955. [Source: Câmara Municipal de Évora (ed.) 2001, p. 116]

Évora, Largo das Portas de Moura with new Palace of Justice, photo after 1963. [Source: Arquivo da Cidade de Évora]

Évora, northern facade of the Palace of Justice with the bridge side-entrance over the decorative square Jardim do Bacalhau, photo by David Freitas, after 1963. [Source: Câmara Municipal de Évora (ed.) 2001, p. 116]

79   Jauss 1931, p. 240.
80   A cidade nos anos 60 2011, p. 15.
81   Cf. A Porta de Moura e o Tribunal 2001, pp. 115–116.
82   Fernandes, Maria 2007, p. 153.

Évora, first draft of a concept for a master plan, Nikita de Groër, 1959. An express ring road was to be built around the historic centre, leaving the latter largely untouched. [Source: Câmara Municipal de Évora (ed.) 2001, p. 108]

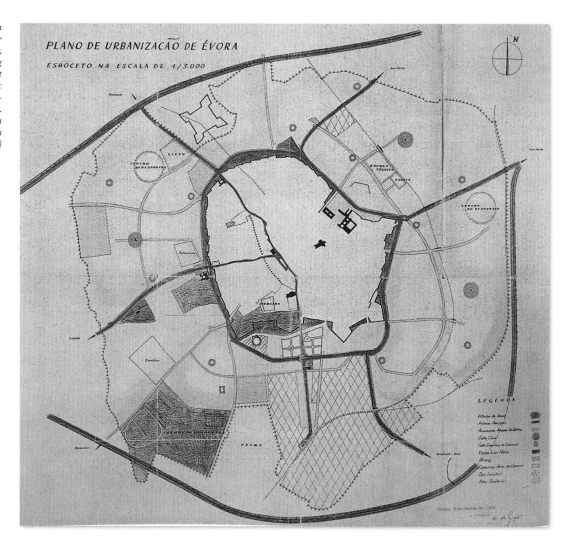

Only a few building monuments outlined in black and the three most important access roads of the Praça do Geraldo, illustrated in red, offer an orientation. Nikita de Groër apparently saw no great need for planning for the historic centre.

Following the approval of Nikita de Groër's planning by the city council in 1959 and by the Ministry of Public Works and Transport in 1963, Évora's historic centre therefore essentially remained a product of the Building Regulation of 1937 and the recommendations of Étienne de Groër from 1942. The as a whole relatively cautious city redevelopment was less due to the strategic interests of the dictatorship than to the pronounced involvement of the educated middle classes, which was, however, not impeded in any way by the dictatorship, but, if anything, supported. The municipal redevelopment policy that was implemented over a number of decades created the foundation for the UNESCO's recognition of Évora's historic centre as a world heritage site in November 1986.[83]

Today Évora possesses a well maintained, although smoothly groomed, historic centre, which is visited by many tourists – the result of a redevelopment of European importance that goes back a long time. It combines very different characteristics in a unique way: the strict maintenance of historic buildings contrasts with the destruction of a number of building complexes that were forced to give way to striking new buildings, which in turn have been integrated remarkably well into the historic centre. This process was accompanied by a policy of "deshaming", the removal of facades from the late 19th century that were perceived as inappropriate. The historical layout of the city was largely maintained in this process although the network of public spaces was extended in some places.

83   A classificação pela UNESCO 2011, p. 17.

Óbidos: "Portuguese Rothenburg" *

The magic of the little town of Óbidos[84] lies in its apparently omnipresent past,[85] which is closely connected with the history of Portugal and its kings and queens.[86] With his breakaway from the royal house of León and the wars of conquest against the Moors Afonso I[87] initiated the founding of the Portuguese empire, of which he was the first king, ruling from 1139 to 1185.[88] The storming of the Moorish Óbidos in 1148 was long regarded in Portugal as a heroic contribution to the Christianisation of the Occident due to the fierce resistance met with.[89] The third king of Portugal, Afonso II, established the tradition that Óbidos was a part of the vested rights of the Portuguese queen by bestowing the town on his wife, Urraca of Castile. Many of the buildings in this little town, such as the churches or the aqueduct and the connected fountains, are due to this particular situation. The town's resistance to the siege by the Count of Bologna in 1246 brought further fame to Óbidos.[90] In the mid-14th century the reputation of the town, which lies 80 kilometres north of Lisbon, was further increased as it served as a sanctuary for the royal family during the outbreak of the plague in the capital.[91]

With the rise of liberalism following the Napoleonic Wars and, above all, with the royal fratricidal war[92] from 1832 to 1834 the rapid decline of the town began.[93] The rich courtly society left for elsewhere. The vacated houses were occupied by the poor from rural regions. Óbidos rapidly became more densely populated than ever before.[94] Although the contemporary beginnings of wanderlust among the rich European upper classes in the 19th century moved Óbidos into international focus, the small numbers of tourists could not stop the decline. In addition to the British and the French, the Italian architect born in Portugal, Alfredo d'Andrade, was interested in the urban monument that was Óbidos.[95] D'Andrade had received the prestigious commission to design the exhibition site for the General Italian Exhibition of 1884 (*L'Esposizione Italiana del 1884*) in Turin. In contrast to the industrial products exhibited, the site was to be constructed in the style of a medieval quarter.[96] In the preliminary stage of his work on the design d'Andrade travelled to Portugal in order to study the medieval architecture and urban construction there – including in Óbidos.[97]

---

84   On the history of Óbidos' urban development cf. Soares/Neto 2013.
85   A linda vila de Obidos ... 24.09.1934, p. 5.
86   Cf. Marinho 2015, pp. 1–2.
87   Afonso I is known in Portuguese documents as Dom Afonso Henriques (King Afonso, [son] of Henry [of Burgundy]).
88   Portugal 1907, p. 184.
89   Ministério das Obras Publicas 1952, p. 6–7.
90   Larcher 1939, p. 24.
91   Soares/Neto 2013, p. 11.

*   Rudolf Wolters called Óbidos the "Portuguese Rothenburg". Diary entry from 10.11.1941, documented in: Düwel/Gutschow 2015, p. 437. Wolters, Albert Speer's most important colleague, visited Portugal with the national socialist travelling propaganda exhibition "Neue Deutsche Baukunst" [New German architecture] at the end of 1941.

92   The fratricidal war, also known as the Miguelite War, was a factional dispute within the Portuguese royal family between supporters of absolutism and supporters of liberalism, which was waged between Ex-King Peter IV and his brother King Michael I.
93   Prista 2013, p. 371.
94   Prista 2013, p. 371.
95   Soares/Neto 2013, pp. 14–16.
96   Ferreira 2016, p. 72.
97   Soares/Neto 2013, p. 16.

Óbidos, View of the castle from the north, photo by the Marques de Abreu, before 1927. [Source: Lino 1927, following p. 592]

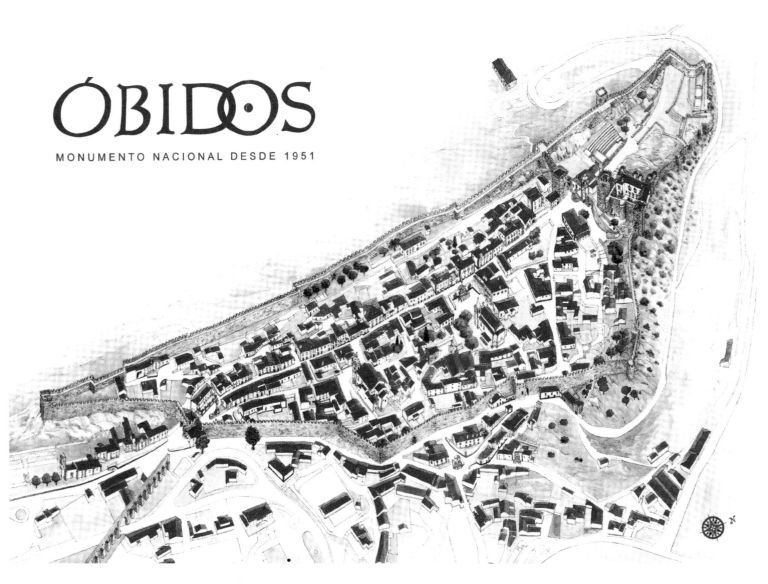

ÓBIDOS

MONUMENTO NACIONAL DESDE 1951

Representation of the historic centre of Óbidos as a national monument. The map, which is currently distributed to tourists, shows the "national monument" declared at the beginning of 1951, one of the first complete, i.e. including the simple historic buildings, protected urban ensembles in Europe.
[Source: Arquivo Municipal de Óbidos]

Discovery of a National Monument

Parallel to the high regard abroad for Óbidos' cultural building heritage, the interest at home in the testimonials to the medieval art of building also grew. The first proposal to place several buildings in Óbidos under conservation protection came in 1880 from the Ministry of Public Works. The Ministry commissioned the Association of Freelance Architects and the Portuguese Archaeological Society to make a list and a map of the buildings which should be classified as national monuments.[98] At the end of the 19th century the demand by the Portuguese scholar, Alexandre Herculano, for the conservation of the country's cultural building heritage in order to strengthen national consciousness enjoyed great popularity.[99] On the eve of the Portuguese revolution, with which the monarchy founded by Afonso I disappeared after almost 800 years, Vicente Almeida d'Eça described the little Portuguese town of Óbidos as a "true museum of national art"[100].

In the summer of 1910 the new republican Ministry of Public Works, Trade and Industry published a decree that classified numerous castles, city walls, palaces, churches, monasteries and other buildings as national monuments. Apart from the Castle and the *Pelourinho*[101] none of Óbidos' buildings were included in the list.[102] In 1920 an article by Leitão de Barros on the Castle of Óbidos was published in the influential daily newspaper *"Diário de Noticias"*.[103] In his observations, Barros took the entire town into consideration and emphasised that in Portugal there were only a very few so well preserved historic centres as that of Óbidos. He recommended conserving the little town as an object of study and as a tourist attraction.[104]

In the first year after the military coup, 1927, when the dictatorship was not yet consolidated, the first issue of the travel guide *"Guia de Portugal. Estremadura, Alentejo, Algarve"* was published. The contribution on Óbidos was written by the architect Raúl Lino, who stated right at the beginning of his article that Óbidos was a part of Portugal which had best conserved its picturesque medieval

character.[105] In addition to the paragraphs on the Castle and the churches Lino dedicated a paragraph of their own to the secular buildings of the town, in which he described the composition of old, white houses, chapels and churches, interrupted by the green of the gardens bordered by walls, as testimonials to more prosperous epochs.[106] In 1928 the Department of Tourism in the Ministry of the Interior officially recognised Óbidos as a "tourism town".[107] This took place on the basis of a law that had been passed during the First Republic for the support of tourism.[108] The recognition meant that the municipality was obliged to set up a commission (*Comissão de Iniciativa e Turismo*) with the task of producing concepts for the development of tourism. Resources were provided for this from a fund that had been created shortly after the declaration of the First Republic in 1911.[109]

The commission began its work at the end of April 1928. One of its first decisions was the publication in 1929 of a tourist guide exclusively for Óbidos and its surrounding area.[110] The preface by Marcelo Caetano, the later successor to Salazar,[111] sounds like a fairy tale. It cleverly combines the history of the town with the most important dates for the country. The text begins quite prosaically with three quotations that describe the uniqueness of the town of Óbidos. In addition to an extract from Raúl Lino's text from 1927, Agnes Goodall is quoted with the words: "It is the quaintest little place in the world, which lets one's thoughts wander to the Middle Ages [...]." Caetano took up the ideas of Goodall and Lino and placed them in contrast to the materialist, heartless, fast-moving present. Óbidos, the place in which the passing of time is hardly perceptible, was celebrated as a relic of the past – as a place for lovers, not for tourists. One can only experience its spirit, according to Caetano, if one succumbs to it. The sight of the castle, this Holy Grail, awakens memories of the holy order which liberated the fortress. The splendid past stood in stark contrast, however, to the sad present, which was characterised by disrepair and decline. Night-time, however, bewitched the little town and the spirits of the past were resurrected. Caetano did not forget one single hero of Óbidos in his story of resurrection. Thus, he emphasised that Afonso I had not only freed Spanish soil from the Moors but had also brought law and order to the town. The place of execution, Largo do Alceide-mor, was a testimonial in stone to this loyal and noble epoch, which had only collapsed in

---

98   Soares/Neto 2013, p. 26.
99   In view of the threat of the deterioration and demolition of Portugals cultural building heritage Alexandre Herculano called in 1838 in the weekly journal "*O Panorama*" for the conservation of the castles, city walls, palaces, churches and monasteries in remembrance of the heroic deeds of Portugal's forefathers, such as the secession from Spain, and of the splendid period of discovery, and at the same time for the recognition of their value for tourism. Cf. Monumentos II 01.09.1838, pp. 275–277.
100   Soares/Neto 2013, p. 25.
101   *Pelourinho* = small pillar. It was erected in front of the Town Hall to illustrate specific municipal rights.
102   Decree of 16.06.1910 on the establishment of national monuments.
103   Leitão de Barros 28.04.1920, p. 20.
104   Leitão de Barros 28.04.1920, p. 20.

105   Cf. Lino 1927, p. 587.
106   Lino 1927, p. 588–589.
107   Decree 15333 of 31.03.1938 on the recognition of Óbidos as a tourism town.
108   Law 1152 of 23.04.1921 on support for the tourism industry.
109   Law of 16.05.1911 on the creation of a department with own resources in the Ministry for Development for the development of tourism.
110   Comissão de Iniciativa e Turismo (ed.) 1929.
111   Marcelo Caetano took over the office of Prime Minister from António Salazar in 1968, which he held until the Carnation Revolution of 1974, which marked the end of the Portuguese dictatorship.

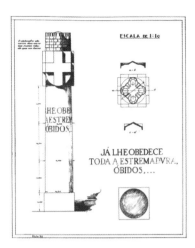

Óbidos, Largo do
Alceide-mor below
the castle, photo by
Alfred Ehrhardt, 1951.
[Source: Alfred
Ehrhardt Stiftung]

Padrão Camoniano in Óbidos,
installation drawing for the Camões
monument, Raúl Lino, 1929–1930.
The monument, in which the lines on
Óbidos formulated by the national
poet Camões are carved in capital
letters, is crowned by a stylised copy
of Óbidos Castle. Below the castle
are four coats of arms, each of
which displays a Christian cross. The
monument illustrates the words of
Portugal's conservative thinkers in
the mid-20th century. Portugal's great
contribution to world history, they
proclaim, was the Christianisation
and thus the civilisation of humanity,
which had its starting-point here in
Western Europe.
[Source: Soares/Neto 2013, p. 42]

Advertising poster "Óbidos – Museum of
Portugal", Abílio de Mattos e Silva, 1931.
[Source: Soares/Neto 2013, p. 164]

the recent light of apparent freedom. But the spirit of the old days still hovered over the ruins. And like a miracle the monument that was Óbidos had been conserved throughout seven centuries of turbulent European history.[112] With this patriotically charged preface Caetano supplied the basis for the interpretation of the history of Óbidos by the official propaganda of the *Estado Novo*.

Parallel to the publication of the tourist guide, the commission decided to erect a memorial stone for the Portuguese national poet, Luís de Camões. In his key work, the Lusiads,[113] Camões alluded to the conquest of the town of Óbidos by Afonso I.[114] The idea of the commission, to increase the awareness of Óbidos by means of a monument to Camões, met with a mixed reception. The discussion ended with the decision by the municipal administration in favour of the monument, which was to be erected in front of the local theatre. Raúl Lino, who had sparked a debate on the Portuguese national style with various writings, including his book "*A casa portuguesa*"[115], was recruited to draw up a plan.[116] The decision in favour of Raúl Lino complied with the idea of linking Óbidos more strongly to Portugal's national identity. The monument was erected in Óbidos between 1931 and 1932. An old house in the Rua Direita, Óbidos' main street, was demolished specifically for this purpose,[117] so that the first thing one sees when one goes through the main gateway into the town is the monument for Camões.

From a National Dream to a Declared National Monument

In 1933, when the *Estado Novo* had officially succeeded the military dictatorship by means of a constitutional referendum, the architect Couto Abreu made a proposal for the rehabilitation of the castle at the behest of the General Directorate for National Buildings and Building Monuments. He first established that the castle was one of the best preserved in the country and then recommended several measures for restoring the original character of the castle. Parallel to the study of Óbidos, further medieval fortifications throughout Portugal were examined with a view to their reconstruction. This was connected to the intention of giving national history a unified, ever recurring picture, the Lusitanian castle, which was to be found in every part of the country.[118]

The application by the municipality that Óbidos' town church, *Santa Maria*, be included in the list of historic monuments was also approved by the General Directorate for National Buildings and Building Monuments in 1933. Against this background, the later president of the regional administration, Albino de Castro, made the first attempt to have the entire town of Óbidos recognised as a national monument.[119] At first his proposal was not considered but nevertheless in 1934 reconstruction activities on Óbidos' town wall were begun under the management of the General Directorate for National Buildings and Building Monuments. The reconstruction, which was completed in 1936, was the first work by the General Directorate on a secular construction that was not a castle.[120]

In September 1934 a full-page article on Óbidos appeared in "*Diario de Lisboa*".[121] Its structure was similar to that of the preface by Marcelo Caetano to the tourist guide to Óbidos from 1929. In rather prosaic language the article describes Óbidos as a medieval town in which time stands still. Óbidos was a museum built of stone, a witness to the long lineage of Portugal's ancient nobility. The article provides a dismal assessment of the state of the castle. The civil war and recent decades had seriously affected the building, "the most important monument of the Portuguese military dictatorship"[122]. But fortunately, it was argued further, the General Directorate for National Buildings and Building Monuments had assumed responsibility for the castle and the fortress walls. Thus, Óbidos would be resurrected and its centuries-old walls would again be constructed in the fashion in which the "undying" verses of the Lusiads sang about them.[123]

112 Cf. Caetano 1929, pp. 4–15.
113 The Lusiads, "*Os Lusíadas*", written by Luís de Camões and first printed in 1572, are considered the Portuguese national epic. They establish an heroic interpretation of the history of the discoveries.
114 Camões 1883, p. 97.
115 Lino 1929.
116 Soares/Neto 2013, p. 40.
117 Soares/Neto 2013, p. 41.

118 Cf. Soares/Neto 2013, pp. 62–68.
119 Prista 2013, p. 372.
120 Soares/Neto 2013, pp. 68–73.
121 A linda vila de Obidos ... 24.09.1934, p. 5.
122 A linda vila de Obidos ... 24.09.1934, p. 5.
123 A linda vila de Obidos ... 24.09.1934, p. 5.

Cartilha
da Uospedagem Portuguesa

EDIÇÃO DO SECRETARIADO DA PROPAGANDA NACIONAL

Title page of a manual of the Office for Propaganda of
the Estado Novo on the management of a hotel, 1941.
[Source: Secretariado da Propaganda Nacional (ed.) 1941]

In March 1939 António Oliveira Salazar officially announced the national celebrations planned for 1940 for the 800th anniversary of the founding of the state of Portugal by the proclamation of the kingdom in 1139 and the 300th anniversary of the regaining of independence from Spain in 1640.[124] In addition to various exhibitions, particularly the exhibition on the Portuguese world (*Exposição do Mundo Português*) in Lisbon,[125] parades were to take place in all the places in Portugal that were of importance for the founding of the nation.[126]

The preparations for the anniversary celebrations had already begun several years before the official announcement. In the spring Minister Duarte Pacheco had authorised 475.000 *Escudos* from the unemployment fund on the basis of a decree from 1932[127] for a unique building programme for the restoration and reconstruction of historic castles, town walls, churches and palaces.[128] Responsible for this programme was the General Directorate for National Buildings and Building Monuments. Óbidos' castle also profited from this programme. The most important measures for the repair and reconstruction of the castle were to be completed by April 1940.[129]

In order to prepare the ground for the anniversary celebrations, between January 1939 and December 1940 a monthly information brochure was published by the festival committee under the direction of António Ferro, the director of the Office for Propaganda.[130] Each issue presented one or two castles that had been included in the castle building programme. Óbidos' castle was described in one of the first issues as one of the oldest and most attractive castles in Portugal. Its history stood not only for the liberation of Portugal by Afonso I, but also for Portugal's national independence. This picturesque, but also archaeologically and historically important building should, as an object of study, perpetuate the memories of Portugal's glorious past.[131]

The remembrance of a great past was always also understood as the promotion of tourism, however, which, in the opinion of António Ferro, was a key industry in Portugal.[132] The participation of the country in the World Exhibition in Paris in 1937 gave Ferro his first opportunity to present his tourism concept to an international public.[133] It was not until the reshuffle of the Cabinet as a result of the start of the war in 1939, however, that the tourism remit was officially transferred to the Office of Propaganda on 1 January 1940.[134] In February, Ferro obtained the necessary power to implement his plans through the formation of the National Tourism Council (*Conselho Nacional de Turismo*), over which he presided.[135]

Óbidos, the "museum of Portugal", with its buildings and its history, proved to be the ideal urban area for António Ferro's project.[136] For him, as the person responsible for propaganda, tourism was the great industry of dreams.[137] Óbidos as the "city of dreams" offered the visitor, in Ferro's view, the opportunity to travel into the past, as in a novel or a history book. In the sense of the motto of the Commission "Óbidos – museum of Portugal" the little town transformed itself into a symbol of Portugal and of tradition. The maintenance of its medieval assets became the guideline for the redevelopment of the historic centre, for the restoration of its monuments and for its touristic transformation. Both public and private houses retained their modest, simple character. The few new buildings that were permitted for the necessary infrastructure had to be built with local materials and in a traditional way.[138]

In the summer of 1940, two days before the great parade for the remembrance of the capture of Óbidos Castle by Afonso I, a new hostel was opened in the town. The *Estalagem do Lidador* was the first attempted implementation of António Ferro's tourism concept. In line with his ideas, the hostel was designed in a modest, rural style without renouncing modern comfort.[139] In the night of 18 to 19 August 1940 it was finally ready: the scene was set for the so often extolled dreams of Óbidos. The spectacle of the conquest took place in the forecourt of the castle and was transmitted throughout the country by the national radio company. Accompanied by an orchestra and the most modern lighting technology the battle was simulated in historical costumes. At midnight the Portuguese actress Palmira Bastos spoke to the audience from one of the castle towers. In her speech, which she held in the name of the town of Óbidos, she pointed out that no other place was as Portuguese as Óbidos. The town was rooted with heart and soul in the blood-soaked earth of the Portuguese whose blood it had absorbed in order to safeguard it in remembrance of the founding of Portugal.[140] Since this time the fortifications of Óbidos are regarded as the "most picturesque in the whole of Portugal".[141]

124   Salazar 1939, p. 2.
125   Cf. Bodenschatz/von Oppen 2019.
126   Salazar 1939, p. 6.
127   Decree 21699 of 19.09.1932 on the creation of the unemployment office within the Ministry of Public Works and Transport.
128   Cf. Oppen 2019, pp. 284–287.
129   Cf. Legislação 1939, p. 22.
130   Costa 2006.
131   Larcher 1939, p. 24.
132   Ferro 1949, p. 38.
133   Acciaiuoli 1998, p. 60.

134   Decree 30251 of 30.12.1939 on the reshuffle of the cabinet as a result of the outbreak of war in 1939.
135   Decree 30289 of 03.02.1940 on the formation of the national tourist council.
136   Soares/Neto 2013, p. 54.
137   Ferro 1949, p. 58.
138   Soares/Neto 2013, p. 54.
139   Lobo 2012, p. 464.
140   O serão medieval de Óbidos 1940, p. 58.
141   National Secretariat of Information (ed.) 1940, p. 79.

The spectacle of dreams (espectáculo de sonho) in front of Óbidos Castle, photo 1940. [Source: O serão medieval de Óbidos 1940, p. 58]

Óbidos Castle, photo by Mario Catharino Cardoso, before 1946. [Source: Marjay 1953, p. 42]

The map of Óbidos from 1948 shows two different protected areas. The dashed line marks the outer border of the area outside the historic centre in which construction is not allowed. The dotted line marks an additional protected area. [Source: Administrative regulation of 18.09.1948 on the outer border of the protected zone outside the town in which construction is not allowed]

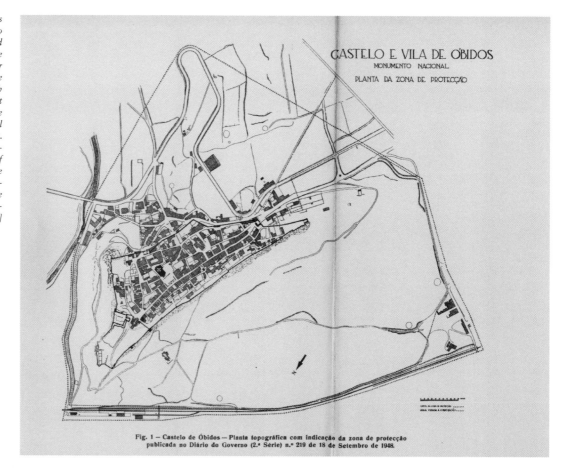

Fig. 1 — Castelo de Óbidos — Planta topográfica com indicação da zona de protecção publicada no Diário do Governo (2.ª Série) n.º 219 de 18 de Setembro de 1948.

A year after the tremendous exertions for the ostentatious anniversary celebrations António Ferro met with the Minister of Public Works and Transport, Duarte Pacheco, in the hostel *Estalagem do Lidador* in Óbidos. Ferro wanted in this way to fulfil a dream: the founding of a national hotel chain, inspired by the Spanish model of the *paradores*.[142] Ferro did not want simply to copy the model but to adapt it to Portuguese reality according to his ideas. Small, simple hostels with charm should be built in the rural style of the local region.[143] In order to implement his plan, however, he needed the influential Minister with his powerful Ministry as a partner. Ferro was obviously able to convince him with his prototype hostel. The two men agreed that the hostels, which Ferro had given the name of *pousada*,[144] would be built by the Ministry of Public Works and Transport, and furnished and run by the Office for Propaganda.[145]

For a while after 1940 the castle was no longer in focus. It was not until 1946 that the work on the empty ruins was taken up again.[146] The reconstruction work on the castle was aimed at installing a regional museum there. After two years of building, however, it turned out that the building was unsuitable for the planned function.[147] The plan was therefore changed. Following the confirmation that the utilisation of the castle as a hostel did not contradict the conditions pertaining to a national monument the transformation of the castle into a *pousada* began.[148] The responsibility for the building of the national hostels was also in the hands of the General Directorate for National Buildings and Building Monuments within the Ministry of Public Works and Transport. With nine guest rooms, Óbidos Castle was opened in 1951 as the first *pousada* in Portugal that was located in a historic building.

Efforts to protect the entire historic centre were intensified parallel to the reconstruction of the castle. Thus, in 1948 an administrative regulation was decided[149] which laid a protective zone around the town of Óbidos, in which construction was not allowed.[150] And at the beginning of 1951 it finally happened: all of Óbidos within the protective zone was declared a national monument as one of the first historic towns in the whole of Europe.[151]

Inner courtyard of Óbidos Castle after its transformation into a pousada, photo 1951. [Source: Como se viaja em Portugal ... 1951]

Picturesque Historic Centre from the Period of the Estado Novo

With the *pousada* Óbidos developed into a popular holiday resort for Portugal's upper middle class in the 1950s. The rural population that had moved there in the middle of the 19th century was increasingly displaced. Many residential buildings now served as weekend homes. As in the epoch of the monarchy, the castle (now *pousada*) was the centre of social life, supported by new restaurants, bars and shops.[152] Today the *pousada* is a luxury hotel under private management, which advertises with the monarchic tradition of the past – Óbidos as a wedding present fit for a queen. The little town is praised as a place of tranquillity and refuge that was much appreciated by the royal court. Due to its medieval architecture, its attractive squares and alleyways, Óbidos – according to the advertising quite in line with bygone propaganda – is an ideal place for tourists.[153] The background to the wonderfully picturesque historic centre remains in the dark, however.

142   *Parador* = Hotel. In 1910 the Spanish government commissioned the development of a concept for a national hotel chain. The first hotel was built in 1926. The success of the first hotel and the great interest aroused by the concept at the Iberoamerica exhibition in 1929/1930 in Sevilla, accelerated the expansion of the national hotel chain *paradores* that was founded in 1928.
143   Raimundo 2015, p. 283.
144   *Pousada* = Place of tranquility.
145   Ferro 1949, p. 65.
146   Mendonça/Matias 2011.
147   Ministerio das Obras Publicas 1952, p. 21.
148   Ministerio das Obras Publicas 1952, p. 21.
149   Administrative regulation of 18.09.1948 on the outer border of the protected zone outside the town in which construction is not allowed, following p. 31.
150   Castelo de Óbidos e todo o conjunto urbana da vila, no date.
151   Decree 38147 of 05.01.1951 on the recognition of the entire town of Óbidos as a national monument.
152   Prista 2013, p. 373.
153   Pousada Castelo de Obidos – Hotel Castelo, no date.

Policy of Urban Renewal

The urban renewal of historic centres in Portugal was essentially a result of the implementation of official programmes by public authorities, which had recourse to relatively effective legal and financial instruments. With the establishment of a Ministry of Public Works and Transport (1932–1946) the decisions on urban development measures were centralised in one single institution, which was led for most of that time by an assertive engineer – Duarte Pacheco (1899–1943) – until his accidental death in 1943. The most important operative arm of the Ministry was the General Directorate for National Buildings and Building Monuments. The instruments of urban development – especially with regard to the master plan and the options for expropriation – were also developed relatively quickly. These included in particular the Legal Decree on the Simplification of Expropriation in the Public Interest (1938). The planned and implemented urban development measures were, finally, the subject of comprehensive propaganda, for which a further central institution was responsible: the Office for National Propaganda (1933–1945 *Secretariado de Propaganda Nacional*, 1945–1968 *Secretariado Nacional de Informação*), which was led by António Joaquim Tavares Ferro (1895–1956).

Particular attention was paid to the transformation of the historic centre of Lisbon, which – especially in the oldest parts of the city, in the quarters of Alfama and Mouraria – was characterised by comprehensive wholesale demolition programmes. There were also projects for the orchestration of Portugal's glorious history. In Lisbon the reconstruction of the historic centre remained rather fragmentary, however. In contrast, small and tiny historic centres such as those in Évora and Óbidos were redeveloped relatively cautiously, and included the reconstruction of historic buildings or parts of buildings that had disappeared. Her, the state aimed early on at the development of tourism and – influenced by the Italian discussion[154] – at a programme of European significance for the preservation of urban historic monuments. Within the framework of this urban renewal policy, which largely preserved the existing historic buildings but also improved and embellished them, a relatively flawless, apparently preindustrial cityscape was created that still delights many tourists today.

Nowhere in Europe was a quantitatively and qualitatively comparable programme of castle reconstruction drawn up and implemented as in Portugal. It served the formation of a Portuguese identity, which was to be constituted through the great stories of the struggle for freedom from the Moors and later the Spanish, but also through the saga of the conquests. In addition, it was to promote tourism, as was the construction of roads in rural areas and the building of modern state hostels – *pousadas*. Numerous castles, admired by visitors as medieval but de facto reconstructed, still provide testimonial today to this prioritisation, with the castle of Lisbon, St. George's Castle (*Castelo de São Jorge*, 1938–1940) at the top of the list.

For the historiography of the urban renewal of historic centres in Europe Portugal was until now a blank page – unjustifiably. The conserving redevelopment of the historic centre of Évora in the 1940s and 1950s must be counted as one of the most important examples of its kind before the beginning of the great epoch of cautious urban renewal (from 1969 onward). It was due primarily to local civil society involvement. In contrast, Óbidos (1951) is an example of historic centre urban renewal from above, but in particular it is also an early example of a monument preservation of the entire historic centre.

---

154 Cf. Aguiar 2013, pp. 56–69.

References

Acciaiuoli, Margarida: Exposições do estado novo 1934–1940. Lisbon 1998

Aguiar, José: Reabilitação ou fraude?
In Revista Património 1/2013, pp. 56–69

Almeida, Rita Frangoso de: Frente ribeirinha. O futuro era em altura. In: Câmara Municipal de Lisboa (ed.): a Lisboa que teria sido. Exhibition catalogue.
Lisbon 2017, pp. 29–42

Araújo, Norberto de: A praça da Figueira que acabou e aquela que a antecedeu. In: Revista Municipal 42/1949, pp. 23–26

O bairro das Minhocas oferece-nos um aspecto de verdadeira miseria citadina. In: Diário de Lisboa from 03.02.1927, p. 5

Bandeira, Filomena: O Teatro Garcia de Resende.
A pertinência de um inventário para avaliação de uma herança. In: monumentos 26/2007, pp. 76–91

Barbosa, José M Pinto: O Ante-Plano de Urbanização de Évora de 1937–39. In: Câmara Municipal de Évora 2001, pp. 94–96

Bodenschatz, Harald/Oppen, Christian von: "Ausstellung der Portugiesischen Welt" 1940. In: Bodenschatz/Welch Guerra (eds.) 2019, pp. 38–51

Bodenschatz, Harald/Welch Guerra, Max (eds.): Städtebau unter Salazar. Diktatorische Modernisierung des portugiesischen Imperiums. Berlin 2019

Branco, Manuel/Gordalina, Rosario/Marques, Lina: Paços de Évora/Paço de D. Manuel/Palácio de D. Manuel. In: Direção-Geral do Património Cultural (ed.): Sistema de Informação para o Património Arquitetónico. Sacavém 2002 (1993). www.monumentos.pt/site/app_pagesuser/ sipa.aspx?id=1185 [12.05.2017]

Caetano, Marcello: Introdução. In: Comissão de Iniciativa e Turismo (ed.) 1929, pp. 4–15

Câmara Municipal de Évora: Regulamento Geral da Construção Urbana para a Cidade de Évora. Évora 1937

Câmara Municipal de Évora (ed.): Riscos de um século: memórias da evolução urbana de Évora.
Exhibition catalogue. Évora 2001

Camões, Luís de: Die Lusiaden. Paderborn 1883

Castelo-Franco, Fernando: O feito do Martim Moniz.
In: Revista Municipal 84/1960, pp. 5–18

Castelo de Óbidos e todo o conjunto urbano da vila. In: Património Cultural. www.patrimoniocultural.gov.pt/en/ patrimonio/patrimonio-imovel/pesquisa-do-patrimonio/ classificado-ou-em-vias-de-classificacao/geral/view/70427 [04.06.2017]

Christino, Ribeiro: Estética Citadina. Lisbon 1923

A cidade nos anos 60. In: Évora mosaico 10/2011, pp. 14–15

A classificação pela UNESCO. In: Évora mosaico 10/2011, pp. 16–17

Clemente, Marta/Vieira, João: Núcleo urbano Núcleo urbano da cidade de Évora/Centro Histórico de Évora/ Núcleo intramuros de Évora. In: Direção-Geral do Património Cultural (ed.): Sistema de Informação para o Património Arquitetónico. Sacavém 2013 (2007). www.monumentos.pt/site/app_pagesuser/sipa. aspx?id=1185 [23.05.2017]

Comissão de Iniciativa e Turismo (ed.): Óbidos-Guia do Visitante. Óbidos 1929

Comissão Municipal de Turismo de Évora (ed.):
Évora. Guia Histórico-Artístico. Lisbon 1949

Como se viaja em Portugal ... In: Panorama 1/1951

A Construção de Equipamentos. In: Câmara Municipal de Évora 2001, pp. 134–139

Costa, Helena Bruto da: Revista dos Centenários.
In: Hemeroteca Municipal de Lisboa. Lisbon 2006.
http://hemerotecadigital.cm-lisboa.pt/FichasHistoricas/ RevistadosCentenarios.pdf [03.06.2017]

David, Celestino Froes/Rodrigues Marcial A. E.: O Grupo Pró-Évora e as Imagens da Cidade no Termo do Século XX. In: Câmara Municipal de Évora 2001, pp. 66–68

Düwel, Jörn/Gutschow Niels: Baukunst und Nationalsozialismus. Demonstration von Macht in Europa 1940–1943. Die Ausstellung Neue Deutsche Baukunst von Rudolf Wolters. Berlin 2015

Fernandes, José Manuel: Martim Moniz, breves reflexões sobre os sucessivos projetos de remodelaçãoo ou renovação urbana. In: Câmara Municipal de Lisboa (ed.): a Lisboa que teria sido. Exhibition catalogue. Lisbon 2017, pp. 81–87

Fernandes, Maria: Os "restauros" do século XX. De 1900 à classificação mundial. In: monumentos 26/2007, pp. 144–155

Ferreira, Teresa Cunha: Paisagem, património, arquitetura. A obra de Alfredo de Andrade em Itália. In: monumentos 34/2016, pp. 72–81

Ferro, António: Turismo Fonte de Riqueza e de Poesia. Lisbon 1949

Fundação Calouste Gulbenkian (ed.): Os Anos quarenta na arte Portuguesa. Vols. 1 to 6. Exhibition catalogue. Lisbon 1982

Groër, Étienne de: Évora. Esquisse du plan d'aménagement. Paris 1942

Os instrumentos fundamentais de protecção e requalificação. In: Évora mosaico 10/2011, pp. 9–10

Jauss, Annemarie: Von einer Studienreise nach Portugal. In: Deutsche Bauzeitung 39–40/1931, pp. 238–240

Larcher, Jorge: Castelos de Portugal. Leiria e Óbidos. In: Revista dos Centenários 5/1939, pp. 21–24

Legislação. In: Revista dos Centenários 4/1939, p. 22

Leitão de Barros: O Castelo de Obidos. Um dos mais belos exemplares da arquitectura militar dos mouros. In: Diário de Notícias vom 28.04.1920, p. 20

A linda vila de Obidos é reintegrada no seu recortado perfil medieval. In: Diario de Lisboa vom 24.09.1934, p. 5

Lino, Raúl: Óbidos. In: Guia de Portugal. Estremadura, Alentejo, Algarve. Lisbon 1927, pp. 587–589

Lino, Raúl: A casa portuguesa. Lisbon 1929

Lisboa Futura. In: Revista Turismo 78/1948, pp. 30–33

Lôbo, Margarida Souza: Planos de urbanização a época de Duarte Pacheco. Porto 1995

Lobo, Susana Luísa Mexia: Arquitectura e Turismo: Planos e Projectos. As cenografias do lazer na costa Portuguesa, da 1.a República à democracia. Doctoral thesis. Universidade de Coimbra 2012

Mangorrinha, Jorge: papéis de(o) Arquitecto na intervenção municipal urbana: notas sobre projectar Lisboa no século XX. In: Cadernos do Arquivo Municipal 3/1999, pp. 218–228

Mangorrinha, Jorge: Lisboa Republicana. In: Cadernos do Arquivo Municipal 9/2007, pp. 113–144

Mangorrinha, Jorge: Da Baixa de Lisboa ao Aeroporto: subsídios para um discurso histórico-iconográfico. In: Cadernos do Arquivo Municipal 10/2009, pp. 155–179

Marinho, Patrícia: Ensaio teórico do Projeto – BEHIND THE WALL. In: Marinho, Patrícia: BEHIND THE WALL. Etnografia audiovisual na Vila de Óbidos (Portugal). Lisbon 2015. https://behindthewallpgcvd.wordpress.com [31.05.2017]

Martins, João Paulo: Arquitectura contemporânea na Baixa de Pombal. In: monumentos 21/2004, pp. 142–151

Mendonça, Isabel/Matias, Cecília: Castelo de Óbidos/ Castelo e cerca urbana de Óbidos/Pousada de Óbidos. In: Direção-Geral do Património Cultural (ed.): Sistema de Informação para o Património Arquitetónico. Sacavém 2011 (1992). www.monumentos.pt/Site/APP_PagesUser/ SIPA.aspx?id=3324 [04.06.2017]

Mesquita, Jorge Carvalho de: Plan de Remodelacion de la "Baixa". Plaza de la Figueira, Rossio, Calle de la Palma, Restauradores, San Lázaro. Lisbon 1950

Ministério das Obras Publicas: Monumentos. Boletim da Direcção Geral dos Edifícios e Monumentos Nacionais. Castelo de S. Jorge 25–26/1941

Ministério das Obras Publicas: Monumentos. Boletim da Direcção Geral dos Edificios e Monumentos Nacionais. Castelo de Obidos 68–69/1952

Monteiro, Maria Filomena/Tereno, Maria do Céu/Tomé, Manuela Maria: Utopia and reality: from Étienne de Groër to the late 20th century. Évora, Portugal. In: Oliveira, Vítor/Pinho, Paulo: Our common future in urban morphology. ISUF 2014, pp. 625–634. https://dspace. uevora.pt/rdpc/bitstream/10174/13378/1/isuf2014.fe.up. pt_ISUF2014%20ebook.pdf [08.03.2021]

Monumentos II. In: Panorama, 01.09.1838, pp. 275–277

National Secretariat of Information (ed.): Monuments of Portugal. Lisbon no date (1940)

As Obras do Estado Novo. In: Câmara Municipal de Évora 2001, pp. 111–126

Oppen, Christian von: Monumentalstadt Lisbon: ein (Papier-)Projekt der Salazar-Diktatur. In: Altrock, Uwe/ Kunze, Ronald/Schmitt, Gisela/Schubert, Dirk (eds.): Jahrbuch Stadterneuerung 2013. Berlin 2013, pp. 265–280

Oppen, Christian von: The Driving Force and Stage of the Portuguese Dictatorship. In: Bodenschatz, Harald/Sassi, Piero/Welch Guerra, Max (eds.): Urbanism and Dictatorship. A European Perspective. Basel 2015, pp. 102–116

Oppen, Christian von: Kleine und kleinste Städte. In: Bodenschatz/Welch Guerra (eds.) 2019, pp. 252–289

Património e Cidade. Mesa-redonda, Universidade de Évora, 2 de Dezembro de 2006. In: monumentos 26/2007, pp. 198–223

Pereira, Paulo: Die Vergangenheit neu erarbeiten. Der Eingriff in das gebaute Kulturerbe. In: Becker, Annette/Tostões, Ana/Wang, Wilfried (eds.): Architektur im 20. Jahrhundert. Portugal. Exhibition catalogue. Munich/New York 1997, pp. 99–110

A Porta de Moura e o Tribunal. In: Câmara Municipal de Évora 2001, pp. 114–116

Portugal. In: Meyers Konversationslexikon. Band 16. Leipzig 1907, pp. 179–187

Um pouco de história. In: Metropolitano de Lisboa. www.metrolisboa.pt/institucional/conhecer/historia-do-metro [02.03.2021]

Pousada Castelo de Obidos – Hotel Castelo. In: www.pousadasofportugal.com/pousadas/obidos [04.06.2017]

Prista, Marta Lalanda: Turismo e sentido de lugar em Óbidos: uma pousada como metáfora. In: etnográfica 17/2013, pp. 369–392

Raimundo, Orlando: António Ferro. O inventor do salazarismo. Alfragide 2015

Um Regulamento Exemplar e um Plano Inexperimente. In: Câmara Municipal de Évora 2001, pp. 91–93

Revista dos Centenários 5/1939

Rodrigues, Marcial A. E.: Acerca do Grupo Pro-Évora e da Defesa do Património Eborense ao Logo do Século XX. In: A Cidade de Évora 5/2001, pp. 415–426

Rodrigues, Paulo Simões/Matos, Ana Cardoso de: Restaurar para renovar na Évora do século XIX. In: monumentos 26/2007, pp. 134–143.

Salazar, António Oliveira: Independência de Portugal. (Nota oficiosa da presidência do conselho). In: Revista dos Centenários 1/1939, pp. 2–7

O serão medieval de Óbidos. In Boletim da Junta de Provincia de Estremadura 1940, p. 58

Secretariado da Propaganda Nacional (ed.): Cartilha da Hospedagem Portuguesa. Lisbon 1941

Simplício, Maria Domingas: Evolução da Estrutura Urbana de Évora: o século XX e a transição para o século XXI. In: A Cidade de Évora 7/2007, pp. 321–360

Soares, Clara Moura/Neto, Maria João Baptista: Óbidos: De "Vila Museu" a "Vila Cultural". Estudos de Gestão Integrada de Património Artístico. Casal de Cambra 2013

Sokol, Hans: Salazar und sein neues Portugal. Graz/Vienna/Cologne 1957

Tostões, Ana: O processo da Baixa. In: Câmara Municipal de Lisboa (ed.): Lisboa. O Plano da Baixa hoje. Exhibition catalogue. Lisbon 2008, pp. 168–229

Vai ser reintegrado no ambiente arquitectónico geral um vetusto edifício de Évora. In: Diário Popular vom 03.11.1965, p. 13

Lisbon: the New St. George's Castle

Crowned with battlements, the outer walls of St. George's Castle reveal themselves as clean and orderly when one enters the castle ruins. An impressive backdrop from the 1940s! The walls stand on fragments of the completely ordinary buildings that stood instead of the castle on the castle hill until 1938 and were then demolished step by step in the search for the weir system from the 12th century. The reconstruction which followed did not aspire to reproduce the original structure of the castle. It was intended, rather, to create the triumphant image of a fortified medieval castle that kept alive the remembrance of the heroic victory over the Moors and thus of the birth of Portugal. Castles were actually restored and reconstructed throughout the country on the occasion of the anniversary celebrations in 1940. Well-known examples are the castles in Guimarães, Óbidos, Tomar and Vila Viçosa. The castle construction programme strongly characterised the redevelopment of the historic centres in many towns. It was certainly the most comprehensive programme of this type in Europe in the period between the two world wars.
[Photo: Harald Bodenschatz, 2013]

Lisbon: Portugal's Capital

An imposing, large medieval castle overlooks the historic centre of Lisbon – St. George's Castle, one of the great attractions of the Portuguese capital, conspicuous from both land and sea. Medieval? The castle is relatively new: it was built in 1940 for the purported anniversary celebrations as a structural testimonial to the dictatorship's claim to power over Portugal and its colonial empire. 1940 was the 800th anniversary of the independence of Portugal – or so the dictatorship claimed – and the 300th anniversary of the regaining of independence from Spain. For these celebrations – the zenith of Salazar's dictatorship – the castle was reconstructed. The castle – the crown of the modern empire with regard to urban development – was to serve for ever as a reminder of Portugal's great history. The price for the reconstruction, which has now been forgotten, was the demolition of entire districts of the historic centre.
[Photo: depositphotos/zastavkin, 2017]

Évora: a New Palace of Justice in the Historic Centre
Évora is an ancient town of extraordinary historical importance in Alentejo. The remains of the Roman Temple of Diana in the town centre are still evidence of that today. The town is also a model case of the comprehensive redevelopment of historic centres during the dictatorship. This included the remarkable attempt to integrate the gigantic structure of a Palace of Justice relatively cleverly into the historic centre without limiting its visibility from various directions. The huge structure is composed of several different parts which interact with their individual surroundings, particularly with a double square and a small green decorative square. The construction of a Palace of Justice was a major urban development task during the Salazar dictatorship. The State demonstrated its presence in a town or city with a Palace of Justice. At that time numerous palaces of justice were built throughout the country. The implantation of such a palace into the historic centre of Évora was achieved relatively well. It was not completed until 1963, however. Since 1986 Évora's historic centre has been a world heritage site.
[Photo: Harald Bodenschatz, 2015]

Óbidos: Camões Monument in the Historic Centre
Óbidos is a picturesque historic town somewhat north of Lisbon and a popular destination for both national and foreign tourists. The little town is often called "the Portuguese Rothenburg" or "the museum of Portugal". The castle ruins in Óbidos were also extended, although later than most of the others. Since 1951 it has served as a special hotel – as a pousada. There is a small historic centre next to the castle, which is completely surrounded by a town wall. The historic centre and the town wall were the subject of intensive redevelopment during the Salazar dictatorship, but visitors do not learn of this. In 1951 the entire "old town" was declared a national monument – as one of the first historic towns in the whole of Europe. In the course of the redevelopment of the historic centre a monument to Portugal's national poet, Camões, was erected between 1931 and 1932, designed by the famous architect, Raúl Lino. Camões' poetic lines on Óbidos are carved on the monument in capital letters. The monument is crowned by a stylised copy of Óbidos Castle. It also bears four coats of arms, each with a Christian cross. The column, like the castle itself, is a building block in the urban construction propaganda of the dictatorship: Portugal, says the message carved in stone, fulfilled and still fulfils a historic mission, namely the Christianisation, and thus the civilising, of the world.
[Photo: Harald Bodenschatz, 2014]

The Urban Renewal of Historic Centres in Franco's Spain

Piero Sassi

On 28th March 1939 General Francisco Franco's Nationalist troops marched into Madrid, the capital city of the Second Republic, which had been under siege since 23rd November 1936. A few days later, on 1st April 1939, Franco proclaimed the end of the so-called Civil War. This marked the beginning of the history of a brutal dictatorship in Spain that only ended with the death of the dictator in 1975. The Nationalists had been given decisive support during the Civil War by Germany's national socialists and Italy's fascists. The *Falange*, a mass organisation initiated in 1933 under the leadership of José Antonio Primo de Rivera on the model of the fascist *camice nere*, the Italian Blackshirts, and the German SA, proved to be a mainstay of the Franco dictatorship, in addition to the military, the Catholic church and the supporters of the monarchy.

Following their accession to power the Nationalists were confronted with the enormous challenge of the reconstruction of the country. This was not only a question of rebuilding the towns and cities, the infrastructure and industrial plants destroyed in the course of the war. Of central importance was also the founding of new institutions, of the backbone of the "New State", as the dictatorship was now called, and the establishment of an economic system suited to the new circumstances. The years that followed coincided with the isolation of the Second World War. Spain's situation deteriorated further following the downfall of its previous allies, Mussolini's Italy and Hitler's Germany. Until the beginning of the 1950s the country continued to find itself in a difficult situation characterised by political isolation and economic autarky.

The transformation of socio-political relationships had major effects on urban development policy, which was also influenced by representatives of the *Falange*. In order to increase agricultural production and to provide food for the country a massive internal colonisation was initiated. At the same time the function of the Spanish cities changed fundamentally – with a few exceptions. In the economic system of the New State they initially lost their priority position over rural regions but they were able to maintain almost unchanged their function as centres of political and military power. The historic centres played a particularly important role in this. Institutions of the regime of both local and national importance were to be concentrated here, both in traditional buildings and in buildings still to be constructed. For this purpose the historic centres had to be transformed into showcases for the New State. The handling of the historic centres also reflected the policy of the dictatorship towards the legacies of Spanish history.

Madrid: a New Crown for the Historic Centre

In the *Plan General de Ordenación de Madrid*, the first master plan for the capital city of the Francoist New State, which was prepared in 1941 to 1946, the "central nucleus" (*núcleo principal*) was Madrid's inner city. This comprised primarily the historic centre, the area within the city walls from the era of Philipp IV, the planned extension from the 19th century (*Ensanche*) and generous vacant lots for a northern expansion of the city. From a political point of view this was the power centre of the dictatorship, the place that was to represent most strongly the character of Madrid as capital city. The most important institutions of the New State were to be housed here, both in old buildings and in ones that were to be newly constructed. In addition, new, spacious apartments had to be created in the inner city for the state-supporting middle classes who found work in the many new institutions. The status of capital city also meant that those places and buildings were to be glorified which could be interpreted as bearers of traditional values or as symbols of historical highlights of Spanish history. A special role was played by the area of the former Arabic city that was conquered in 1086 (today the area around the Cathedral – Plaza de la Armería – Royal Palace) and above all the city facade on the bank of the Manzanares river. The built structure of the historic centre was to be maintained without any great changes and, where necessary, modernised with small adjustments.[1]

The discussion on the urban renewal of the historic centre, which began in Madrid together with the preparations for the new master plan, put things on the agenda that had already been under discussion for decades. Examples were the modernisation of streets that were not suited to motor vehicle traffic, the rehabilitation of old apartments with a poor state of hygiene, and above all the decentralisation of the functions that were regarded as unsuitable for the historic centre, such as trading facilities.[2] The planning institutions of the New State wished to prove their implementation abilities by finding a rapid solution to these old problems. Among the few large urban development projects that were planned for the historic centre in the first phase of the dictatorship, the transformation of the Plaza de España must be highlighted due to its importance for the entire city.

It was intended that the Plaza de España be understood as part of the Gran Vía, the most important urban development project for the historic centre of those years. The development of this axis had begun at the beginning of the 20th century with a massive street breakthrough.[3] The Gran Vía had already established itself as the most important shopping street in the capital before the siege of Madrid by the Francoists. The final section in the north-western part of the historic centre was not finished, however, and would only be completed after the Civil War. For the city as a whole the street was part of a connection that ran through the entire inner city, from the Puerta de Alcalá and the Retiro-Park in the east through the historic centre to the university town in the northwest. The Gran Vía was renamed Avenida de José Antonio following the Nationalists' accession to power in honour of the founder of the *Falange*.

The north-western end of the Gran Vía was crowned by the redevelopment of the Plaza de España begun in 1943. The city administration, the *Ayuntamiento de Madrid*, was responsible for its implementation, for which – according to the official information in 1948 – 3,764,645 *pesetas* were planned.[4] The green areas on the plaza were redesigned and two high-rise buildings were erected, first the *Edificio España* and later, in the second half of the 1950s, the *Torre de Madrid*. The *Edificio España* was designed by the architects Joaquín and Julián Otamendi Machimbarrena, and the *Torre de Madrid* by the architect Julián Otamendi Machimbarrena and the engineer José Otamendi Machimbarrena. Both large buildings were financed by private capital. The ostentatious *Edificio España* was the highest building in Spain (117 metres) at the time of its inauguration (1953) and provided space for different functions: apartments, a luxury hotel, commercial facilities and offices. The building site, which at the time was considered enormous, and on which 500 building workers were employed daily, was one of the largest in Madrid at the end of the 1940s and was intended to exemplify the modernisation programme to which the regime aspired for the entire country. The cost of the high-rise building – according to official estimates from 1950 – was roughly 200,000,000 *pesetas*.[5]

Further, though smaller, urban development projects in the historic centre during the first phase of the dictatorship were the redevelopment of two squares, the famous Puerta del Sol and the Plaza de Oriente with the renovation of the Royal Theatre (*Teatro Real*).[6] The Puerta del Sol is considered today to be the square with the greatest degree of centrality in the city and is the most popular place for political activities. This is explained by the fact that the seat of the Government of the Autonomous Community of Madrid is located there, in the building of the *Real Casa de Correos* [Royal House of the Post Office], and that of the Ministry of Finance is not far removed, in the Calle de Alcalá, but also due to the large-scale open space, which easily serves

1 Junta de Reconstrucción de Madrid 1943, I-4 and I-6, p. 8.
2 Diéguez Patao 1991, p. 69.
3 Cf. Reforma de la Calle de la Princesa, Gran Madrid 3/1948, p. 40.

4 Reforma de la Calle de la Princesa, Gran Madrid 3/1948, p. 41.
5 El Edificio España y los jardines de palacio, Gran Madrid 12/1950, pp. 26–27.
6 On the redevelopment of the Puerta del Sol cf. Herrero Palacios 1951, pp. 2–18.

The historic centre of Republican
Madrid during the siege in the Civil
War. Photo probably 1937. On the
banner are the words "¡No pasarán!"
("They shall not get through!") in
capital letters. This battle cry from
a radio message by Dolores Ibárruri
in the summer of 1936 did not stand
up to history. Nevertheless, it is still
used today in many countries as a
call for active resistance to the extreme
right wing.
[Palmero/Arjona/Fernández/Ruiz (eds.)
2005, p. 14]

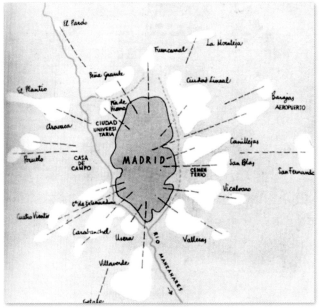

Diagram of the settlement structure
envisaged in the master plan with a
central core (dark grey) and satellite
towns (white), City Development
Office for Madrid and the
surrounding area, 1953.
[Source: Comisaría General para la
Ordenación Urbana de Madrid y sus
Alrededores 1953, p. 13]

Master plan for
Madrid: Subplan
no. 75, western
part of the historic
centre with the area
Cathedral – Plaza de
la Armería – Royal
Palace, the royal
theatre and the Plaza
de Oriente, the rede-
velopment of which
was envisaged. Agency
for the reconstruction
of Madrid, 1943.
[Centro de Docu-
mentación de la
Consejería de Medio
Ambiente, Ordenación
del Territorio y
Sostenibilidad,
Madrid]

Plaza de España after the completion of the Edificio España and the final section of the Gran Vía, photo c. 1953. [Source: Comisaría General para la Ordenación Urbana de Madrid y sus Alrededores 1953, p. 51]

The Edificio España and the Torre de Madrid rise above the historic centre, seen from the Plaza de Oriente. On the left-hand side the much lower buildings of the Royal Palace can be seen. Photo probably from the 1960s.
[Source: Postcard, Piero Sassi collection]

Plaza de España shortly after completion, on a postcard from 1961. In the centre is the Edificio España and on the left the Torre de Madrid, at that time the highest building in Spain.
[Source: Postcard, Piero Sassi collection]

Calle de Alcalá after the redevelopment of the street in 1949.
Photo presumably 1949.
[Source: Reforma de la Calle de Alcalá, Gran Madrid
9/1950, p. 6]

The Foreign Ministry (Ministerio de Asuntos
Exteriores), housed in the Palacio de Santa Cruz
from the 17th century, photo 1950, shortly after
the extension of the palace.
[Source: La ampliación del edificio del Ministerio de
Asuntos Exteriores, Gran Madrid 11/1950, p. 17]

as a point of reference. The Plaza de Oriente, for its part, increases the urban appeal of the Royal Theatre. Of course, these projects cannot compete in their importance for the city as a whole with the construction of the final section of the Gran Vía and the transformation of the Plaza de España. These and other, less well-known, projects contributed, however, to the modernisation of public spaces and the image of the historic centre, which was able nevertheless to maintain its structural character.[7]

Finally, the locating of government functions in the historic centre must not be forgotten. Some of the regime's institutions moved into old buildings which had to be extended or restructured. Even these small projects, which are hardly paid any attention in the professional discussion, must be understood as urban development projects of the dictatorship. They were concentrated primarily on prominent palaces in the historic centre and changed the character of streets and quarters. Eminent architects were commissioned for the reconstructions and extensions. Several institutions of the regime moved into historic buildings in the Calle de Alcalá, between the Puerta de Alcalá and the Puerta del Sol, for example. These included the Party House (*Secretaría General del Movimiento*) and the Ministry of Finance. The latter remained in its historic seat, the palace *Real Casa de la Aduana* from the 18th century, which was extended in 1944 following the demolition of the neighbouring building.[8] Historically speaking the Calle de Alcalá was

one of the most representative locations in the inner city of Madrid; its roadway and open spaces were modernised and adapted for motor vehicle traffic in the course of the 1940s.[9] Further examples are the expansion of the *Palacio de Santa Cruz* from the 17th century near to the Plaza Mayor, which was completed in 1950 under the direction of the brothers Pedro and José Maria Muguruza,[10] and the extension and reconstruction of the *Palacio de la Marquesa de la Sonora* from the 18th century (1942–1947), the seat of the Ministry of Justice.[11]

The situation of Madrid under the Franco dictatorship offered – according to Gaspar Blein in 1943, the head of the department for architecture in the city administration (*Dirección de Arquitectura del Ayuntamiento*) – optimal conditions for "a [radical] redevelopment [of the historic centre], which in the era of democratic governments, when 'a fanatical respect for individual freedom ruled unchallenged', would never have been implementable [...]."[12] In fact, however, Madrid – in contrast to Mussolini's Rome, Stalin's Moscow, Salazar's Lisbon and Hitler's Berlin – was spared wholesale demolition in the historic centre. This can only partially be explained by the symbolic role of the historic centre. Much more important was the prevailing shortage of housing and building materials following the Civil War.

7   For an overview of the planned measures cf. Ordenación general de la zona interior de Madrid, Gran Madrid 9/1950, pp. 8–10.
8   Ministerio de Hacienda y Función Publica, no date. On the project cf. also Durán Salgado 1944, pp. 426–435.
9   Cf. Reforma de la Calle de Alcalá, Gran Madrid 9/1950, pp. 2–7.
10 Ministerio de Asuntos Exteriores y de Cooperación 2013.
11 Cf. Laso Gaite, no date.
12 Quoted in Diéguez Patao 1991, p. 74.

Toledo: Place of Pilgrimage for Heroic Remembrance

Toledo, a city about 70 kilometres southwest of Madrid and of exceptional importance for the history of Spain, became a Nationalist place of pilgrimage immediately after the Civil War in the newly created commemorative landscape. The city already possessed a valuable urban heritage before the Civil War and was closely connected with the history of the *Reconquista*, the reconquest of the territory that had been under Arabian rule for centuries by Spanish rulers under the banner of Christendom by 1492.[13] The events of the Civil War consolidated Toledo as the central place of commemoration for the Francoist New State. After the Republican forces had succeeded, shortly after the beginning of the insurrection in 1936, to repulse the attempted coup in Toledo, the Nationalists retreated to the monumental fortress of the city (*Alcázar*). Here they put up resistance under the leadership of Colonel José Moscardó during a two-month siege until the city was captured by the Nationalists.[14] There is no secure information on the course of the conflict or on the balance of power between Republicans and Nationalists. It is a fact, however, that the history of the defence of *Alcázar* was manipulated by the dictatorship's propaganda to such an extent that a "Francoist myth" concerning the "heroic defenders of the fortress" was created, as the historians Walther L. Bernecker and Sören Brinkmann call it.[15]

The events of Toledo were paid great attention in the media, not only in Spain but also abroad.[16] They became, for example, the subject of the famous film "*Sin novedad en el Alcázar*" ("The Siege of the Alcazar", 1940),[17] a Spanish-Italian production that was translated into many different languages – including German – and was awarded the Coppa Mussolini at the International Film Festival in Venice. Several works published in Hitler's Germany also reported on the siege of *Alcázar*, for example "*Kriegsschule Toledo* [War school Toledo]"[18] (1937) and "*Das*

Heldenlied vom Alkazar [The heroic ballad of Alkazar]"[19] (1937). Almost two decades after the events, in 1955, José Moscardó, who was the main hero in the official interpretation by the New State, was honoured in the Federal Republic of Germany with the *Bundesverdienstkreuz* [Federal Cross of Merit].[20] Beyond the propagandistic patina surrounding the story of the defence of *Alcázar* the violent conflict over Toledo left a largely destroyed historic centre.

Due to the wish of the regime to immortalise the "epic"[21] of the siege and to anchor *Alcázar* as a place of pilgrimage in the New State, the attention of the new planning institutions immediately after the Civil War was concentrated on the city and its reconstruction. Toledo was therefore already declared a "historic-artistic monument" ("*Monumento histórico-artístico*") in 1940 by way of decree.[22] The entire historic centre was thus placed under a preservation order. A few years later a master plan (1945) was presented, among the aims of which were the protection and maintenance of the urban built heritage and the reconstruction of the historic centre.[23]

The defining element of the plan is a new system of centres. The historically most important places in the historic centre were to be connected to one another and made more accessible to the public. The most important of these centres was *Alcázar*. The fortress stands on the highest point in Toledo and thus dominates the entire historic centre. This massive construction, one of the best known examples from the Spanish Renaissance, was built in the 16th century under Charles V as a royal residence. From 1875 – and up until the Civil War – *Alcázar* housed the Infantry Academy, in which the later dictator Franco was trained as a young cadet between 1907 and 1910.[24] Following the siege of 1936 the facility was largely destroyed. Although the reconstruction officially began already in 1940, the ruins of the *Alcázar* remained until the mid-1950s. They received a museum on the siege and were considered "a touristic, patriotic destination"[25]. The rituals of this type of tourism were reminiscent of the traditional Christian pilgrimage.[26]

13 A reconstruction of the history of Toledo from the perspective of the institutions of the dictatorship is provided by Fernández Vallespín 1942, pp. 167–186 and Dotor 1954, pp. 61–72.
14 On the importance of the capture of Toledo for the Civil War cf. Prutsch 2012, pp. 153–154.
15 Bernecker/Brinkmann 2011, p. 196.
16 On the use of the image of *Alcázar* in Spanish media cf. Sánchez-Biosca 2000, pp. 143–157.
17 The film "*Sin novedad en el Alcázar*" (in the Italian version "*L'assedio dell'Alcazar*") was shot by the Italian director Augusto Genina in Italy (film city *Cinecittà* in Mussolini's Rome) and in Spain (Toledo) and appeared in the cinemas in 1940. The film deals with the siege of *Alcázar* during the civil war (1936) from the perspective of the Nationalists. The wording of the title could easily be understood by contemporaries as an answer to the US American anti-war film "All Quiet on the Western Front" (in German: "*Im Westen nichts Neues*", in Spanish: "*Sin novedad en el frente*") of 1930 which, like the novel of the same name by Erich Maria Remarque from 1928, had been combatted by right-wingers a few years earlier.
18 Dietrich 1937.
19 Menke [1937] 1939.
20 Straßennamen. Weniger Franco-Militärs 09.09.2015.
21 Arrarás 1941, p. 2.
22 Decree of 09.03.1940 on the recognition of the cities of Santiago and Toledo as historic-artistic monuments.
23 Cf. Plan General de Ordenación de Toledo, Revista Nacional de Arquitectura 40/1945.
24 On Franco's training in the Infantry Academy in Toledo cf. Collado Seidel 2015, pp. 28–33.
25 Basilio 2006, p. 117.
26 Basilio 2006, p. 120–123.

Toledo before the Civil War. The Alcázar sits enthroned above the historic centre. Postcard probably from the 1940s, photo beginning of the 1930s. [Source: Postcard, Piero Sassi collection]

Toledo before the Civil War. Zocodover Square in the historic centre, with the Alcázar looming in the background. Photo beginning of the 1930s. [Source: Fernández Vallespín 1941, p. 10]

Toledo after the Civil War. In the front the destroyed Zocodover Square can be seen, and behind it the ruins of the Alcázar, photo 1941. [Source: Fernández Vallespín 1941, p. 11]

The historical reconstruction of the fortress was finally completed in 1957.[27] The pressures on the dictatorship to adjust to the new relationships of the postwar period probably contributed to the acceleration of the reconstruction. In 1953 the treaties with the USA and the Vatican marked the beginning of an international opening. A few years later, with the government reshuffle in 1957, the radical change in the relationships of power among the supporting forces of the regime found its culmination in the rise of the technocrats from Opus Dei. In this context the ruins of *Alcázar* lost part of their symbolic importance. Furthermore, the fortress stood within the historic centre of Toledo that had been placed under a preservation order in 1940. In this extremely central and visible location a ruin of such a monumental dimension formed a marked contrast to the rest of the historic centre. And not least, the reconstruction of the 1950s fitted into the chequered history of the fortress, which was characterised by repeated attacks, destruction and reconstruction. Following the reconstruction *Alcázar* continued to be closely bound to Spain's military history. A branch of the Army Museum of Madrid was located in the fortress, and a newly built crypt contains the tombs of Nationalists who participated in the defence of *Alcázar*.[28] These include the remains of Colonel José Moscardó, who died in 1956. The open spaces around the fortress were also redesigned in order to improve the visibility and accessibility of the complex.

Other important parts of the historic centre in Toledo were also reconstructed, particularly the central Zocodover Square and sections of the city wall. The Infantry Academy was relocated to a new complex built in the 1940s outside the historic centre on the opposite bank of the Tagus river. The historic centre of Toledo was, finally, recognised as a world heritage site by UNESCO in 1986 and is visited today by numerous tourists from home and abroad. The *Alcázar* is one of the major tourist attractions. In 2010 the fortress was enlarged by a new building on its northern side and is today the seat of the Army Museum. In view of the central role played by Alcázar in the propaganda of the Franco dictatorship it is surprising that the permanent exhibition of the museum presents the history of the Civil War and the Nationalist insurrection in an uncritical way.[29]

27 Basilio 2006, p. 127.
28 Basilio 2006, p. 127.
29 Cf. for example Museo del Ejército, no date.

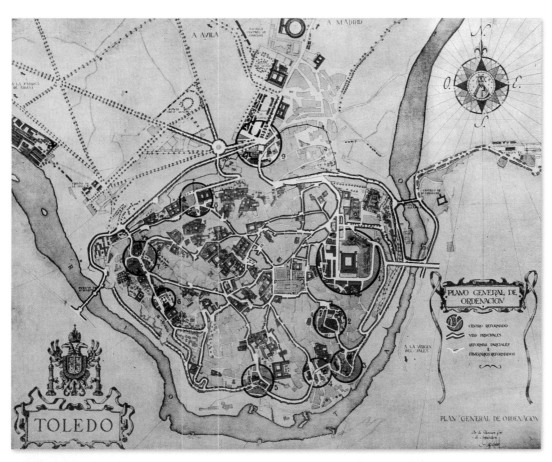

Master plan of Toledo: system of the centres, 1945. On the right, in the eastern part of the historic city, the centre of Alcázar can be seen.
[Source: Plan General de Ordenación de Toledo, Revista Nacional de Arquitectura 40/1945, p. 139]

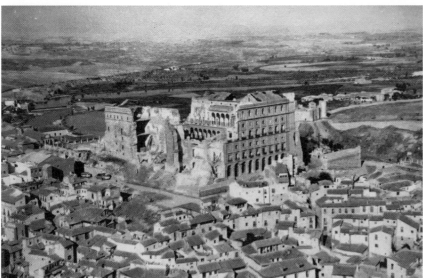

The ruins of Alcázar following the siege. Postcard probably from the 1940s.
[Source: Postcard, Piero Sassi collection]

Alcázar in the process of reconstruction, photo probably end of the 1950s.
[Source: Photo, Piero Sassi collection]

Barcelona: a New Gothic Quarter*

Catalonia, and particularly Barcelona, was considered an enemy under the dictatorship. This can be explained, first of all, by the aspirations to autonomy that had characterised the history of Catalonia in the previous decades and which contradicted the centralism of the New State. The key role played by Catalonia as a bulwark of the Republican army in the Civil War certainly also contributed. In this period Barcelona served as the seat of the Republican government for more than a year (1937–1938), after first Madrid and then Valencia had to be abandoned. And last but not least, the Catalan industrial city was considered historically as one of the centres of the conflicts between trades union organised workers and rulers, as the events of the "tragic week" (*Semana Trágica*) in 1909[30] had shown. During the Franco dictatorship, political opponents and

30 During the "tragic week" in the summer of 1909 numerous workers were killed in street fights in Barcelona.

* In this section the Castilian name of the Gothic Quarter, Barrio Gótico, is used, which was also used in the official documents of the Franco dictatorship, which banned the Catalan language from all official publications.

Plan for Barcelona: excerpt from the map of the existing functions, 1954. The historic centre going back to the Middle Ages can easily be recognised, surrounded by the large-scale geometrically planned spaces of the city expansion in the second half of the 19th century that is connected with the name of Cerdá. The historic centre was characterised by a clearly predominant residential utilisation (red) as well as the presence of public (yellow with red cross-hatching) and religious (white with red cross-hatching) facilities. [Source: Comisión Superior de Ordenación Provincial/Oficina de Estudios del Excmo. Ayuntamiento de Barcelona 1954b, section II, chapter VII. Departament de Territori i Sostenibilitat. Arxiu de Planejament Urbanístic]

forms of expression of Catalan culture were the victims of massive oppression in Barcelona and Catalonia.[31] Even although the urban development measures in Barcelona during the period of autarky proved to be relatively modest, the planning for Barcelona and the industrialisation of the urban region, the most important expression of which was the master plan for Barcelona and the surrounding area (*Plan de Ordenación de Barcelona y su Zona de Influencia, 1945–1953*), influenced the long-term development of the planning discipline in Franco's Spain.

Barcelona's historic centre, defined by the position of the city wall that was torn down in 1854, is characterised by a densely built, mixed-use urban structure. Next to simple historic houses, which were largely occupied by poorer sections of the population, institutions of importance to the urban region were also to be found, such as the city hall (*Ayuntamiento*), the seat of the provincial council (*Diputación de Barcelona*) and the Cathedral. Although in the new master plan the redevelopment of the historic centre was of secondary importance, nevertheless remarkable urban development projects were implemented in Barcelona's historic centre during the dictatorship. These had often already been developed before the Civil War. It is therefore hardly surprising that they are not regarded today as products of the Franco dictatorship. The institutions of the New State, however, which took responsibility for them and partially redefined them, made an important contribution to their implementation.

They included above all the completion of the Gothic Quarter, the construction of which had begun in the 1920s under the dictatorship of Primo de Rivera, the father of the founder of the *Falange*.[32] With this project it was attempted for touristic purposes to emphasise the Gothic character of the Cathedral's surroundings by means of reconstructions and invented Gothic building elements. Even the name "Gothic Quarter" ("*barrio gótico*") for the area

31 Following the accession to power of the Francoists numerous streets and squares in Barcelona were renamed in order to suppress the Catalan language and culture and to glorify the victors of the civil war. Thus today's Avenida Diagonal (in Catalan Avinguda Diagonal), the most important axis in the city expansion of the 19th century, was named Avenida del Generalísimo Franco from 1939 to 1979. In this chapter we use the names – where they are known – of places, streets and squares in the form which was usual during the Franco dictatorship.

32 The construction of the Gothic Quarter has recently been paid greater attention by the professional community. Cf. Cócola Gant 2010; Cócola Gant 2014; Cócola Gant/Palou-Rubio 2015, pp. 461–482; Garcia-Fuentes 2016, pp. 95–117. The discussion on the Gothic Quarter has suffered somewhat due to the fact that this case has been exaggerated and usually not placed in the context of similar projects in other countries. On this cf. also Bodenschatz 2019, pp. 121–122.

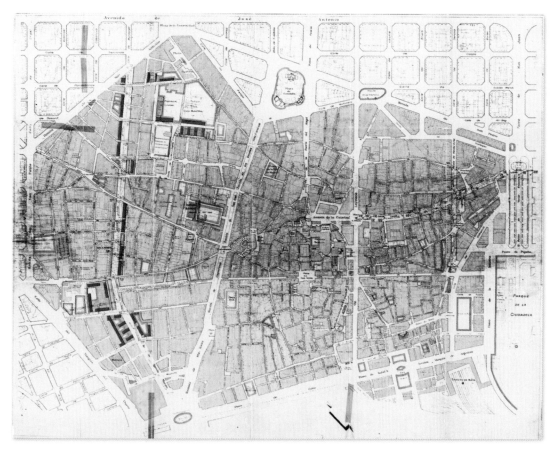

Partial building plan for the historic centre, 1959. On the right we can see the Vía Layetana, one of the great new axes of the historic centre that was constructed at the beginning of the 20th century. This street crosses in the middle with the Avenida de la Catedral, an extended square opposite the Cathedral, which was completed at the beginning of the 1950s as one of the most important measures in the construction of the Gothic Quarter. The partial building plan envisages the extension of the square via a huge breakthrough through the historic structure of the city to the location of the World Exhibition in 1888 at the right-hand edge of the planning area. This was never implemented, however.
[Source: 1959/000061/B P.P. CASC ANTIC. Registre de planejament urbanístic de Catalunya]

around the Cathedral was first established during the dictatorship of Primo de Rivera, when it replaced the traditional name of "Cathedral Quarter" ("*barrio de la Catedral*").[33] The urban development measures that were implemented during the autarky were made possible by public funds at a time when poverty was widespread in Barcelona and in the entire country.[34] They were implemented by an autonomous institution and independently of city-wide planning. The construction of the Gothic Quarter was therefore dealt with explicitly neither in the master plan for Barcelona and the surrounding area (1953) nor in the partial building plan for the historic centre presented in 1956 and approved with some changes in 1959.[35]

Beginning of the Urban Renewal of the Historic Centre before the First World War

The history of the creation of the Gothic Quarter must be seen within the framework of the process of redevelopment of the historic centre initiated by Ildefonso Cerdá's extension plan. Until into the second half of the 19th century the most important institutions and the majority of the residents were concentrated in the historic centre. This changed in 1854 with the demolition of the old city wall and in 1859 with the extension plan. The traditional city now became the old city and was to become part of a growing, modern city in the surrounding urban region. The urban structure characterised by narrow streets and a densely built environment was to be connected to the city extension of the 19th century by the breakthrough of three new axes. The most important of these was the Vía Layetana[36], which had been laid out at the beginning of the 20th century. It traversed the historic centre and connected the urban extension of the 19th century via the Plaza Urquinaona in the north with the harbour to the south of the historic centre

---

33 Cf. Florensa Ferrer 1958, p. 3.
34 Ganau 2008, pp. 821–822.
35 On the partial building plan for the historic centre cf. Comisión Técnica Especial de Urbanismo – Oficina de Estudios [Barcelona] 1956.

36 Today in Catalan Via Laietana. The street was renamed Via Durruti in 1936 in honour of the anarchist resistance fighter Buenaventura Durruti (1896–1936). The axis kept this name throughout the Civil War until the capture of Barcelona by the Francoists in January 1939.

Demolition work for the breakthrough of the Vía Layetana. The tunnel for a new underground railway line traversing the historic centre was located under the new axis. Photo 1912. [Source: Busquets 2004, p. 201]

Photomontage by the tourism society of Barcelona (Sociedad de Atracción de Forasteros) representing the emerging Gothic Quarter, Pere Català Pic, 1935. The new quarter was quite fittingly presented as a conglomeration of Gothic buildings and parts of buildings surrounding the Cathedral. [Garcia-Fuentes 2016, p. 110]

and provided a representative setting for new office buildings. In the course of the demolitions, roughly 10,000 predominantly poorer residents lost their homes in the historic centre between 1908 and 1913 and had to move to the permanently growing barracks quarters on the periphery of the city.[37] Major building monuments also fell victim to the radical demolitions. Since the loss of an important part of the historic city provoked sharp criticism in professional circles, it was decided to study and document the buildings to be demolished before or during the breakthrough. The most important architectural elements – and in some cases even entire houses – were salvaged and stored by the city administration – at first with the objective of putting them on display in various museums.[38]

Together with the breakthrough of the Vía Layetana, the redesigning of the area around the Cathedral had been the most important aim of the redevelopment of the historic centre since the mid-19th century. The Cathedral (*Catedral de la Santa Creu i Santa Eulàlia*), which was largely built in the course of the 14th century on top of the remains of a Roman temple, stood in a central area of the historic city, to the west of the emerging Vía Layetana. For the local elites at the end of the 19th century this large church was one of the

most important symbols of Barcelona and the redevelopment of the surrounding quarter was intended to be an expression of the rise of the industrial metropolis. Part of this overall project, first and foremost, was the completion of a worthy main facade for the Cathedral. The building monument, which had thus increased in importance, was also to be laid open and made more visible for visitors by the demolition of several simple houses. The new facade was built between 1860 and 1912 in a Gothic form, which was intended to connect the new design with the original project.[39]

In the second half of the 19th century and the early decades of the 20th, several proposals for the redevelopment of the area surrounding the Cathedral were put forward by well-known Catalan experts such as, for example, the urban planner Lluís Domènech i Montaner, most of which recommended the laying out of new squares.[40] These were intended, together with the new facade that was created in that period, to emphasise the outstanding role of the Cathedral in the city. The debate on the construction of a Gothic Quarter around the Cathedral only began at the beginning of the 20th century, however. Now the architectural elements salvaged in the course of the demolition work for the breakthrough of the Vía Layetana confronted the city

37 Cócola Gant 2014, p. 102.
38 Ganau 2008, p. 808.

39 Cf. Ganau 2008, p. 804.
40 Cf. Garcia-Fuentes 2016, pp. 101–102.

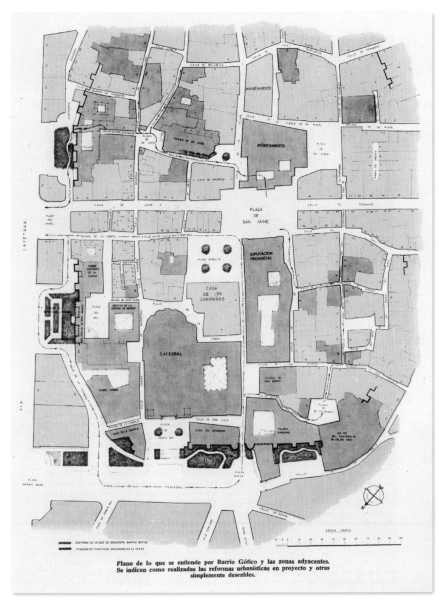

Plan of the Gothic Quarter, 1958. The blue line shows the borders of the Barrio Gótico; the red line shows the tourist routes. [Source: Florensa Ferrer 1958, p. 4]

The neo-Gothic facade of the Cathedral, built between 1860 and 1912. Postcard, probably beginning of the 20th century. [Garcia-Fuentes 2016, p. 97]

Plan for the transformation of the area surrounding the Cathedral, Joan Rubió i Bellver, 1927. The project was composed on behalf of the Province of Barcelona (Diputación de Barcelona) and was never approved. The concept envisaged the demolition of a major part of the residential buildings from the 19th century, which were to be replaced by open spaces and new buildings to be constructed in a Gothic style. On the top right the proposal for the redevelopment of King's Square (Plaza del Rey) can be seen. [Source: Tarín 17.08.2015]

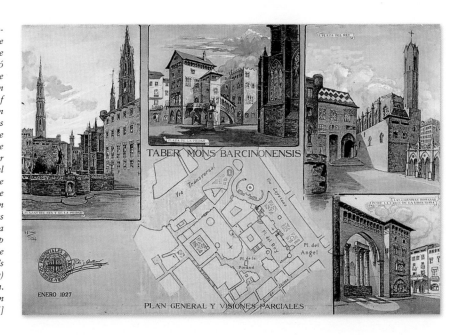

administration and the experts with the question of their future use. Their sheer quantity was far too great for the capacity of the museums, but also for the available storage. The first proposal for the use of all the salvaged elements to construct a medieval quarter was made in 1908, i.e. from the period at the beginning of the demolition work for the breakthrough of the Vía Layetana, and was presented by the Artists' Association of Barcelona (*Associació d'Artistes de Barcelona*) and the Architects' Association of Catalonia (*Associació d'Arquitectes de Catalunya*).[41]

From a historical point of view the Gothic style was closely connected with the phase in the 13th and 14th centuries in which Barcelona rose to become one of the most important ports in the Mediterranean[42] – an international prestige that the progressive industrial development promised to restore. From the perspective of the Catalan movement, which had been gaining in political power since the second half of the 19th century, the construction of a Gothic Quarter therefore meant the emphasising of an important chapter in Catalan history.[43]

Creation of the Gothic Quarter during the Dictatorship of Miguel Primo de Rivera

In the first two decades of the 20th century a lively discussion developed in Barcelona on the construction of the Gothic Quarter in which eminent urban planners and intellectuals participated with various projects. It was not until the dictatorship of Miguel Primo de Rivera (1923–1930), however, that the way was paved for the implementation of this ambitious undertaking. It was intended that Barcelona – following its own tradition – should be the location in 1929 for the most important international event of that period in Spain, the World Exhibition, an event that was intended to show Spain in a new light, as a modern country which could look back on a glorious history. Now those in power regarded the construction of a Gothic Quarter in the area surrounding the Cathedral less as a symbol of Catalan identity and more as an instrument for presenting the history and the urban heritage of Spain to its international visitors. With the same objective, the *Pueblo Español* (Spanish village) was also constructed in 1929, a large-scale open-air museum which allowed the public to visit different buildings and public spaces defined as typically Spanish, such as a Plaza Mayor, on the site of the World Exhibition.

For the reconstruction of the urban heritage of the historic centre a new government agency within the city administration of Barcelona was set up in 1927, the Agency for the Maintenance and Restoration of Historic Monuments (*Servicio de Conservación y Restauración de Monumentos Históricos*). This agency also – and above all – took on the planning and management of the urban development measures that were intended to make the creation of the Gothic Quarter possible. From this time onward, and for the next four decades, the Catalan architect Adolfo Florensa Ferrer shaped the construction of the Gothic Quarter in various leading functions, together with the historian Agustín Durán Sanpere.[44]

The Completion of the Gothic Quarter during Franco's Dictatorship

Between 1927 and 1939, when the Nationalists under Franco seized power, it had only been possible to implement a few urban development measures, the most important of which were on King's Square (Plaza del Rey) to the east of the Cathedral. The Gothic Quarter did not yet exist as a coherent ensemble. This undertaking was adopted by the institutions of the New State and gained new momentum in the early years of the dictatorship. The Barrio Gótico as we know it today was largely constructed in the years of autarky. In the course of the transformation of Barcelona's city administration the competences of the Agency for the Maintenance and Restoration of Historic Monuments were passed to the new Agency for Artistic and Archaeological Buildings (*Servicio de Edificios Artísticos y Arqueológicos*).[45] Adolfo Florensa Ferrer and Agustín Durán Sanpere, the two central figures in the era of the dictatorship of Primo de Rivera, who had been dismissed from their positions during the Civil War (1936–1939),[46] were able to assume their functions once again following the creation of the New State. Florensa became the Head of the Agency for Artistic and Archaeological Buildings and held this position until 1959.[47]

The urban development measures implemented in the 1940s and 1950s still mark the appearance of the Gothic Quarter today. These included, above all, the completion of King's Square (Plaza del Rey) and the layout of the Avenida de la Catedral. King's Square is spread out in the immediate surroundings of the Cathedral. Here stood the historic buildings of the Royal Palace (*Palacio Real Mayor*), which had been built between the beginning of the 14th and the middle of the 16th century and were now due to be restored. Only the south-eastern side was occupied by simple residential

41 Garcia-Fuentes 2016, p. 105.
42 Ganau 2008, p. 812.
43 Garcia-Fuentes 2016, p. 106.

44 Cócola Gant 2014, pp. 169–170.
45 Cócola Gant 2014, p. 169.
46 Cócola Gant 2014, p. 230.
47 Cócola Gant 2014, p. 191.

buildings from the 19th century. These were expropriated by the Agency for the Maintenance and Restoration of Historic Monuments at the end of the 1920s and demolished.[48] In order to emphasise the medieval or Gothic character of the square, the *Casa Padellás* was to be reconstructed on this now vacant lot,[49] a Gothic palace built at the end of the 15th century which had been removed from an area bordering on the Vía Layetana. The reconstruction of the building monument dragged on from 1931 to 1943.[50] In 1943 the Historical Museum of the City (*Museo de Historia de la Ciudad*) opened its doors in the Casa Padellás under the direction of Agustín Durán Sanpere. It made it possible to visit the remains of the Roman city under the square that had been excavated and examined during the reconstruction.[51]

The Avenida de la Catedral, the spacious square that stretches out in front of the Cathedral, today one of the most often visited places in the city, was laid out during the Franco dictatorship following the demolition of buildings from the 19th century. *The Casa del Gremio de los Zapateros* (House of the Shoemakers' Guild), an important building monument from the 16th century, was originally in the demolition area envisaged for the breakthrough. The most important building elements of this house were salvaged and stored. The main facade was rebuilt at the end of the 1950s on the Plaza de San Felipe Neri, to the southwest of the Cathedral.[52] The expropriations and demolitions carried out from 1943 on benefitted from the damage suffered by the building substance during the Civil War. The official reason for these measures was the occasion of the International Eucharistic Congress in 1952, which numerous international tourists were expected to attend.[53]

A few years later the new square ensemble was extended by the construction of the building of the Chamber of Architects of Catalonia (*Colegio de Arquitectos de Cataluña*) on its southwest side. The building was constructed according to plans by the architect Xavier Busquets Sindreu between 1957 and 1962. His sober building volumes and his modern stylistic idiom form a striking contrast to the surrounding of the Gothic Quarter. The frieze on the main facade was decorated with motives designed by Pablo Picasso. The Spanish painter, one of Franco's best known opponents, was condemned by the new rulers following the coup to a sort of damnatio memoriae and lived at that time in exile in France. It was not until the beginning of the 1960s that his artistic works were officially rehabilitated in Spain.[54] The *Colegio de Arquitectos de Cataluña* was not only a

48   Cócola Gant 2014, pp. 170–171.
49   Cf. Florensa Ferrer 1958, p. 18.
50   Font, no date.
51   On the outstanding significance of the remains of the Roman city for the touristic development of the Gothic Quarter cf. Durán Sanpere 1953, pp. 6–7.
52   Cf. Florensa Ferrer 1958, p. 19.
53   Cócola Gant 2014, p. 194.
54   Cf. Leere Wand 03.11.1969.

Freed archaeological remains under King's Square, part of the Historical Museum of the City (Museo de Historia de la Ciudad). Photo probably c. 1966.
[Source: Florensa Ferrer 1966, p. III]

King's Square after the reconstruction. The facade of the ceremonial hall (in the centre) was decorated in the course of the reconstruction with Gothic rose windows (top) and three-light mullioned windows (below). Photo c. 1958.
[Source: Florensa Ferrer 1958, p. 7]

Inner courtyard of the Casa Padellás. The late Gothic palace was built at the end of the 15th century and was in a state of decay at the beginning of the 20th century. In 1931 the monument in the immediate vicinity of the nascent Vía Layetana was dismantled. Photo 1908.
[Source: Font, no date]

Reconstruction of the Casa Padellás, inner courtyard. The palace was rebuilt between 1931 and 1943 on the south-eastern side of King's Square as a significant building block of the Gothic Quarter. Photo 1931.
[Source: Font, no date]

Gothic Quarter, aerial photograph from the west, photo probably mid-1950s.
1. Plaza del Angel;
2. San Justo Church;
3. City Hall;
4. building of the provincial government;
5. San Felipe Neri Church;
6. Bishop's Palace;
7. Plaza Nueva;
8. Avenida de la Catedral;
9. Cathedral;
10. Plaza de Berenguer el Grande.
In the foreground on the left the Avenida de la Catedral is beginning to emerge following the demolition of residential buildings.
[Source: Florensa Ferrer 1958, pp. 11–12]

Avenida de la Catedral after its completion. In the foreground the remains of the Roman city wall that were freed by the demolition work can be seen. Photo probably c. 1966.
[Source: Florensa Ferrer 1966, p. VII]

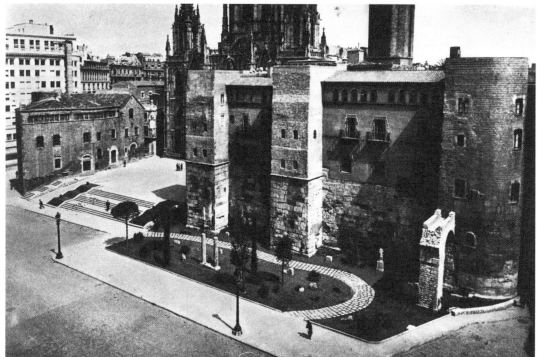

prominent place of debate among experts in the New State but also a centre of intellectual resistance to the Franco dictatorship.[55] The construction of the seat of the Chamber of Architects at the end of the 1950s was a significant break with the urban development policy of monumentalising the Gothic Quarter. At the beginning of the 1960s Franco's Spain found itself in the middle of a rapid process of international opening and of economic upswing. The historic centre of the Catalan metropolis was now not only to reflect the city's glorious history but also to present to the world the image of a modern country.

Building of the Chamber of Architects of Catalonia (Colegio de Arquitectos de Cataluña), built between 1957 and 1962 according to plans by the architect Xavier Busquets Sindreu. The austere volumes of the protruding structure were decorated with figures taken from drawings by Pablo Picasso. The building stands opposite the Cathedral, to which it is in clear contrast. Photo mid-1960s. [Source: Postcard, Piero Sassi collection]

The Gothic Quarter – Model of the Embellishing Urban Renewal of Historic Centres

The process of construction of the Barrio Gótico lasted until the end of the 1960s. There was never a master plan.[56] The creation of the new quarter proved, rather, to be the product of many individual measures, a result of additive urban development. These ranged from the furnishing of historic buildings with Gothic elements such as stairways, portals and window frames, through the demolition of simple residential buildings to the reconstruction of building monuments that had been torn down in other locations in the historic centre – particularly in the demolition area along the Vía Layetana. A central role was also played by the archaeological diggings coordinated by Agustín Durán Sanpere, which accompanied the building work throughout and made the remains of the Roman town accessible. The Gothic Quarter had already established itself as a tourist attraction in the 1950s, as Adolfo Florensa Ferrer emphasised in his "*Nombre, Extensión y Política del 'Barrio Gótico'*", a fundamental work on the history of the origins of the Quarter which was published in 1958.[57] In order to enable the implementation of such an ambitious undertaking as the Gothic Quarter, a considerable – and increasing – control by the institutions involved under the Franco dictatorship was required.

In principle, however, the policy regarding historic centre redevelopment remained unchanged for many decades because the institutional framework and the central actors behind the construction of the Gothic Quarter changed little in the course of the political upheavals of the 20th century. Since the second half of the 19th century the institutions responsible had already been pursuing the monumentalisation of the historic nucleus and the displacement of the poorer strata of the population by means of the demolition of simple housing from the 19th century. The arrangement of the Avenida de la Catedral was already envisaged in the

Plan Cerdá (1859) but could not be implemented until the end of the 1940s within the framework of the preparations for the International Eucharistic Congress (1952). A remarkable continuity in urban development policy can be seen in particular since the period of the dictatorship of Primo de Rivera, when the construction of the Gothic Quarter was begun for the occasion of another large international event, the World Exhibition of 1929. This project was reinterpreted several times, but it was never stopped.

Today the Gothic Quarter is one of the most popular attractions in the city, if not *the* most popular, and is visited daily by thousands of Spanish and international tourists. Most of them are unaware, however, that the medieval character of the area surrounding the Cathedral was essentially created in the course of the 20th century. The fact that the Franco dictatorship made a major contribution to the creation of the Gothic Quarter is largely unknown.

Title cover of the architectural guide to the Gothic Quarter written by Agustín Durán Sanpere, 1953. The photo shows the equestrian statue on the Plaza de Berenguer el Grande to the east of the Cathedral on the Vía Layetana. [Source: Durán Sanpere 1953]

THE GOTHIC DISTRICT OF BARCELONA

A. DURAN SANPERE

---

55 Cf. COAC, no date.
56 Garcia-Fuentes 2016, p. 111.
57 Cf. Florensa Ferrer 1958, p. 6. Cf. also Durán Sanpere 1953.

Zaragoza: "Spiritual Centre of Spanishness"*

Statue of the Emperor Augustus, the founder of Zaragoza. The bronze statue, a copy of the "Augusto di Prima Porta", was given to Franco by Mussolini, his Italian ally, and delivered to Zaragoza in 1940. [Source: García Belenguer 1949, p. 457]

Zaragoza, the contemporary capital city of the northern autonomous community (*Comunidad Autónoma*) of Aragon, has been of considerable political importance ever since it was founded by the Romans. Built in the first century BC in a strategic position at the confluence of the rivers Ebro and Gállego, the then colony of Caesaraugusta fulfilled a military function in the Roman Empire. Later Zaragoza established itself as one of the spiritual centres of Spanish Christianity. In 1927 the city became home to the General Military Academy (*Academia General Militar*). The leadership of the Spanish army was trained here during both the Spanish dictatorships of the 20th century, first that of Miguel Primo de Rivera and then that of Francisco Franco. Franco had already been the head of the Academy before the coup, from 1928 to 1931, in a decisive phase of his rapid military career.[58] The history of Zaragoza, which was often celebrated as glorious, left not only a dazzling reputation but also a remarkable urban development heritage. When the Civil War began, the city found itself in an area controlled by the Francoists. Not far from the front line, Zaragoza was strategically important and became one of the most important centres of weapon production for the Francoists.[59]

Following the Civil War, Zaragoza's prominent older history and the importance of its younger history contributed to its rise to one of the most significant spiritual and military centres of the New State. It was intended, for example, that the baroque church *Catedral del Pilar,* one of Zaragoza's two cathedrals, should provide space for large religious events of local and national importance. The General Military Academy, which had been closed during the Republic (1931), was reinaugurated in 1940 and was able to recover its pre-eminence as a centre of military training. The outstanding role of Zaragoza for the New State was emphasised by generous urban development projects. These included the creation of the Plaza of the Cathedrals (Plaza de las Catedrales) in the historic centre.

Zaragoza's Roman origin was also reflected in the urban structure of its historic centre. The first Roman settlement was originally surrounded by a wall and was divided by the two axes *Cardo* and *Decumanus.* Since the Middle Ages new central functions had been located in the historic centre, particularly the two cathedrals in the north, the *Catedral del Salvador* (*"la Seo"*) and the *Catedral del Pilar ("el Pilar").* Following the accession to power of the Nationalists the historic town centre became the spiritual centre of the New State precisely because of these two cathedrals. This was to be emphasised in the early years of the dictatorship by the largest and most important urban renewal project in a historic centre of the Francoist era: the construction of the Plaza of the Cathedrals (*Plaza de las Catedrales,* also known as *Plaza del Pilar*).

The plaza was among the few Spanish projects that were regarded by the institutions of the New State in 1942 as being suitable to be shown in the Spanish parallel exhibition to the National Socialist urban development exhibition "*Neue Deutsche Baukunst*" ("*Nueva Arquitectura Alemana*" ["New German Architecture"]) in Madrid.[60] The aim of the project was the creation of a worthy arena for the most prominent religious institutions of the city, where mass events could also take place.[61] The baroque *Catedral del Pilar* was one of the largest church buildings in Spain and traditionally one of the main locations of Spanish Christianity. In 1949 it was designated a "sanctuary of the race and a national temple"[62] by the then Mayor of Zaragoza, José María García Belenguer (1949–1954). The church was built around a column (*Pilar*), on which according to legend the apostle James had seen the Virgin Mary in the first century AD. Its interiors were decorated with frescoes by the painter Francisco Goya. In the New State the Catedral

---

58 On Franco's work as Head of the General Military Academy in Zaragoza cf. Collado Seidel 2015, pp. 56–60.

59 Monclús 1994, p. 256.

*   Borobio et al. 1942, p. 32. A comprehensive overview of the history of Zaragoza's urban development is provided by Monclús 1994, pp. 238–265.

60 Cf. Exposición de Trabajos en la Dirección General de Arquitectura, Revista Nacional de Arquitectura 10–11/1942, pp. 2–3.

61 Cf. Borobio 1941, p. 39.

62 García Belenguer 1949, p. 458.

Draft plan for the Plaza of the Cathedrals (here called Avenida de Nuestra Señora del Pilar), architect Regino Borobio, probably 1937. [Source: Borobio 1941, p. 45]

Draft of a new master plan for Zaragoza, 1943. In the centre, in the northern part of the historic centre, the breakthrough to the Plaza of the Cathedrals can be seen. [Source: Yarza et al. 1949, annex]

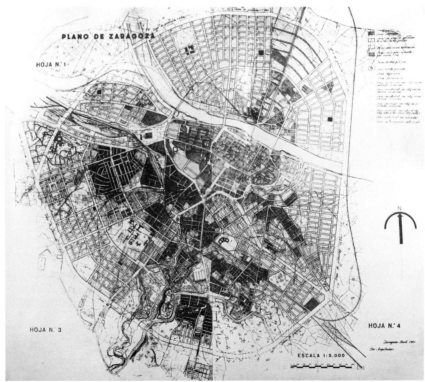

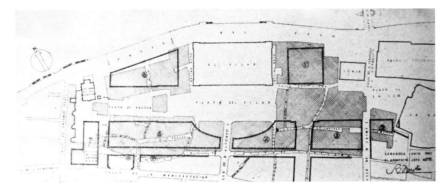

Plan for the layout of the Plaza of the Cathedrals (here called Avenida de Nuestra Señora del Pilar), architect Regino Borobio, 1937. The areas affected by demolition are crosshatched. [Source: Borobio 1941, p. 40]

Partial area of the later Plaza del Pilar before the demolition work, photo c. 1941. [Source: Borobio 1941, p. 44]

Plaza del Pilar after the demolition work, photo c. 1941. [Source: Borobio 1941, p. 44]

Plaza of the Cathedrals: concept for a new city hall (Casa Consistorial), architects Mariano Nasarre, Alberto de Acha and Ricardo Magdalena, contribution to the architectural contest (first prize), 1941. [Source: Concurso de anteproyectos de Casa Consistorial de Zaragoza, Revista Nacional de Arquitectura 9/1942, p. 3]

del Pilar and the new plaza were intended to emphasise the role of Zaragoza as "Spiritual Centre of Spanishness"[63].

The new plaza counts as one of the most important urban development projects of the New State during the early years of the dictatorship and was presented accordingly in 1941 in the first issue of the specialist journal "*Revista Nacional de Arquitectura*", the leading specialist journal of the New State.[64] Nevertheless, it can only be regarded as a product of the Franco dictatorship to a limited extent. The undertaking was based on an older proposal by the Zaragoza Architects' Association from 1916, which had envisaged a better connection between the two existing squares, the Plaza del Pilar and the Plaza de La Seo. Regino Borobio was commissioned with the preparation of a concept for the new plaza in 1936, shortly after Zaragoza had been captured by the Nationalists. At that time Borobio was the Head of the Department of Architecture in Zaragoza's city administration and in the following years he would leave a strong imprint on the development of the town. A few months later, in 1937, Borobio presented the final project.[65] This was then integrated into the plans that the institutions of the New State had prepared for Zaragoza, for example the plan for the transformation of the inner city from 1939 (*Plan de Reforma Interior*) and in the draft for the new master plan from 1943 (*Anteproyecto de Ordenación General de Zaragoza*). The drafting process was regarded at the beginning of the 1940s as a model of fruitful cooperation between the planning institutions of the central state and the local city administration.[66]

The Plaza of the Cathedrals altered fundamentally the northern part of the historic centre between the Roman city wall in the north and the *Catedral del Salvador* in the northeast. Two squares became one single square, an open space 500 metres long and 50 metres wide,[67] one of the most extensive squares in Europe. The elongated form with its greenery made the plaza into something in between a traditional square and a boulevard. Its layout required a ruthless, wholesale clearing, for which a significant part of the densely built, mixed-use area of the historic centre was sacrificed. In 1941 for the implementation of the project 224 properties were expropriated and costs of 9,740,143.98 *pesetas* calculated.[68]

63 Borobio et al. 1942, p. 32.
64 Cf. Borobio 1941, pp. 39–46.
65 Borobio 1941, pp.39–40.
66 Cf. Borobio et al. 1942, p. 35.
67 Borobio 1941, p. 40.
68 Borobio 1941, p. 44. The sum refers to the costs for expropriation, demolition, the provision of street lighting and the connecting of the properties to the water and wastewater network. The costs for the construction of the new buildings are not included here.

Plaza de las Catedrales, photo 1960s.
[Source: Postcard, Piero Sassi collection]

Monument to the Fallen, built according to plans by the architects Enrique Huidobro Pardo, Luis Moya Blanco and Ramiro Moya Blanco, and the sculptor Manuel Álvarez Laviada, completed in 1954. The memorial formed the head of the new plaza at its northwestern end before it was removed in 1991 and relocated to the cemetery of Torrero on the southern periphery of the city. Photo probably 1960s. [Source: Vázquez Astorga 2006, p. 302]

The borders of the plaza were also redesigned. The prominent historic buildings, the two cathedrals, a third church, the *Iglesia de San Juan de los Panetes*, and the mercantile exchange (*Lonja*) from the 16th century were supplemented by new buildings in which further central functions were housed. These included the City Hall (*Casa Consistorial*), for which an architectural contest was announced.[69] This contest was won by the proposal by the architects Mariano Nasarre, Alberto de Acha and Ricardo Magdalena, who were also commissioned with the elaboration of the final project. Another important building, the Guesthouse del Pilar (*Hospedería del Pilar*), was designed by the brothers Regino and José Borobio. With regard to the architecture, both buildings were characterised by arcades on the ground floor, which was presumably an attempt to capture the overdimensional space better by means of an ordering architectural element. The austere stylistic form of the new buildings is based on simple and almost unadorned facades, which are reminiscent of the traditional brickwork facades of the historic buildings and emphasise the desired harmony of the urban ensemble. Both of the new buildings therefore placed themselves in the building tradition of Zaragoza, the central characteristic of which the urban planner Pedro Bidagor defined as "Aragon sobriety" ("*sobriedad aragonesa*"[70]).

Today only fragments of the transformations of the Franco era can still be recognised. Following the demise of the dictatorship the Plaza of the Cathedrals was repeatedly altered and lost its connective character. An underground car park was built and the war memorial, the head of the square, was replaced directly opposite the remains of the Roman wall by a futuristic fountain. There is also nothing left of the gardens that originally significantly characterised the Plaza.

As in the case of the redevelopment of the historic centre of Brescia with the construction of Victory Square (Piazza della Vittoria) in Mussolini's Italy in 1929–1932, the significant changes in the historic centre of Zaragoza were limited to the area of the Plaza de las Catedrales.[71] Apart from that there were only a few small redevelopment measures. On the southern periphery of the historic centre the Plaza de España, into which the axis of the Paseo de la Independencia enters, was redesigned. Noteworthy here are the ostentatious building of the *Banco de España*, which was built between 1933 and 1936 according to plans by the architects Juan de Zavala and Romualdo de Madariaga y Céspedes, and the renewal of the facades of existing buildings in a traditional style. It was intended for the historic centre to be connected at its northern edge with the General Military Academy by means of a monumental north-south axis, the Avenida de los Héroes[72] (Heroes' Avenue), according to a concept drawn up in about 1950 by the architect José de Yarza. The project was never implemented, however.

69 On the architectural contest cf. Concurso de anteproyectos de Casa Consistorial de Zaragoza, Revista Nacional de Arquitectura 9/1942.
70 Bidagor 1949, p. 460.
71 On the redevelopment of the historic centre of Brescia cf. Bodenschatz 2011, pp. 298–299.
72 On the project of the Avenida de los Héroes cf. Monclús 1994, p. 260.

Santillana del Mar: a National Monument

During the Franco dictatorship, even small towns were recognised as national monuments and placed under a preservation order. An outstanding example in this respect was the medieval township of Santillana del Mar near Santander, a stop along the Way of St. James, the pilgrimage route to Santiago de Compostela. The little town also profited from the discovery of the nearby Cave of Altamira in 1879. Its layout evolves along a main street with an erratic direction, which splits into two lines in its central section, and in its complex course connects the two most important squares – the square at the collegiate church and the Plaza Mayor with the town hall and state hotel (*parador*). On 27th July 1943 the town as a whole was declared a historic-artistic monument (*Monumento Histórico Artístico*) per decree due to its particular "beauty reminiscent of past epochs" and thus placed under the control of the Ministry of Education (*Ministerio de Educación Nacional*).[73]

In order to enable longer tourist stays in Santillana del Mar a state hotel was opened there in 1946, the *Parador Nacional de Gil Blas*. The creation of state hotels (*paradores*) in small and medium-sized towns such as Santillana del Mar and Granada (*Alhambra*) is one of the building blocks of the policy towards historic town centres of the Franco dictatorship that can still be seen today. The first *paradores* had already been set up in different regions of Spain in the second half of the 1920s, at that time under the dictatorship of Miguel Primo de Rivera. These were renovated building monuments, the use of which was intended to promote the tourist sector in those areas in which private investors were not yet active. Well known architects participated in the planning of the *paradores*. The hotels were managed during the early years of the Franco dictatorship by the General Directorate for Tourism (*Dirección General del Turismo*), a state institution that was subordinated to the Ministry of the Interior (*Ministerio de la Gobernación*). They were therefore under the sphere of influence of the *Falange*.

Santillana del Mar is one of the oldest examples in Europe of an entire historic centre being covered by urban heritage conservation. A Spanish travel guide from 1973 (1st edition 1950) described Santillana as "one of the most attractive urban heritage monuments that exist in Europe", the highlight among its buildings being the collegiate church, "one of the best examples of Romanesque art in Spain".[74] The little town had 4,172 inhabitants in 2018[75] and is today among the most popular tourist destinations in Cantabria.

---

73 Decree of 27.07.1943 on the recognition of the entire built area of Santillana del Mar (Santander) as a historic-artistic monument.

74 Quotes from: España Turística [1952] 1973, p. 399.
75 Demografía de Santillana del Mar (Cantabria), no date.

Santillana del Mar: main street, with the collegiate church in the background. Photo c. 1965.
[Source: Postcard, Harald Bodenschatz collection]

Santillana del Mar: Front view of the collegiate church. Photo c. 1965.
[Source: Postcard, Harald Bodenschatz collection]

*Santillana del Mar, c. 1948, a
few years after its recognition
as a historic-artistic national
monument. On the left-hand side
stands the Romanesque collegiate
church Colegiata de Santa Juliana
with attached monastery.
[Source: Muguruza 1948, p. 485]*

*Map of the state hotels of the General
Directorate for Tourism, 1948. The
paradores are highlighted by light-
coloured dots.
[Source: Mapa de España con los
paradores y albergues de la Dirección
General de Turismo, Revista Nacional
de Arquitectura 84/1948, p. 472]*

*Santillana del Mar:
state hotel Parador
Nacional de Gil Blas,
inaugurated 1946.
[Source: Muguruza
1948, p. 484]*

Policy of Urban Renewal

The historic centre projects in the capital cities of other dictatorships, particularly in Italy, Germany and Portugal, were known in Franco's Spain and were published and discussed in detail in the specialist journals.[76] Nevertheless, the policy of the Franco dictatorship towards the historic centres was an exception. In Spain the most important redevelopment projects were not concentrated in the capital, Madrid, but in other, primarily medium-sized towns. This particularity has a number of different reasons. Certainly, the lack of resources and the acute housing shortage were important, because they hindered the planning institutions from conducting radical demolitions in Madrid's historic centre. Even more important, however, was the great weight attached to medium-sized towns in the socio-political programme of the New State. Finally, a special role was played by the historic centre of Barcelona, the Catalan industrial metropolis that was long neglected during the dictatorship. Here, referring to earlier periods, but with a different focus, the area around the Cathedral was reconstructed into a "Gothic Quarter".

The result of these particular circumstances was a network of small and medium-sized towns with historic centres that demonstrated throughout the country the energy of the New State. The subject of the most important urban redevelopment projects was the historic centres of those cities that were considered particularly loyal to the regime. These were above all the cities that were of importance during the Civil War, such as Salamanca and Zaragoza, and those which had supported the Nationalists from the very beginning or which lay in the territory controlled by the Francoists. Toledo with its *Alcázar*, the stage of fierce conflict between Nationalists and Republicans, also belonged to this group, however, as did Granada with its castle steeped in history, the Alhambra. A special case is Santander, a city which remained in the background in the early years of the dictatorship. After its historic centre had burned down in February 1941, however, the reconstruction of Santander's historic centre became a flagship of the New State.

The maintenance and cautious redevelopment of small historic centres were part of the urban redevelopment programme of the Franco dictatorship. They were intended to form a new landscape which reflected those traditional Spanish values with which the programme of the New State wished to be connected. Later, small historic towns, such as the medieval Santillana del Mar were to serve as destinations for tourism, but this did not experience an upswing until the 1960s and then made a significant contribution to the international opening up of Spain after the period of autarky.

The maintenance of the urban heritage formed an important part of the socio-political programme of the Franco dictatorship. The institutions of the New State had already paid great attention to the protection and maintenance of Spanish building monuments during the Civil War. However, even although the renewal of historic centres must be counted among the most important urban development policy projects of the New State, they were not, as a rule, new creations of the Franco dictatorship. Some projects were based on older proposals that had long been under discussion before the accession to power of the Nationalists. This is true, for example, of the layout of the Plaza of the Cathedrals in Zaragoza. Others were based on planning instruments that were created during the Second Republic. One example of this is the maintenance of the medieval township of Santillana del Mar, which was based on the Law on the Protection of the National Artistic Heritage (*Ley relativa al Patrimonio Artístico Nacional*)[77]. This law was passed in May 1933, during the Second Republic under the left-wing government headed by Manuel Azaña, and remained the most important instrument for the protection and preservative redevelopment of the Spanish historic centres during the dictatorship.[78] The law made it possible to declare and preserve not only individual buildings as building monuments, but also extensive areas of historic centres as national monuments. In a performance report from 1949 the Ministry of Education, which was responsible for the preservation of monuments, lists the following historic centres or parts of town centres (*conjuntos* – ensembles), which had been placed under a preservation order by 1945: Santiago (09.03.1940), Toledo (09.03.1940), Alberca (06.09.1940), Segovia (12.07.1941), Santillana del Mar (27.07.1943), Guadalupe (27.09.1943) and Ciudad Rodrigo (29.03.1944).[79] Other projects arose from emergencies. This was the case in the reconstruction of Toledo. However, the relatively rapid implementation of these projects was only possible due to the particular circumstances of the Franco dictatorship.

The history of the urban renewal of historic centres in Madrid, Toledo, Barcelona, Zaragoza and Santillana del Mar shows in an exemplary manner how complex and in

---

76   Cf. for example on Berlin, Bidagor 1941, pp. 3–25; on Rome Polazzo 1948, pp. 386–392.

77   Cf. Law of 13.05.1933 on the national artistic heritage.

78   A broad overview of instruments and projects for the maintenance of the urban heritage during early Francoism is given in the publication by Casar Pinazo/Esteban Chapapría (eds.) 2008.

79   Ibáñez Martín 1950, no page number.

part contradictory the policy of the Franco dictatorship with regard to historic centres was. In contrast to other areas of urban development policy such as the planning of the cities, in the case of the reconstruction and redevelopment of historic centres the control by the institutions of the central state stepped somewhat into the background. The Ministry of Education (*Ministerio de Educación Nacional*) certainly played a central role in the maintenance of the urban heritage, but the individual projects were the result of the cooperation of a large number of actors, laws and planning instruments, which differed from town to town and depended on local circumstances. Nevertheless, they also demonstrated characteristics of a common urban development policy for the historic centres.

The policy towards the historic centres was largely characterised by small interventions. Fundamental transformations of historic centres by means of large-scale demolitions were an exception in Franco's Spain. This was partly due to the difficult economic situation in the period of autarky (1939–1959). The widespread housing shortage among the low-income groups of the population, which afflicted not only the capital in that period but also other towns, and the lack of financial and material resources made large breakthrough projects impossible. These would not only have required huge resources. In most cases they would have led to a significant loss of affordable housing in inner-city areas and would thus have placed the planning institutions with the difficult challenge of resettling the residents. The construction of the Plaza of the Cathedrals in Zaragoza and the breakthrough of the Gran Vía in Salamanca were among the few examples of wholesale reconstruction in those years. In addition, the historic centre of Santander was rebuilt following a huge fire. These striking cases were distinguished by peculiar features such as the alignment with traditional urban construction elements, particularly in the case of the *Plaza Mayor*. From an architectural point of view the widespread utilisation of traditional building materials and decorative elements demonstrated the attempt to integrate the new constructions harmoniously into the historic built environment of the old towns.

The legacies of the Franco dictatorship's numerous projects for the urban renewal of historic centres are still visible today. They are often places that are visited by tourists and are host to important political, cultural and economic functions. However, the fact that they are the products of a dictatorship usually remains undetected.

References

La ampliación del edificio del Ministerio de Asuntos Exteriores. In: Gran Madrid 11/1950, pp. 17–18

Arrarás, Joaquín: La nueva Acrópolis. In: Reconstrucción 9/1941, p. 2–8

Basilio, Miriam: Peregrinaje al Alcázar de Toledo: ritual, turismo y propaganda en la España de Franco. In: Medina Lasansky, D./Mclaren, Brian (eds.): Arquitectura y turismo – Percepción, representación y lugar. Barcelona 2006, pp. 115–130

Bernecker, Walther L./Brinkmann, Sören: Kampf der Erinnerungen. Der Spanische Bürgerkrieg in Politik und Gesellschaft 1936–2010. Heidelberg 2011

Bidagor, Pedro: Reformas urbanas de carácter político en Berlín. In: Revista Nacional de Arquitectura 5/1941, p. 3–25

Bidagor, Pedro: Sobriedad y ritmo, características de la arquitectura de Zaragoza. In: Revista Nacional de Arquitectura 95/1949, pp. 460–462

Bodenschatz, Harald: Brescia – Modell der Altstadt-sanierung. In: Bodenschatz, Harald (ed.): Städtebau für Mussolini. Auf der Suche nach der neuen Stadt im faschistischen Italien. Berlin 2011, pp. 298–299

Bodenschatz, Harald: Abbruch und Erhalt. 150 Jahre Planungsgeschichte der europäischen Altstadt. In: Forum Stadt 2/2019, pp. 113–133

Bodenschatz, Harald/Sassi, Piero/Welch Guerra, Max (eds.): Urbanism and Dictatorship. A European Perspective. Bauwelt Fundamente. Basel 2015

Borobio, Regino: Proyecto de Plaza de Nuestra Señora del Pilar, en Zaragoza. In: Revista Nacional de Arquitectura 1/1941, pp. 39–46

Borobio, Regino/Acha, Alberto/Beltrán Navarro, José/Magdalena, Ricardo/Nasarre, Mariano: Plaza de las Catedrales en Zaragoza. In: Revista Nacional de Arquitectura 10–11/1942, pp. 32–37

Busquets, Joan: Barcelona – La construcción urbanística de una ciudad compacta. Barcelona 2004

Casar Pinazo, José Ignacio/Esteban Chapapría, Julián (eds.): Bajo el signo de la victoria. La conservación del patrimonio durante el primer franquismo (1936–1958). Valencia 2008

COAC: Historia del Colegio de Arquitectos de Catalunya, no date. www.arquitectes.cat/es/coac/historia [10.12.2019]

Cócola Gant, Augustín: El Barrio Gótico de Barcelona. Planificación del pasado e imagen de marca. Doctoral thesis. Universitat de Barcelona 2010. http://diposit. ub.edu/dspace/bitstream/2445/35609/1/ACG_TESIS.pdf [25.12.2018]

Cócola Gant, Augustín: El Barrio Gótico de Barcelona. Planificación del Pasado e Imagen de Marca. 2nd edition. Barcelona 2014. https://agustincocolagant.net/wp-content/uploads/2015/03/Barri_gotic.pdf [25.12.2018]

Cócola Gant, Augustín/Palou-Rubio, Saida: Tourism promotion and urban space in Barcelona. Historic perspective and critical review, 1900–1936. In: Documents d'Anàlisi Geogràfica 3/2015, pp. 461–482. http://orca.cf.ac.uk/79027/1/DAG%2B61%283%29%2B461-482%20Comp.pdf [25.12.2018]

Collado Seidel, Carlos: Franco. General – Diktator – Mythos. Stuttgart 2015

Comisaría General para la Ordenación Urbana de Madrid y sus Alrededores: Planeamiento Urbanístico de Madrid. Document in the annex to Gran Madrid 23/1953

Comisión Superior de Ordenación Provincial/Oficina de Estudios del Excmo. Ayuntamiento de Barcelona: Plan de Ordenación de Barcelona y su Zona de Influencia. Barcelona 1954a

Comisión Superior de Ordenación Provincial/Oficina de Estudios del Excmo. Ayuntamiento de Barcelona: Plan de Ordenación de Barcelona y su Zona de Influencia – Memoria. Barcelona 1954b

Comisión Técnica Especial de Urbanismo – Oficina de Estudios [Barcelona]: Plan Parcial de Ordenación del Casco Antiguo de Barcelona. Barcelona 1956

Concurso de anteproyectos de Casa Consistorial de Zaragoza. In: Revista Nacional de Arquitectura 9/1942, Special issue for the architectural contest for a new city hall in Zaragoza

Decree of 09.03.1940 on the recognition of the towns of Santiago and Toledo as historic-artistic monuments (Decreto de 9 de marzo de 1940 declarando Monumentos histórico-artísticos las ciudades de Santiago y Toledo). In: www.boe.es/datos/pdfs/BOE/1940/109/A02657-02658.pdf [23.08.2017]

Decree of 27.07.1943 on the recognition of the entire built area of Santillana del Mar (Santander) as a historic-artistic monument (Decreto de 27 de julio de 1943 por el que se declara Monumento histórico artístico toda la zona edificada de Santillana del Mar (Santander)). In: www.boe.es/datos/pdfs/BOE//1943/215/A07554-07554.pdf [17.07.2018]

Demografia de Santillana del Mar (Cantabria), no date. www.foro-ciudad.com/cantabria/santillana-del-mar/habitantes.html#EvolucionGrafico [23.09.2019]

Diéguez Patao, Sofía: Un nuevo orden urbano: "el Gran Madrid" (1939–1951). Madrid 1991

Dietrich, Erich: Kriegsschule Toledo – Des jungen Spaniens Heldenkampf vom Alkazar. Leipzig (2nd edition) 1937

Dotor, Angel: Ciudades monumentales – Toledo, la imperial, o la historia hecha ciudad. In: Reconstrucción 124/1954, pp. 61–72

Durán Salgado, Miguel: Proyecto de un edificio para ampliación del Ministerio de Hacienda. In: Revista Nacional de Arquitectura 36/1944, pp. 426–435

Durán Sanpere, Agustín: El Barrio Gótico de Barcelona. Barcelona 1952. English: The Gothic Quarter of Barcelona. Barcelona 1953

El edificio España y los jardines de palacio. In: Gran Madrid 12/1950, pp. 26–27

España Turística: Guías Afrodisio Aguado. 9th edition. Madrid [1952] 1973

Exposición de Trabajos en la Dirección General de Arquitectura. In: Revista Nacional de Arquitectura 10–11/1942, pp. 2–3

Fernández Vallespín, Arístides: Orientaciones sobre la reconstrucción de Toledo. In: Reconstrucción 9/1941, pp. 9–15

Fernández Vallespín, Arístides: Pasado y presente de Toledo. In: Reconstrucción 23/1942, pp. 167–186

Florensa Ferrer, Adolfo: Nombre, Extensión y Política del "Barrio Gótico". Barcelona 1958

Florensa Ferrer, Adolfo: Conservación y Restauración de Monumentos Históricos. Barcelona 1966

Font, Francesc: Casa Padellàs. In: Barcelona entre muralles, no date. www.barcelonaentremuralles.com/sebreelprojecte.cfm [08.11.2019]

Ganau, Joan: Reinventing Memories: The Origin and Development of Barcelona's Barri Gòtic, 1880–1950. In: Journal of Urban History 5/2008, pp. 795–832

García Belenguer, José María: Zaragoza. In: Revista Nacional de Arquitectura 95/1949, pp. 457–459

Garcia-Fuentes, Josep María: Reinvenzione del barri gòtic di Barcellona – Sull'interpretazione creativa del passato. In: Cutolo, Davide/Pace, Sergio: La scoperta della città antica – Esperienza e conoscenza del centro storico nell'Europa del Novecento. Macerata 2016, pp. 95–117

Herrero Palacios, Manuel: Reforma de la Puerta del Sol. In: Gran Madrid 13/1951, pp. 2–18

Ibáñez Martín, José: Diez años de servicios a la cultura española, 1939–1949. Madrid 1950

Junta de Reconstrucción de Madrid: Plan General de Ordenación de Madrid. 28 de marzo de 1943. Documented in: Sambricio, Carlos (ed.): Plan Bidagor 1941–1946. Plan General de Ordenación de Madrid. Madrid 2003, pp. 120–301

Laso Gaite, Francisco: Edificio del Ministerio de Justicia: su historia, no date. www.mjusticia.gob.es/cs/Satellite/Portal/1292344046409?blobheader=application%2Fpdf&blobheadername1=Content-Disposition&blobheadername2=EstudioDoctrinal&blobheadervalue1=attachment%3B+filename%3D1968_0759.pdf&blobheadervalue2=1288775090601 [26.01.2017]

Law of 13.05.1933 on the national artistic heritage (Ley de 13 de mayo de 1933 relativa al Patrimonio Artístico Nacional). In: www.boe.es/datos/pdfs/BOE/1933/145/A01393-01399.pdf [08.07.2017]

Leere Wand. In: Der Spiegel of 03.11.1969. www.spiegel.de/spiegel/print/d-45464976.html [15.11.2019]

Mapa de España con los paradores y albergues de la Dirección General de Turismo. In: Revista Nacional de Arquitectura 84/1948, p. 472

Medina Warmburg, Joaquín: Projizierte Moderne. Deutschsprachige Architekten und Städtebauer in Spanien (1918–1936). Dialog – Abhängigkeit – Polemik. Frankfurt am Main 2005

Menke, Willibrord: Das Heldenlied vom Alkazar – Aus Francos Freiheitskampf um Spanien. Paderborn (2nd edition) [1937] 1939

Ministerio de Asuntos Exteriores y de Cooperación: Palacio de Santa Cruz. Madrid 2013. www.exteriores. gob.es/Portal/es/Ministerio/Historia/Sedes/Paginas/ PalacioDeSantaCruz.aspx [26.01.2017]

Ministerio de Hacienda y Función Publica: Breve Historia del Ministerio de Hacienda y Función Pública, no date. www.minhafp.gob.es/es-ES/El%20Ministerio/ Historia%20del%20Ministerio/Paginas/Historia.aspx [26.01.2017]

Monclús, Francisco Javier: Zaragoza. In: Guàrdia, Manuel/Monclús, Francisco Javier/Oyón, José Luis (eds.): Atlas histórico de ciudades europeas, Vol. I, Península Ibérica. Barcelona 1994, pp. 238–265

Muguruza, José María: Parador Nacional de Gil Blas. Santillana del Mar (Santander). In: Revista Nacional de Arquitectura 84/1948, pp. 483–485

Museo del Ejército: Historia del Alcázar, no date. www. museo.ejercito.es/exposiciones/exposicion_permanente/ recorrido_tematico [25.08.2017]

Ordenación general de la zona interior de Madrid. In: Gran Madrid 9/1950, pp. 8–10

Palmero, Fernando/Arjona, Daniel/Fernández, Silvia/ Ruiz, Fátima (eds.): La Batalla de Madrid – Noviembre 1936. Reihe: La Guerra Civil Española mes a mes, Vol. 7. Madrid 2005

Plan General de Ordenación de Toledo. In: Revista Nacional de Arquitectura 40/1945. Special issue on the master plan for Toledo

Polazzo, Terzo Antonio: La Avenida de la Conciliación, en Roma. In: Revista Nacional de Arquitectura 82/1948, pp. 386–392

Prutsch, Ursula: Iberische Diktaturen.
Portugal unter Salazar, Spanien unter Franco.
Innsbruck/Vienna/Bolzano 2012

Reforma de la Calle de Alcalá. In: Gran Madrid 9/1950, pp. 2–7

Reforma de la Calle de la Princesa. In: Gran Madrid 3/1948, pp. 40–44

Remarque, Erich Maria: Im Westen nichts Neues. Berlin 1929

Sambricio, Carlos: Madrid, vivienda y urbanismo. 1900–1960. Madrid 2004

Sánchez-Biosca, Vicente: La imagen documental del Alcázar – Entre la obscenidad y el mito. In: Archivos de la filmoteca: Revista de estudios históricos sobre la imagen 35/2000, pp. 142–157

Sassi, Piero: A new master plan for the "Gran Madrid capital de España" after the Civil War. In: Hein, Carola (ed.): International Planning History Society Proceedings, 17th IPHS Conference, History-urbanism-Resilience, TU Delft 17–21 July 2016. Delft 2016, Vol. IV, pp. 357–367. https://journals.library.tudelft.nl/index.php/iphs/article/ view/1301/1896 [20.03.2018]

Sassi, Piero: Erneuerung der Altstädte. In: Welch Guerra, Max/Bodenschatz, Harald (eds.): Städtebau als Kreuzzug Francos. Wiederaufbau und Erneuerung unter der Diktatur in Spanien 1938–1959. Berlin 2021, pp. 220–245

Straßennamen. Weniger Franco-Militärs. In: Junge Welt of 09.09.2015. www.jungewelt.de/m/artikel/271595. stra%C3%9Fennamen-weniger-franco-milit%C3%A4rs. html [23.08.2017]

Tarín, Santiago: Un barrio no tan Gótico. In: La Vanguardia – Barcelona of 17.08.2015. www.lavanguardia.com/local/barcelona/20150817/ 54435852924/barrio-no-tan-gotico.html [02.10.2019]

Terán, Fernando de: Historia del urbanismo en España III: Siglos XIX y XX. Vol. 3. Madrid 1999

Vázquez Astorga, Mónica: Los monumentos a los caídos: ¿un patrimonio para la memoria o para el olvido? In: Anales de Historia del Arte 16/2006, pp. 285–314

Welch Guerra, Max/Bodenschatz, Harald (eds.): Städtebau als Kreuzzug Francos. Wiederaufbau und Erneuerung unter der Diktatur in Spanien 1938–1959. Berlin 2021

Yarza, José de/Beltrán, José/Borobio, Regino/Mantecón, Miguel/Mercadal, Vicente: Ordenación urbana de Zaragoza. In: Revista Nacional de Arquitectura 95/1949, pp. 481–488

Films

All Quiet on the Western Front. Directed by Lewis Milestone, screenplay by Maxwell Anderson, George Abbott, Del Andrews and C. Gardner Sullivan, music by David Broekman; s/w; 136 minutes. USA 1930

L'assedio dell'Alcazar. Directed by Augusto Genina, screenplay by Augusto Genina and Alessandro De Stefani, music by Antonio Veretti; s/w; 98 minutes. Italy/Spain 1940

Madrid: Capital of Spain
The historic centre of Madrid was hardly affected by the large urban redevelop-
ment projects that were planned following the Civil War for the transforma-
tion of the new Francoist capital. In this regard the renovation of the Plaza
de España (centre left in the photo) represents one of the few exceptions.
Important components of the project were two high-rise buildings inaugurated
in the 1950s: the Edificio España (117 Meter), completed in 1953, and the
Torre de Madrid (l42 Meter), inaugurated in 1957, two works by the brothers
Otamendi Machimbarrena, which at that time were among the highest build-
ings in Europe. They offered an extensive programme of functions, including
hotel rooms, luxury apartments, shops and offices. The high-rise buildings were
erected by the Compañía Inmobiliaria Metropolitana, which was financed by
Basque capital, one of those private enterprises, the extensive power of which
in the Francoist capital was conspicuous. The Edificio España and the Torre
de Madrid still dominate the entire historic centre today, including the highly
symbolic Royal Palace from the 18th century (on the right in the front).
[Photo: picture-alliance/Bildagentur-online/Rossi, 2008]

Barcelona: International Industrial Metropolis
During the Franco dictatorship the embellishing redevelopment of the historic
centre proved to be a central element of the urban development policy for the
international industrial metropolis of Barcelona. It followed up on the urban
redevelopment of the period of the first Spanish dictatorship in the 20th cen-
tury, that of Miguel Primo de Rivera (1923–1930). For four decades, from the
end of the 1920s to the end of the 1960s, the area around the Cathedral was
reconstructed with the objective of developing its medieval character and pre-
senting to international visitors the impression of a coherent Gothic Quarter.
In this context King's Square (Plaza del Rey, see photo), where the city's His-
torical Museum was inaugurated in 1943, was also reconstructed. The ceremo-
nial hall (in the centre) was embellished with Gothic decorative elements. On
the opposite side, the reconstructed Casa Padellás, a Gothic palace that was –
literally – dismantled in a demolition area, replaced simple houses from the
19th century. Today the Barrio Gótico has a fixed place in the destination pro-
gramme of millions of international tourists who flock every year to Barcelona.
The circumstances of its creation in the 20th century under the dictatorships of
Primo de Rivera and Franco are only known to a few, however.
[Source: MUHBA Museo de Historia de Barcelona]

Santillana del Mar: a National Monument
The maintenance of the urban heritage was one of the main aims of the New
State's urban development policy. Not only prominent individual building
monuments were placed under protection. Already in the early years of the
dictatorship several historic centres were declared aggregate monuments that
were considered to be built symbols of traditional Spanish values. During the
1960s the urban heritage of the historic centres developed into an engine for
tourism. The little town of Santillana del Mar was recognised as a national
monument per decree in 1943 as one of the first historic towns in a European
context. Today the little medieval town in the northern region of Cantabria is
a popular tourist destination. An integral part of the route of the Spanish and
international visitors is the walk along the main street (see photo),
which leads to the square in front of the Romanesque collegiate church
Colegiata de Santa Juliana (in the background).
[Photo: Harald Bodenschatz, 2009]

Zaragoza: "Spiritual Centre of Spanishness"
In the period of autarky (1939–1959), which was characterised by poverty and
housing shortages, there were hardly any large projects of area-wide demolition
in Franco's Spain. The construction of the Plaza of the Cathedrals (Plaza de
las Catedrales) in Zaragoza is a special case. The cornerstone of the design for
this immense open space was the connecting of the historic church squares in
front of the city's two cathedrals, the baroque Catedral del Pilar (front left in
the photo) and the Catedral del Salvador (in the background). The demolition
of the extensive area of the historic centre that separated the two squares was
completed a few years after the accession to power of the Nationalists. The
plan had already been drawn up during the Civil War by Regino Borobio, an
eminent expert under the Franco dictatorship. The new Plaza de las Catedrales
was intended to emphasise the character of Zaragoza as the spiritual centre
of the New State and to provide a suitable setting for religious mass events.
Carefully planned gardens originally marked the profile of the Plaza de las
Catedrales, reminiscent of a traditional boulevard. These were removed after
the dictatorship in the context of the car-friendly urban redevelopment that
transformed the plaza into a bleak, overdimensional open space.
[Photo: iStock/saiko3p, 2019]

Urban Renewal of Historic Centres in Dictatorships: An Integral Part of the European History of Urban Development*

Harald Bodenschatz

The urban renewal of historic centres was not invented by the dictatorships. Ever since the industrialisation and the explosive growth of towns and cities the question has moved into the foreground as to what should be done with the old towns and cities that had become historic centres in the course of the massive urban expansion in the decades before the First World War. These were now regarded as a problem: the wealthy social strata had moved out of the historic centres, modern traffic could not find enough space, and the new centrality of the historic centres could not be used for new city functions because the streets were too narrow, the plots too small, the houses too humble and their residents too poor. On the other hand, some historic centres and some historic districts or even some historic buildings were excellently predestined to serve as reminders of a good, glorious, heroic past. Numerous politicians and professional experts were therefore convinced that the historic centres required special treatment in the context of urban development.

Against this background the historic centres experienced both destruction and preservation, and both of these were an expression of the new epoch, of a new way of dealing with the traditional city. Destruction and preservation (combined with a radical change in usage) were two sides of a modernisation process and their prioritisation depended on local and national factors, and of course on the circumstances of the time. Decisive for the specific form were without doubt the relationships of production of the historic centre redevelopment: private-sector (primarily via the market), municipal-economy (primarily managed by the local authorities) or state-controlled redevelopment (primarily in dictatorships).

The urban renewal of historic centres under the dictatorships examined in this volume must be embedded in the roughly 150-year-old history of the modern redevelopment of historic centres in Europe. In order to do this it is necessary, first of all, to define a periodisation according to actors and planning objectives in order to clarify the dominant motives and circumstances in each case which then led to the very different measures. It should be noted, however, that important prerequisites for a systematic review are still missing: we still only have fragments of the history of the planning of the urban renewal of historic centres in Europe. It is therefore appropriate to concentrate first on the larger towns and cities because these were usually the ones to which attention was paid and which also served as models.[1]

---

* This text is a significantly revised version of Bodenschatz 2019, pp. 113–133.

1 An earlier partial overview was provided by Schulz 1988. There are already some recent studies which enrich this field of research across periods, cf. for example Cutolo/Pace 2016; Enss/Vinken (eds.) 2016. Cf. also the somewhat older, exemplary longitudinal study on Berlin: Goebel 2003. On further strategic considerations regarding the urban renewal of historic centres cf. Altrock 2016.

The Urban Renewal of Historic Centres before the First World War

The starting-point is the period around 1860, when a new era of urban development was heralded with great plans – plans which have either enthralled or horrified the chroniclers of town planning up until the present day, which set the towns and cities affected thoroughly in motion and still characterise them today. Paris was restructured from 1852 onwards, the construction of Vienna's Ring Road began in 1858, Barcelona was massively extended as of 1859 and in 1862 Berlin, the capital city of Prussia, was presented with the highly controversial Hobrecht Plan. All these plans aimed at a new city that was developed by new actors, that was intended for new social strata, and which de facto departed from the old absolutist urban development. But what was to happen to the old, outdated, pre-industrial cities? The plans for Berlin, Barcelona and Vienna offered at best an indirect answer to this question. They more or less ignored the historic cities, which only became historic centres due to the planned extensions. However, they did enable the construction of new housing with which the housing in the historic centres could not compete, and thus created important preconditions for the exodus of wealthier social strata from the historic centre and therefore for its socio-economic transformation.

Only in Paris was the transformation of the pre-industrial city not only planned but also comprehensively implemented in a breath-taking manner: by the construction of an abundance of new streets across the city.[2] Only under the dictatorial regime of Napoleon III was it possible to radically challenge the existence of the old, historic city. This required not only an expropriation law but also political relationships that allowed the application of this law on a large scale. The construction of the new streets was financed by a modern business model – with levies on the increases in land value that were due to the plans.

The construction of the new streets meant the creation of completely new, linear, broad public spaces. The boulevards offered pedestrians and vehicles ample space and facilitated the construction of magnificent, multi-storey buildings that were socially graded according to the number of storeys and offered the new bourgeoisie representative housing including servants' quarters. In addition there were other facilities that served this social class such as theatres and railway stations. Military considerations also played a role. Whoever lived on a boulevard was in the immediate vicinity of the historic city, which still existed but had been moved to behind the boulevards. In this way, an urban habitat in, and at the same time beyond, the historic city was created for the emerging bourgeoisie, a social class which in the USA and in the United Kingdom had already begun to leave the historic centres and move to the suburbs. Paris thus became the cult location of historic centre transformation and the Paris model of historic centre redevelopment became the example that was invoked again and again but was never attained elsewhere before the First World War.

2   Numerous studies in many languages deal with the case of Paris, including a publication that provides enlightening information on the reception of Haussmann's work in the Nazi era: Waetzoldt 1943.

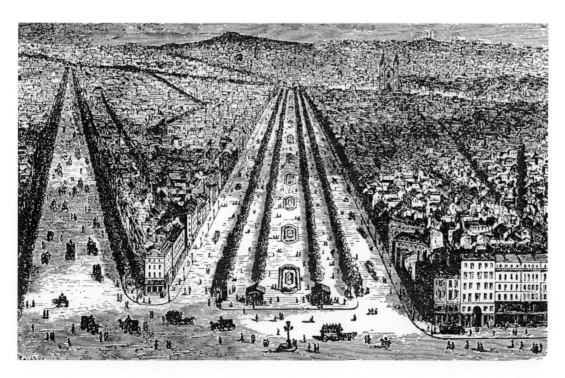

The Paris model: new spaces in the old city, 1863. The new Boulevard Richard Lenoir, the width of which is exaggerated here, offered a stage for the new, privileged social classes. The old city continued to exist behind the boulevard. [Source: Benevolo 1976, p. 790]

The London model: step-by-step transformation of the old city into a business city ("The City"). The picture shows the construction of the Victoria Embankment near Charing Cross in the 1860s. The small buildings in the foreground had to give way shortly afterwards to the construction of a new street. [Source: Stamp 1986, p. 166]

The transformation of Paris under the management of the Prefect Georges-Eugène Haussmann supplied not only a model with regard to spatial design, but also an example with regard to favourable circumstances and successful implementation practices – last but not least for the dictatorships of the first half of the 20th century.

The comprehensive social and functional occupation of the territory of the historic centre by the new bourgeoisie following the partial demolition and new construction under the command of the state distinguished the Paris type of historic centre redevelopment from the London type of formation of a "business city", which – via the private property market – crowded all residential use out of the old city, which then developed into a monofunctional business, administrative and entertainment centre. It was the private-sector London model[3], not the state-controlled Paris model, which characterised the development of the historic centres of the new expanding European cities up until the First World War. The formation of a "business city" was also easier to establish step-by-step as a fragmented development by private investors.

This process was already long underway in London when Paris was radically reconstructed. The transformation of a historic town into the centre of a city was a process of unbelievable momentum that called the very foundations of the old town into question. In the course of the formation of a "business city" the historic town had to assume three completely new responsibilities: (1) to provide locations for central functions such as banks, department stores, entertainment venues etc., (2) to provide space for the new mass transport and (3) to represent the new city of the middle classes at home and abroad. The historic town was only suited to these three tasks to a limited degree. Where the

implementation of the gradual formation of a "business city" reached its limits, the private-sector redevelopment of historic centres required the public authorities to play an active role with regard to demolition. These were often not in a position, however, to implement such measures. The instruments for such demolition work were limited: expropriations were usually only possible for the construction of roads, and they had to be appropriately compensated. Above all, however, they had to find a political majority. For city governments dominated by landowners expropriations were not a popular procedure.

This had serious consequences for the transformation of the historic town into a centre. Where the daily processes of the formation of a "business city" did not function, where there were too many small properties for a single private investor to be able to purchase them all, and where the alleys and crossings were so small that the development of modern city functions was impossible, these parts of the historic town became home to the poorest sections of the population. The new centre was therefore by no means identical with the new business city. Rather, there was a difficult coexistence there between glittering splendour and slums – a subject that was often discussed in the specialist literature.[4] The removal of the slums thus became the fourth task of historic centre redevelopment.

In view of this situation what did the formation of a "business city", London's model of historic centre redevelopment, mean for the old town? There was broad consensus only over the fact that large, splendid buildings of the past, which could also be used for representation, should be preserved – the large churches, castles and palaces. Only the third task, the representation of the new elites in the growing city, offered these buildings some protection. Simple buildings, in contrast, had no lobby. At best, a few tears were shed over the demolition of picturesque corners.

New Appreciation of the Historic Centres in Professional Circles

Long before the First World War critical positions had already been formulated taking the experiences made with the massive processes of destruction in the historic cities as the starting-point for concepts for the more preservative redevelopment of historic centres. The work of Charles Buls, the mayor of Brussels from 1881 to 1889, attracted great interest.[5]

With explicit reference to Charles Buls, in 1913 the Italian Gustavo Giovannoni developed a concept for

3 There are also many studies dealing with the case of London. An impression of the fragmentary building changes is presented by Stamp 1986.

4 Cf. for example Eberstadt 1917, p. 358.
5 On the creative programme of the Mayor of Brussels cf. Buls 1893; cf. also Smets 1995.

Fundamental works on urban construction with regard to the redevelopment of historic centres: "Handbuch des Städtebaues" by Cornelius Gurlitt, 1920; "Innere Stadt-Erweiterung" by Otto Schilling, 1921; "Vecchie città ed Edilizia nuova" by Gustavo Giovannoni, 1931. [Source: Collection Harald Bodenschatz]

the redevelopment of historic centres[6], which he called *diradamento*, thinning out. Giovannoni was one of the most important European experts in this field. He differentiated between artistic restoration, which was intended to reconstruct the original appearance of a historic building, and adaptive restoration, which was intended to bring the historic buildings closer to modern requirements. New buildings should take the "atmosphere" of a quarter into consideration in order to achieve harmony between old and new.

Positions such as these did not play any great role until after the First World War. The war changed the relationships of production, but also the objectives, although in a different manner to that often assumed. Due to the weakness of the economy the process of the formation of a "business city" was slowed down considerably, particularly in Germany. As David Koser quite recently showed in his doctoral thesis on the development of the Berlin city centre[7], after 1918 only a few individual reconstruction measures were carried out there – a completely new situation, contradicting the impressions that our books on architecture suggest.

The relative standstill of historic centre redevelopment also conformed to something else, however: a new appreciation of the historic city. It was in the years between the First and the Second World War that the historic building stock attracted fresh attention and in some cases was treated in a less destructive way. Gustavo Giovannoni was paid greater attention in Italy after the First World War and was only then able to implement his concept, at least fragmentarily. In 1931, in the middle of the epoch of Mussolini's dictatorship, he presented one of the most important books on the redevelopment of historic centres: *Vecchie città ed Edilizia nuova.*[8]

In 1920 in Germany Cornelius Gurlitt published a fundamental work, "*Handbuch des Städtebaues*".[9] It contains a chapter "*Die Planbildung im Stadtkern*" [Planning in the city centre], which ends with the following demand: "careful maintenance of the historic town for the purpose of preserving it in its old structural essence and thus for the middle classes and through these for retail trade."[10] Remarkable here, and in the case of other experts, is the linking of urban development aspects to social and economic aspects – a perspective which seems particularly appropriate in the case of the redevelopment of historic centres. Gurlitt also emphasises, however, that preservation is inconceivable without the public authorities. This concerned not only the question of the instruments, such as local laws against disfigurement, and it concerned not only preventive urban planning that was intended to reduce the pressure related to traffic and functions on the historic centre. It also concerned the preservation measures themselves, which often could not be financed by the private owners. Precisely this appeal to the public authorities found a higher acceptance after the First World War in the context of an urban development that was to a greater extent in the hands of the local – and later national – authorities than the private-sector urban development of before 1914.

One year after the publication of Gurlitt's work a second major work appeared in Germany, which for the first time dealt with the actual subject of city redevelopment: "*Innere Stadt-Erweiterung*"[11]. Its author, Otto Schilling, described the process of the formation of a "business city" or the redevelopment of historic centres with all its consequences in detail, systematically and using the examples of selected cities, primarily large German cities, but also Paris. The introduction to this work was written by Cornelius Gurlitt. What was not mentioned in either of the books was the question as to how the considerable destruction wrought by the First World War in the cities of some countries should be dealt with.

6 Cf. Giovannoni June 1913, pp. 449–472; Giovannoni July 1913, pp. 53–76. On Giovannoni cf. also Zucconi 2014 and Tragbar 2016.
7 Koser 2017.
8 Giovannoni 1931. This fundamental programmatical work is undeservedly little known outside of Italy.

9   Gurlitt 1920.
10 Gurlitt 1920, p. 287.
11 Schilling 1921.

Ambivalent Appreciation of the Historic Centres between the Wars

After the First World War the treatment of the historic centres became even more differentiated. For almost all these more or less preservative or reconstructive variations public funds were now made use of. They were an expression of a publicly controlled urban development, usually the redevelopment of the historic centre under the management of the local authority, which with the ascent of the dictatorships was replaced by the redevelopment of the historic centres under the management of the central government. The bodies responsible for the different varieties of historic centre redevelopment were therefore not the same as those responsible for the market-related formation of a "business city" of before the First World War. This also meant, however, that they were subjected to quite different pressure regarding their justification. The reasons given for the measures were primarily based on the policy of remembrance: by the evoking and emphasising of the great past of a city or a nation. They were also intended, however, to promote tourism, to pave the way for the new, private mass transport and above all to bring the new middle classes back into the historic centres – both to live and to work. In the cities of the dictatorships this policy of remembrance was accompanied by large-scale destruction and displacement, for example in Rome, Moscow and Berlin. In contrast, many smaller towns in the dictatorships were the subject of less brutal redevelopment projects – for example, in Bergamo and Siena in Italy and Évora in Portugal. Some historic centres or historic quarters were placed under preservation orders – examples from before the end of the Second World War are Santiago de Compostela, Toledo and Santillana del Mar in Spain. The variations described in the following are not absolutely distinct and partially overlap one another, and they all have the objective of a new, better historic centre that is more modern and more artistically attractive, and that is suitable for the representation of constructed history.

One of the most spectacular answers to the destruction of the First World War was given by Belgium. Ypres, an important medieval town, was virtually obliterated in 1914 to 1917. In 1919 it was decided to reconstruct the town in a way as faithful as possible to the original. The ruined town was then almost completely reconstructed.[12]

On a large scale, buildings that no longer, or only partially, existed were rebuilt to their original state, whether this was verified or simply presumed, i.e. they were de facto constructed anew. Until now this aspect has been completely ignored by the historiography of planning with regard to

Portugal. There, in the late 1930s during Salazar's dictatorship city walls and castles were restored or newly built on an almost unbelievable scale, not only in Lisbon. In that city, St. George's Castle, which had virtually disappeared and been reshaped by new buildings, was reconstructed following extensive demolition work, enriched with historical spolias and set in a kind of park. A side-effect of such practices was the elimination of slum areas. There were similar projects throughout the country, including Guimarães.[13]

A further variation, which remained largely unknown until recently, was the new creation of apparently medieval, new buildings, which were often constructed in place of demolished historic buildings or as an addition to them. There were, of course, earlier examples of this, for example in the venerable English town of Chester in the 19th century. Significant in this regard is the construction of the "Gothic Quarter" in Barcelona, which as such was an "invention" and was enriched by freely created neo-Gothic components from the end of the 1920s until into the 1950s. The surroundings of the cathedral in Porto in Portugal were redesigned in a similar way. Examples of this variation can also be found in Mussolini's Italy.[14] They include, for example, the construction of the district to the west of the Piazza Maggiore in Bologna. One remarkable case is the construction of a previously non-existent, apparently medieval, new street in Weimar in the Nazi era, which was designed to provide replacement housing for the demolitions necessary for the construction of the *Gauforum* – a model of national socialist historic centre redevelopment.[15]

The historic centres in the capital cities of the dictatorships, in particular, were to be crowned by spectacular, large new buildings. The most significant example can be found in Moscow. There, in the immediate neighbourhood of the historic nucleus of the old town, the Kremlin, it was intended to build a new central urban baton that was to represent the entire capital city, and even the entire Soviet Union and the communist world movement: the Palace of the Soviets. In Rome the most important building of the dictatorship was planned next to the new triumphal boulevard of Italian fascism, the Via dell'Impero: the *Palazzo del Littorio*. Only in Berlin was there a different decision: the city's old town and the entire historic centre were not regarded as a sufficiently representative location. In this case, the most monumental and highest building of the dictatorship, the Great Hall, was to be built outside of the city centre, as the crowning of a completely new centre. None of these three projects was implemented. In contrast, an ostentatious city crowning was realised in Madrid, the centre of the Franco dictatorship, although not until after the end of the Second

---

12 Cf. Baert 1999.

13 In national socialist Germany, too, the reconstruction of castles was important. Cf. Scheck 1995, pp. 97–113.

14 For Italian examples, such as Arezzo, cf. Tragbar 2009, pp. 189–210.

15 Cf. Bodenschatz 2016, pp. 25–27.

Ypres: historical reconstruction after the First World War; here the Boterstraat near the Grote Markt in 1923.
[Source: Baert 1999, p. 183]

Guimarães: aerial photograph of the cleared castle hill, photo c. 1960. In the foreground the new building of the Palace of the Dukes of Bragança is visible. Behind it the restored chapel São Miquel stands out from the dark field. In the upper centre of the picture the massive reconstructed castle keep can be seen.
[Source: Paço dos Duques de Bragança 1999, p. 55]

Porto: Terreiro da Sé, photo, 1955. The square in front of the cathedral in Porto was redesigned for the anniversary celebrations in 1940. The spatial composition of historical components such as the memorial column (on the right) and the fortified tower (Torre de Angulo, partially visible on the left) and contemporary additions such as the equestrian staircase and the balustrade presented a neo-medieval stage setting for the medieval spectacle (Acto Medieval) that took place on 7th June 1940. For that day the avant-corps of the cathedral was freed of the extensions added in later centuries.
[Source: Arquivo Municipal do Porto]

Weimar: View of X-Straße from the "Gauforum", constructed 1936–1940 according to plans by the architect Willem Bäumer, c. 1941.
[Source: Hoefer 1941, p. 515]

*Moscow: planned Palace of the Soviets in the centre,
the Kremlin on the left. Outside of the Kremlin only new
buildings are to be seen; the old city has disappeared.
[Source: Atarov 1940, following p. 146]*

World War. In the centre of the Spanish capital, within the framework of the reconstruction of the Plaza de España that had begun in 1943, two high-rise buildings that towered over the city were built by the private sector during the 1950s: the *Edificio España* and the *Torre de Madrid*. They also served as a symbol of economic upswing.

The remembrance of an allegedly heroic and splendid national history was cultivated in dictatorships to a much greater extent than elsewhere. This was particularly true of the historic cities in Italy, especially Rome. The testimonials to the imperial Rome of antiquity were to be uncovered. The cultic presentation of buildings as testimonials to past greatness also took place in Germany, for example in the transformation of the Braunschweig Cathedral[16] and in Lisbon in the transformation and uncovering of the Hieronymites Monastery. In Portugal the programme for the reconstruction of castles served the remembrance of a splendid history. In Moscow the Kremlin, as a testimonial to a great past, also became the seat of government of the Soviet dictatorship. In Spain the redevelopment of historic centres such as those of Toledo and Zaragoza also served the evocation of national greatness.

Extensive demolition programmes were implemented especially in the dictatorships for the policy of remembrance, but also for traffic and for the removal of undesirable buildings. In Rome, for example, the largest wholesale demolition programme in Europe in the interwar period was implemented in the area surrounding the Capitol, not only in order to place the noble ruins of antiquity on display but also in order to construct a boulevard between Mussolini's seat of government and the Colosseum. Again, less wealthy layers of the population were displaced. It is still little known that a large part of Old Berlin was destroyed. The basis for this was, as ever, wide-ranging expropriation, accelerated in this case by the theft of Jewish property.[17] There were also particularly extensive demolitions in Moscow's historic centre. Even the stage-setting reconstruction of castles in Portugal often meant the demolition of historic districts.

Translocation was one possible way of saving historic buildings, even if at another location. In the Soviet Union there was a particular variation of translocation: in the course of the extension of one of Moscow's most important arterial roads, Gorky Street, existing historic stately buildings that were to be preserved were moved in a complicated process and placed on a new site behind the new residential

16 Cf. Scheck 1995, pp. 175–179.

17 Cf. Stadtmuseum Berlin (ed.) 2013.

Braunschweig: invoked in the era of National Socialism as a "shrine of German history". The reconstruction of the historic centre was accompanied and supported by the cult of Henry the Lion, who with a glance towards the east had "won new lands for Germanity". In front of the most important building in the historic centre, the Cathedral of St. Blasius, stands the "brazen lion", victory sign of the Duke, placed there in 1166. In the cathedral itself is the tomb of Henry the Lion, which was redesigned in the Nazi era. The transformation of the interior of the cathedral was a central component of the redevelopment of the historic centre in that period.
[Source: Illustrirte Zeitung of 28th March 1935. Magazine on Braunschweig, p. 398]

Lisbon: Demolition of unwelcome historic buildings in 1939 in the district of Belém. The objective was the freeing of the Hieronymites Monastery, a testimonial to Portugal's golden age, to which the Salazar dictatorship related. The monastery itself was comprehensively restored. In the process, the tombs of the contemporary – and present-day – national heroes Vasco da Gama and Luís de Camões were again placed on show in the monastery church in 1940. Today the monastery is a world heritage site.
[Source: FCG – Biblioteca de Arte e Arquivos]

Rome: Wholesale demolition between the monument for Vittorio Emanuele II (Altar of the Fatherland) and the Colosseum, proudly presented in the newspaper "La Domenica del Corriere" of 9th October 1932.
[Source: Insolera/Sette 2003, p. 80]

Moscow: Translocation of valuable buildings, here: moving of a building in Gorky Street, c. 1938.
[Source: Bodenschatz/ Post (eds.) 2003, p. 229]

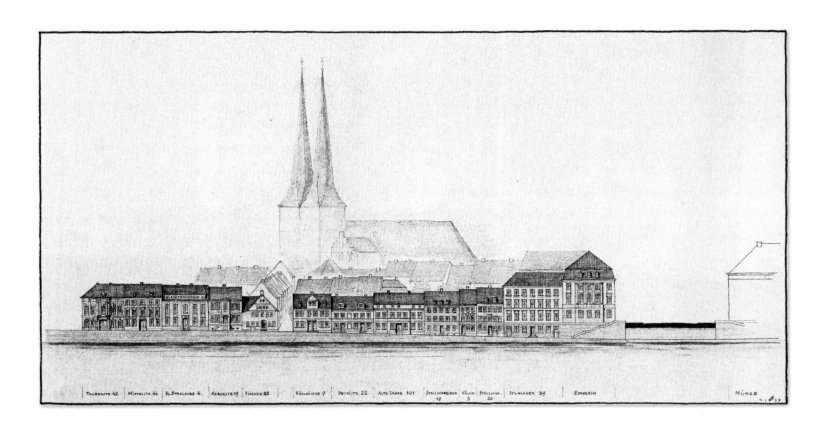

Berlin: View of the planned Museum of Architecture of the Old Town, 1937, not implemented. Around the St. Nicholas Church historic houses that had been the victims of demolition in other parts of the old city were to be rebuilt.
[Source: Landesarchiv Berlin, F Rep. 270-03, No. 684, Bl. 5]

palaces.[18] The new elites of the Stalin era moved into the residential palaces. In Berlin it was intended during the Nazi era that the district around the Church of St. Nicholas be developed into a kind of medieval museum of architecture with buildings that had been torn down elsewhere in the course of the redevelopment of the historic centre.

Wartime Destruction, Reconstruction and Wholesale Demolition

In a terrible way, the Second World War turned the new, although often questionable, appreciation of the historic centres into an act of destruction. Precisely because they were regarded as something special, as a reference point for national identity, they became the objective of destructive bombings. After the end of the war the destruction of the historic centres was often regarded as an "opportunity" for modern reconstruction. In the 1950s and 1960s the historic centres, which were regarded as backward, were confronted with wholesale demolition programmes. In the shadow of this development stood the quite impressive attempts to reconstruct the historic centres or to lead the way into the future without widespread destruction.

The almost complete obliteration of the historic town of Guernica (Basque: Gernika), the mythical place of the Basque people, by German and Italian fighter planes in April 1937 was the very first bombing and destruction of this type.[19] It was followed by the devastating attack by the German Luftwaffe on Coventry in 1940, the bombing of Lübeck and Rostock by the Royal Air Force and in turn of Bath, Canterbury, Exeter, Norwich and York, all in 1942, by the German Luftwaffe, and finally in 1944/1945 there was the extensive destruction not only of Dresden and Le Havre by Allied aircraft. In this context we must also remember the destruction of Warsaw and Gdańsk by the German Wehrmacht and the destruction of historic cities in the Soviet Union, such as Belarusian Minsk in 1941.

Following the destruction of historic towns and cities in the Second World War the questions were posed: how should the historic centres be reconstructed? What does a centre of tomorrow look like? The historical reconstructions of the "old towns" of Warsaw and Gdańsk are famous, although these do not take their already considerably altered state at the time of their destruction into account but, rather, a purified pre-industrial state. In the Soviet Union triumphant new building dominated, for example in Minsk. Whereas in the dictatorships urban development was organised by the national state, in Western countries the reconstruction was managed at a local level. In Rotterdam and Coventry the

Gernika/Guernica: Francoist reconstruction. New main street with city hall, c. 1945. [Source: Reconstrucción 55/1945, p. 231]

Warsaw: Reconstruction of the historic centre, here Piwna Street 1945 (top) and after the reconstruction (bottom). [Source: Ciborowski, Adolf: Warschau. Zerstörung und Wiederaufbau der Stadt. Warsaw 1969, p. 89]

Minsk: Triumphant new construction – Stalin Prospekt, photo c. 1957. In the badly damaged Belarusian "city of heroes" a new centre was built in the pattern of Stalinist urban development. The most important main street was the new Stalin Prospekt planned in 1950. [Source: Sovetskaia arkhitektura 1917–1957 1957, no page number]

18 Cf. Ott 2003, pp. 226–230.
19 Cf. Bodenschatz/Welch Guerra 2012, pp. 279–292.

184

Rotterdam: Modern new construction of the centre, photo c. 1957. Original caption: "One lives in the centre of the city again. Higher and lower buildings alternate in a composition with open spaces."
[Source: Rotterdam 1957, p. 11]

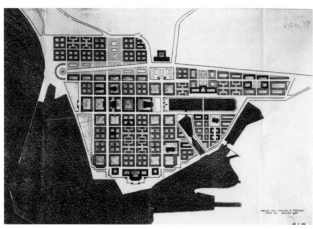

Le Havre: New construction from one mould. The destroyed Le Havre was rebuilt in 1945–1964 according to plans by Auguste Perret. These were guided by the forms of traditional urban construction but gave no consideration to the historical layout of the city and did not aim at the reconstruction of historic buildings. In 2005 the ensemble was designated a UNESCO World Heritage Site. [Source: La ville moderne en Europe 1996, p. 178]

Bad Godesberg, Bonn: a programme of extensive demolition. The planning began in June 1962, inspired by the choice of Bonn as the capital of the Federal Republic. The degree of destruction of the town in the Second World War was 6.5 per cent. [Source: Deutsche Akademie für Städtebau und Landesplanung (ed.) 1970, p. 156]

destruction was utilised for reconstruction that was modern and car-friendly. In Germany, in addition to more or less free reconstruction such as in Freudenstadt, Münster, Donauwörth and Neumarkt in der Oberpfalz (Upper Palatinate) there was also modern new construction such as in Kassel and Stuttgart. Above all in (East) Berlin the historic centre was subjected to radical change – a decision that was only possible in a dictatorship because of the necessary seizure of private property, and which has given rise to conflict up to the present day.[20]

But what should be done with the historic towns that survived the war? In the 1950s and 1960s these were often subjected, at considerable cost, to a car-friendly transformation. There now came a fourth great wave of destruction that differed considerably from the first wave, the formation of a "business city" before the First World War, from the second wave, the wholesale demolition in the large cities during the dictatorships, and from the third wave, the bombing in the Second World War. In a programme supported by both local and national governments the historic centres, regarded as being no longer up-to-date, were damaged by the car-friendly extension of major thoroughfares

20 Cf. Bodenschatz 2018, pp. 167–184.

redevelopment of historic centres in the Federal Republic of Germany, for example in the model towns of Bamberg, Lübeck and Regensburg, and indirectly also to a certain extent in the GDR.

Even before the European Architectural Year in 1975 it also became clear that the change towards preservative redevelopment was not a top-down change of paradigm but was supported by numerous civil society and intermediate initiatives such as citizens' action groups and local monument preservation offices. In the GDR the many action groups for the rescue of the historic centres were part of the great protest movements of 1989.

The pioneers of a cautious redevelopment of historic centres could not yet have foreseen, however, that in the course of the success of this variation the historic centres themselves would change radically, although their buildings remained the same. During the postwar decades the historic centres were relatively normal residential areas. This was true even

Cáceres: a historic Spanish town, protected in its entirety as a monument since 1949.
[Source: Ibáñez Martín 1950]

and main squares or – as in Bad Godesberg – even directly obliterated by means of comprehensive demolition programmes. In the 1950s, however, entire historic centres were also placed under preservation orders – again in dictatorships such as Spain and Portugal, although usually in small towns. In 1949 during the Franco era the historic town of Cáceres in the southern Spanish region of Extremadura was declared a national monument and 1986 it was named a World Heritage Site. The small historic town of Óbidos in Portugal was comprehensively restored and reconstructed with government funding during the Salazar epoch and was finally declared a national monument in 1951.

Cautious Urban Renewal since the 1970s

In the 1960s, against the background of experience with the destructive redevelopment of historic centres in the postwar period, the long era of cautious historic centre redevelopment began, which found a starting-point that was admired worldwide in the Bologna model. In Bologna the entire historic centre, including the simpler buildings, was discovered as an ensemble worth preserving, not only by monument conservators but also by architects, town planners and local politicians.[21] As part of the redevelopment of the historic centre of Bologna destroyed historic buildings were also reconstructed – typologically reconstructed, as it was then called. The Bologna model proved yet again that neither in the case of demolition nor in the case of preservation was the issue simply one of buildings and public spaces, but always also one of the economy and society. In this sense the Bolognese plan for social housing construction in the historic centre, linking social and town planning objectives programmatically and explicitly, represented a climax in the planning history of historic centre redevelopment. It was also a climax for municipal urban development. The Bologna model also characterised the

The Bologna model: internationally respected project of cautious historic centre redevelopment. Image of the cover of the journal "Bauwelt" by Peter Debold and Astrid Debold-Kritter from the year 1974, which essentially founded the German enthusiasm for Bologna.
[Source: Bauwelt 33/1974, cover]

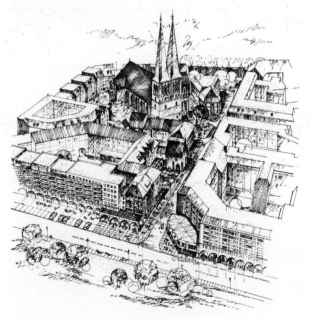

East Berlin: free reconstruction of the medieval Nikolaiviertel (Nicholas quarter) according to plans by Günter Stahn, drawing from 1982.
[Source: Stahn 1985, p. 72]

21 Cf. Bodenschatz/Harlander 2015, pp. 357–376.

of places such as the Tuscan San Gimignano. This began to change rapidly in the 1970s. A space came into existence that was clearly delimited from the rest of the town or city and presented a setting for tourism, local remembrance policy, and particular residents and usage. This trend was intensified by the gradual withdrawal of the public sector from the redevelopment of historic centres, and especially from the modernisation of older residential buildings. The local authority (in the West) or national government (in the East) redevelopment of historic centres was increasingly replaced by private-sector redevelopment. The unmistakable success of preservative urban redevelopment led, finally, to developments that opened up new areas of dispute – not only on the use of the historic centre as a setting for events of all kinds, but also to initiatives that propagated, often successfully, the new construction of historic quarters such as in Dresden, in Potsdam, in Frankfurt am Main, in Berlin and in Lübeck. Under state control this already happened in the 1980s, in East Berlin, where within the framework of the exuberant 750-year anniversary celebrations the Nikolaiviertel (Nicholas Quarter) was newly constructed in a free form according to plans by Günter Stahn.

Frankfurt am Main: on 28th September 2018 the completely new historic centre (more precisely: a part of the historic centre) that had been reconstructed from 2012 to 2018 was inaugurated. [Photo: Harald Bodenschatz 2018]

Outlook

Today we can look back on a period of a good 150 years of a broad and bewildering spectrum of the urban renewal of historic centres in Europe. This included the comprehensive appropriation of the pre-industrial town – also as a place of residence – by new upper classes (Paris and Moscow), the formation of a "business city" that displaced residents (London), historical reconstruction (Ypres and Warsaw), enthusiastic appreciation (Barcelona), the forcible uncovering of testimonials to past greatness (Rome, Lisbon and Porto), the (planned) implantation of massive buildings (Moscow and Rome), the translocation of historic buildings (Moscow), the placing of entire towns under preservation orders (Óbidos and Santillana del Mar), modified reconstruction (Gernika), purifying reconstruction (Münster and Donauwörth), car-friendly new construction (Kassel and East Berlin), ostentatious new construction (Minsk and Rostock), wholesale demolition (Bad Godesberg), preservative and socially oriented redevelopment combined with typological reconstruction (Bologna), the approximate reconstruction of vanished historic quarters (Berlin, Dresden, Potsdam and Frankfurt am Main). In addition, there was a supplementary typology of the treatment of public spaces, which were exposed to far more changes in the last 150 years than buildings were. These concerned not only the historical layout of the towns, but also, and above all, the image and features of traditional streets, pathways and squares. All these variations could be summarised by a socio-economic typology: private-sector, local authority or national redevelopment of historic centres.

The historic city centres in Europe were massively destroyed in the last 150 years. Dictatorships and war, in particular, but also the formation of a "business city" and individual mass transport furthered comprehensive demolition. The year 1942, when Europe suffered the bombing and destruction of numerous historic towns and cities, can probably be regarded as the worst year of destruction in the entire long history of European towns and cities. Beyond the destruction caused by war, the most important precondition for the comprehensive destruction of historic centres was above all the increased ease of the seizure of private real estate property – primarily during the dictatorships. On the other hand, it was also the dictatorships that out of their own interest for the first time implemented more or less preservative redevelopment measures on a larger scale, particularly in smaller towns. And it is the seizure of irresponsibly treated property that can also save historic buildings.

Particularly after the First World War, when the appreciation of the historic centres was increasing, a broad spectrum of new architecture came to the fore in historic centres that challenges the present narrow view of "contemporary architecture": in addition to less radical "modern" buildings there were numerous regional, from restrained to effusive neomedieval, "atmospherically" adapted, neo-realistically traditional, but also historically reconstructive or simplistically reconstructive varieties of style. All these building forms, and certainly not only those that are in unmistakable contrast to the historic buildings, are "contemporary" or "modern" unless one is an advocate of a cultural conflict position that is unjustified in this field, and until into the 1960s they were also an answer to the unpopular architecture of the period before the First World War.

The urban renewal of the historic centres never affected only buildings and public spaces, but also always affected the people who lived there, the "social structure". From the beginning it was an objective to eliminate poor districts, often called slums, which in turn were a result of the segregating spread of the cities outwards during the late 19th century. In some cases replacement housing was provided for those displaced (for example in England), but often it was not. The displacement of the poor from the historic centres was also an important goal of historic centre redevelopment during the dictatorships, particularly in the Soviet Union, Italy and Germany. It continued to play a major role after the Second World War, even in the socialist states, for example in the highly regarded preservative redevelopment of the historic centre of Kraków.

The urban renewal of historic city centres in the European dictatorships is a part of the history of European urban development and not an outlier, even though it is a specific part. What is specific is not so much the spectrum of objectives, but rather their composition and the intensification of the individual goals, and in particular the central state intervention as well as the creation and utilisation of instruments, which made an effective redevelopment of the historic city centres possible in the first place: the elimination of regional autonomy and the extensive application of expropriation. The redevelopment of historic city centres as a daily field of action of urban development on a larger scale and with a systematic methodology originated in the period of dictatorships, war and reconstruction. The question poses itself repeatedly, and today in an especially pointed way: what is an appropriate way of dealing with the structural testimonials of the dictatorships in our historic centres? Preserve them, reflect upon them, seize the opportunity and re-interpret them!

References

Altrock, Uwe: Altstadterneuerung. Zwischen Bewahrung, Revitalisierung und Rekonstruktionismus. In: Enss/Vinken (eds.) 2016, pp. 219–232

Atarov, Nikolaj: Dvorec Sovetov. Moscow 1940

Baert, Koen et al.: Ieper, de herrezen stad. Koksijede 1999 Bauwelt 33/1974

Benevolo, Leonardo: Storia della Città. Rome/Bari 1976

Bodenschatz, Harald: Weimar. Modellstadt der Moderne? Ambivalenzen des Städtebaus im 20. Jahrhundert, published by the Klassik Stiftung Weimar. Weimar 2016

Bodenschatz, Harald: Berlin Mitte: The product of two dictatorships. In: Hökerberg, Håkan (ed.): Architecture as propaganda in twentieth-century totalitarian regimes. History and heritage. Florence 2018, pp. 167–184

Bodenschatz, Harald: Abbruch und Erhalt. 150 Jahre Planungsgeschichte der europäischen Altstadt. In: Forum Stadt 2/2019, pp. 113–133

Bodenschatz, Harald/Harlander, Tilman: 40 Jahre Stadterneuerung Bologna, in: Forum Stadt 4/2015, pp. 357–376

Bodenschatz, Harald/Welch Guerra, Max: Guernica/Gernika: Bild, Zerstörung und Wiederaufbau. Ein vergessenes Kapitel europäischer Städtebaugeschichte. In: Forum Stadt 3/2012, pp. 279–292

Bodenschatz, Harald/Post, Christiane (eds.): Städtebau im Schatten Stalins. Die internationale Suche nach der sozialistischen Stadt in der Sowjetunion 1929–1935. Berlin 2003

Buls, Charles: Esthétique des villes. Brussels 1893

Ciborowski, Adolf: Warschau. Zerstörung und Wiederaufbau der Stadt. Warsaw 1969

Cutolo, Davide/Pace, Sergio: La scoperta della città antica. Esperienza e conoscenza del centro storico nell'Europa del Novecento. Macerata 2016

Dendooven, Dominiek/Dewilde, Jan: The Reconstruction of Ieper. Ypres 1999

Deutsche Akademie für Städtebau und Landesplanung (ed.): Deutscher Städtebau 1968. Essen 1970

Eberstadt, Rudolph: Handbuch des Wohnungswesens und der Wohnungsfrage. 3rd edition. Jena 1917

Enss, Carmen M./Vinken, Gerhard (eds.): Produkt Altstadt. Historische Stadtzentren in Städtebau und Denkmalpflege. Bielefeld 2016

Giovannoni, Gustavo: Vecchie città ed edilizia nuova. In: Nuova Antologia, 1st June 1913, pp. 449–472

Giovannoni, Gustavo: Il "diradamento" edilizio dei vecchi centri. Il quartiere della Rinascenza in Roma. In: Nuova Antologia, 1st July 1913, pp. 53–76

Giovannoni, Gustavo: Vecchie città ed Edilizia nuova. Turin 1931

Goebel, Benedikt: Der Umbau Alt-Berlins zum modernen Stadtzentrum. Planungs-, Bau- und Besitzgeschichte des historischen Berliner Stadtkerns im 19. und 20. Jahrhundert. Berlin 2003

Gurlitt, Cornelius: Handbuch des Städtebaues. Berlin 1920

Hoefer, Friedbert: Die Bauten der Altstadtsanierung in Weimar. In: Moderne Bauformen. Monatshefte für Architektur und Raumkunst 12/1941, pp. 513–538

Ibáñez Martín, José: Diez años de servicios a la cultura española, 1939–1949. Madrid 1950

Illustrirte Zeitung, 28th March 1935. Magazine on Braunschweig

Insolera, Italo/Sette, Alessandra Maria: Roma tra le due guerre. Cronache di una città che cambia. Rome 2003

Koser, David: "Abbruch und Neubau". Die Entstehung der Berliner City. Berlin 2017

Ott, Steffen: Der Umbau der historischen Innenstadt. In: Bodenschatz/Post (eds.) 2003, pp. 213–236

Paço dos Duques de Bragança. In: Direcção-Geral dos Edifícios e Monumentos Nacionais: Caminhos do Património. Lisbon 1999, pp. 52–55

Reconstrucción 55/1945

Rotterdam. Der Neubau einer Stadt. Rotterdam 1957

Scheck, Thomas: Denkmalpflege und Diktatur. Die Erhaltung von Bau- und Kunstdenkmälern in Schleswig-Holstein und im Deutschen Reich zur Zeit des Nationalsozialismus. Berlin 1995

Schilling, Otto: Innere Stadterweiterung. Berlin 1921

Schulz, Hartmut: Stadterneuerung im europäischen Ausland und in den USA. In: Neuer Mierbach, Therese/Kopetzki, Christian (eds.): Stadterneuerung als Teil großstädtischer Entwicklungspolitik in der Weimarer Republik und im Nationalsozialismus. Teil C: Exkurs. Kassel 1988, pp. 1005–1099

Smets, Marcel: Charles Buls. Les principes de l'art urbain. Liège 1995

Sovetskaia arkhitektura 1917–1957 [Soviet architecture 1917–1957]. Moscow 1957

Stadtmuseum Berlin (ed.): Geraubte Mitte. Die "Arisierung" des jüdischen Grundeigentums im Berliner Stadtkern 1933–1945. Berlin 2013

Stahn, Günter: Das Nikolaiviertel am Marx-Engels-Forum. Berlin 1985

Stamp, Gavin: The Changing Metropolis. Earliest photographs of London 1839–1879. Harmondsworth 1986

Tragbar, Klaus: Dante und der Duce. Zu den politischen Motiven der Umgestaltung historischer Städte in der Toskana. In: Mattioli, Aram/Steinacher, Gerald (eds.): Für den Faschismus bauen. Architektur und Städtebau im Italien Mussolinis. Zürich 2009, pp. 189–210

Tragbar, Klaus: Die Entdeckung des ambiente. Gustavo Giovannoni und sein europäischer Kontext. In: Enss/Vinken (eds.) 2016, pp. 29–41

La ville moderne en Europe. Visions urbaines d'artistes et d'architectes 1870–1996. Paris 1996

Waetzoldt, Wilhelm: Paris. Die Neugestaltung des Stadtbildes durch Baron Haussmann. Leipzig 1943

Zucconi, Guido: Gustavo Giovannoni. A Theory and a Practice of Urban Conservation. In: Change Over Time. March 2014, pp. 76–91

Register of Persons

Authors

Prof. Dr. Harald Bodenschatz *1946, town planner and social scientist; from 1995 to 2011 University Professor for the Sociology of Planning and Architecture, Technical University (TU), Berlin; now Associate Professor at the Center for Metropolitan Studies, TU Berlin, and member of the Bauhaus Institute for the History and Theory of Architecture and Planning, Bauhaus-Universität Weimar. Research projects and publications on urban development, including urban development in the dictatorships in Germany, Italy, Portugal, Spain and the Soviet Union.

Dr. Christian von Oppen *1971, architect; from 2007 to 2014 research associate, Design and Urban Development, Bauhaus-Universität Weimar; member of the Bauhaus Institute for the History and Theory of Architecture and Planning, Bauhaus-Universität Weimar; from 2014 to 2018 research associate, Center for Metropolitan Studies, TU Berlin; principal author of the book "Städtebau unter Salazar: Diktatorische Modernisierung des portugiesischen Imperiums 1926–1960" [Urban development under Salazar: dictatorial modernisation of the Portuguese Empire 1926–1960] (eds.: H. Bodenschatz/M. Welch Guerra). Since 2018 participation in the development of the Berlin urban quarter "Am Tacheles" and since 2019 project director at pwrdevelopment.

Steffen Ott *1965, town planner; 2000–2001 research associate in the specialist field "The sociology of planning and architecture", TU Berlin; co-author of the book "Städtebau im Schatten Stalins: Die internationale Suche nach der sozialistischen Stadt in der Sowjetunion 1929–1935" [Urban development in Stalin's shadow: the international search for the socialist city in the Soviet Union 1929–1935] (eds.: H. Bodenschatz/C. Post). Founder and director of SPOK Planergemeinschaft (1994–2011) and DOST GmbH (1997–2015); senior consultant to the Belhasa Group of Companies Dubai/UAE (2012–2020); board member and senior adviser of APEX Capital Ventures Hong Kong (since 2012). Since 2020 senior consultant at ATLES Dubai/UAE and founder and director of APEX International Projects Dubai/UAE.

Dr. Christiane Post *1961, art historian; since 2010 private lecturer in Art at the Faculty of Design and Art, Bergische Universität Wuppertal; 2012/2013 substitute professor, Chair of Art History, Akademie der Bildenden Künste, Nuremberg; from 2014 to 2016 guest professor and managing director of the Institute for Art in Context, University of the Arts, Berlin; co-editor and author of the book "Städtebau im Schatten Stalins: Die internationale Suche nach der sozialistischen Stadt in der Sowjetunion 1929–1935" [Urban development in Stalin's shadow: the international search for the socialist city in the Soviet Union 1929–1935].

Piero Sassi *1984, urban researcher; since 2013 research assistant, Chair of Spatial Planning and Spatial Research, Bauhaus-Universität Weimar, and coordinator of the network UEDXX (Urbanism of European Dictatorships during the XXth Century Scientific Network); principal author of the book "Städtebau als Kreuzzug Francos. Wiederaufbau und Erneuerung unter der Diktatur in Spanien 1938–1959" [Urban development as Franco's crusade. Reconstruction and redevelopment under the dictatorship in Spain 1938–1959] (eds.: M. Welch Guerra/H. Bodenschatz). Member of the Bauhaus Institute for the History and Theory of Architecture and Planning.

Prof. Dr. Max Welch Guerra *1956, political and planning scientist; since 2003 University Professor for Spatial Planning and Spatial Research, Bauhaus-Universität Weimar; director of the Bauhaus Institute for the History and Theory of Architecture and Planning; head of the degree programmes B.Sc. and M.Sc. in Urbanism. Project director of the international research association urbanHist (History of European Urbanism in the 20th Century). Research projects and publications on the area of tension between spatial planning and politics, and on urban development and urban planning in the dictatorships in Germany, Portugal and Spain.

The *Deutsche Nationalbibliothek* lists this publication
in the *Deutsche Nationalbibliografie*; detailed bibliographic
data are available online at http://dnb.d-nb.de.

ISBN 978-3-86922-205-9 (English)
ISBN 978-3-86922-005-5 (German)

© 2021 by DOM publishers, Berlin
www.dom-publishers.com

Design
Inka Humann

Cover Design
Masako Tomokiyo

Translation
Irene Wilson

Printing
Tiger Printing (Hong Kong) Co., Ltd.
www.tigerprinting.hk

This publication is an outcome of urbanHIST, a project that
has received funding from the European Union's Horizon 2020
research and innovation programme, Marie Skłodowska-Curie
actions, grant agreement No 721933.